DEMOCRACY AND GREEN POLITICAL THOUGHT

The green movement has posed some tough questions for traditional justifications of democracy. Should the natural world have rights? Can we take account of the interests of future generations? Do we need to replace existing institutions to deal with the ecological crisis? But questions have also been asked of the greens. Could their idealism undermine democracy? Can greens be effective democrats?

In this book some of the leading writers on green political thought analyse these questions, examining the discourse of green movements concerning democracy, the status of democracy within green political thought, and the political institutions that might be necessary to ensure democracy in a sustainable society. The debates are not simply about the compatibility of democracy with green ideas, but also about how best to define democracy itself.

The authors suggest that greens still have considerable work to do in fleshing out the weaker elements in their conceptions of democracy. In particular, representative institutions would still have an important role to play in any green democracy. But taking green ideas seriously does require reconsideration of some of the central foundations of liberal democracy, including the scope of the moral community and the privileged status of the atomised individual citizen, divorced from nature.

Contributors: Wouter Achterberg, John Barry, Neil Carter, Peter Christoff, Andrew Dobson, Brian Doherty, Robyn Eckersley, Marius de Geus, Michael Kenny, Mike Mills and Michael Saward.

EUROPEAN POLITICAL SCIENCE SERIES
Edited by Hans Keman
Vrije University, Amsterdam
On behalf of the European Consortium for Political Research

The European Political Science Series is published in Association with the European Consortium for Political Research – the leading organisation concerned with the growth and development of political science in Europe. The series will present high-quality edited volumes on topics at the leading edge of current interest in political science and related fields, with contributions from European scholars and others who have presented work at ECPR workshops or research groups.

SEX EQUALITY POLICY IN WESTERN EUROPE
Edited by Frances Gardiner

DEMOCRACY AND GREEN POLITICAL THOUGHT

Sustainability, rights and citizenship

Edited by
Brian Doherty and
Marius de Geus

London and New York

First published 1996
by Routledge
11 New Fetter Lane, London EC4P 4EE

Simultaneously published in the USA and Canada
by Routledge
29 West 35th Street, New York, NY 10001

Routledge is an International Thomson Publishing company

Typeset in Baskerville by
Ponting–Green Publishing Services, Chesham, Bucks
Printed and bound in Great Britain by
TJ Press (Padstow) Ltd, Padstow, Cornwall

British Library Cataloguing in Publication Data
A catalogue record for this book is available from the
British Library

Library of Congress Cataloging in Publication Data
A catalogue record for this book has been requested

ISBN 0–415–14411–6 (hbk)
ISBN 0–415–14412–4 (pbk)

CONTENTS

CONTENTS

Part III The institutions of a green democracy

CONTRIBUTORS

Wouter Achterberg is a Senior Lecturer in the Department of Practical Philosophy at the University of Amsterdam.

John Barry is a Lecturer in Politics at Keele University.

Neil Carter is a Lecturer in Politics at the University of York.

Peter Christoff is a Graduate Research Student at Melbourne University.

Andrew Dobson is a Professor of Politics at Keele University.

Brian Doherty is a Lecturer in Politics at Keele University.

Robyn Eckersley is a Senior Lecturer in Politics at Monash University.

Marius de Geus is a Lecturer in Political Science at the University of Leiden.

Michael Kenny is a Lecturer in Politics at Sheffield University.

Mike Mills is a Senior Lecturer in Politics and Modern History at London Guildhall University.

Michael Saward is a Lecturer in the Department of Social Policy at Royal Holloway and Bedford New College, University of London.

SERIES EDITOR'S PREFACE

The world today is facing many severe problems: armed conflict afflicts many places, famine and fatal diseases are on the increase, economic conditions are worsening in the North and especially the South, and – last but not least – ecological problems are deep-seated and have become a public concern and a political issue for which there is no easy answer.

Particularly in democracies, keeping track of problems and tackling them by political means also appear to have become more problematic than ever. It is even doubtful whether liberal democracies are still capable, within the confines of the nation-state, of coping with these problems by means of public regulation and related policy making.

It is therefore highly appropriate to launch the new *European Political Science Book* series at this time, with a volume on the relationship between ecological problems and democracy. The series is the result of a collaboration between the European Consortium for Political Research and Routledge Publishers. Addressing this topic and related issues from the perspective of political theory is clearly a task for political scientists, who are able to combine a thorough analysis with a concern for the world which we all share.

This volume therefore sets a good example of what we are trying to achieve with this series. That is, a political science which not only deals with issues and topics that are relevant at the moment, but that is at the same time based on thorough analysis and which incorporates recent theoretical insights supported by convincing arguments and evidence.

The authors of this first volume of the new series attempt to go beyond short-term green issues and behind the sometimes volatile public concern about the environment, to the essential question of how to cope with ecological problems that confront us all but which in practice cannot be solved by groups or nations acting in isolation. For this, and other wide-ranging problems, we need collective action based on worldwide consensus and co-operation. This raises questions, *inter alia*, about the efficacy of liberal democratic rule.

The strength and attractiveness of the approach adopted throughout this volume is that the authors do not attempt to present clear-cut answers or come up with idealistic solutions. Rather they discuss the (omnipresent) problems of democratic decision making in terms of normative dilemmas and appropriate political strategies. The options for choice and possibilities for democracy in relation to 'green' concerns are rigorously discussed, and draw extensively on the tools of political theory. In this sense most of the contributions to this volume go beyond 'mere' environmentalism or green 'sloganeering'.

In Part I the key value of world survival is discussed in relation to 'communitarianism' and other ideas about local governance and decentralised control (e.g., 'bio-regionalism'). These are compared with other environmentalist theories urging democratic centralism and the need of a 'strong state' to enhance effective political action.

This discussion naturally spills over into questions that are central to democratic theory – in particular, the range and scope of liberal democracies which are (still) territorially limited and based on aggregated individual choices and preferences. What is the role of citizenship in modern times? It appears from this analysis that one needs to rethink the relationship between a really sustainable environment and the degree of autonomy of citizens in order to combine green concerns with democratically legitimated public action.

In Part III, therefore, the institutions of democracy are at the centre of the discussion. This raises questions about justifiable public interference with individuals, the range of legitimate state intervention and the universality of ecological problems. These are questions to which there are no easy answers and which even raise doubts – as the editors do – about the extent to which it is possible to fuse green political thought with the theory and practice of liberal democracy.

These are only some of the vital and thought-provoking questions considered throughout this volume from different angles and perspectives. There can be no final answers in this area. It is precisely the recognition of this, together with their thoughtful consideration of the range of possible answers, which makes this collection of essays essential reading, not only for political scientists, but for all those citizens concerned about a sustainable environment within a viable democracy.

Professor Dr Hans Keman,
Series Editor,
Haarlem, 1996

ACKNOWLEDGEMENTS

The chapters in this book are taken from a workshop on Green Politics and Democracy at the Conference of the European Consortium for Political Research (ECPR) in Madrid in April 1994 and we would like to thank the ECPR and the British Academy for their financial assistance to the participants. Many excellent papers from that workshop are not included in this collection, not for reasons of quality, but because the central themes that emerged in our discussions concerned questions of political theory and ideology rather than public policy. We would like to express our gratitude to Detlef Jahn, Alfe-Inge Jansen, Volkmar Lauber, Paul Lucardie, Carina Lundmark, Oddgeir Odjborn and Stephen Young for contributing through their involvement in the workshop to the debates in this book.

Jill Allaway and Teresa Steele helped to prepare the final version of this manuscript and kept the book on the road when it might otherwise have faltered. John Barry and Andy Dobson also deserve our thanks for offering advice and comments when they were most needed. And Caroline Wintersgill, our editor at Routledge, was more committed, patient and encouraging than we had any right to expect.

Brian Doherty
Marius de Geus

INTRODUCTION

Brian Doherty and Marius de Geus

Greens may lack formal political power but the impact of their ideas has been remarkable. As recently as the 1970s greens were dismissed as doomsayers, yet now green ideas are taken seriously, and those who place their faith in technological and market-driven solutions to ecological problems are on the defensive. Above all, it is recognition of the need to ensure sustainability that has provided the basis for increased acceptance of the importance of green ideas. Democracy is perhaps the only other term which has such a universal and unrivalled status, but just as there are many ways to be democratic there are also many ways in which to be 'green'. It is not surprising, therefore, that there are numerous ways of being a democratic green.

Amongst those writing from an ecological standpoint there have been two standard and contradictory responses to the relationship between green politics and democracy. From green parties and radical green movements has come a stress on the need for participatory democracy. The liberal democratic state is seen as incapable of enabling the new ethic of responsibility which would be necessary if the behaviour of individual citizens was to become governed by ecological priorities. Only by challenging material inequalities and bureaucratic hierarchies will a new communitarianism emerge that will be powerful enough to overcome the atomised self-interest of individual consumers. As well as new participatory forms of politics, the radical green argument also calls for institutional decentralisation. Decentralised production and decentralised politics are linked in this argument because greens believe that an ecologically sustainable society will have to be small-scale and self-reliant.

In contrast, from 'survivalists' has come a contradictory argument that sees democracy as an obstacle to dealing with the ecological crisis. In the 1970s writers such as William Ophuls (1977) and Robert Heilbroner (1974) argued that the ecological crisis could be tackled only by a strong government that would be prepared to curb the freedom of individual citizens in order to prevent ecological degradation. This was based on the assumption that individuals were most likely to act in their own interests, even if this

1

threatened the current or future existence of the population as a whole. Only a strong government would be able to act in the collective interest.

These two alternatives have represented the principal arguments heard within green movements since the early 1960s. However, they are not necessarily the only arguments, as the contributions to this book show. The evolution of green parties and movements and the growth of writing on green political theory have paralleled each other but not always overlapped. Yet, in one respect, regarding the increased acceptance of the institutions of representative democracy, they have tended to converge. Thus, both green movements and theorists of green politics seem to be less concerned with alternatives to liberal democratic institutions than they were in the 1970s and 1980s. Instead, there is a greater interest in establishing a more secure place within liberal democracy for ecological politics and supplementing representative democracy with other forms, rather than replacing it. This is at most a trend and it does not characterise all green movements, nor is it necessarily the only refrain from theorists writing on green politics. Yet, it is identifiable in a number of shifts in the discourse of green activists themselves and of those writing on green theory. For instance, criticism of the state is now much more muted, and green anarchism no longer seems to be hegemonic. It is no longer as plausible to claim that greens are mostly anarchistic (Dobson 1990; Goodin 1992). Second, there is a greater interest within green movements in achieving interim practical policy changes (Dalton 1994).

For the greens, the main reason for these shifts was that as their arguments became more influential following new evidence about climate change and other effects of pollution at the end of the 1980s, greens themselves received more attention. They not only had to alter their emphasis from demanding recognition of problems to providing solutions, but also had to develop new relationships with both political opponents and the general public. Most greens had believed that their vision of a different kind of society would seem more attractive once there was greater awareness of the scale of the ecological crisis. When this did not happen, and when the rise in support for green issues and parties reached a plateau, they were forced to reconsider their strategies.

This produced a certain kind of realism about liberal democracy, which has meant that the accent is now less on absolute rejection. Nevertheless greens are still radicals and their radicalism on issues such as the scope and depth of democracy still distinguishes them from those environmentalists who do not link their defence of the natural environment to any wider project for political change. Even if they no longer want to do away with liberal democracy greens do want to change it in radical ways. Of course, despite its hegemony in the post-1989 period, liberal democracy is not the only form of democracy and while greens may be more prepared to accept its institutional forms, they remain sceptical about its ethos and practices.

The traditional liberal eschewal of any role for the public sphere beyond the defence of the rights necessary to allow individuals to pursue their own version of the good life now seems increasingly questionable. For greens, the ecological crisis has exposed the extent to which liberal democracy has never questioned the domination of nature by humanity.

Not all the contributors to this volume endorse the radicalism of the greens. There are no proposals to do away with liberal democracy, rather there is a general interest in how green politics raises normative and analytic questions which might call for changes in our understanding of the form and scope of democracy. The three areas of analysis are the discourse of green movements on democracy, the status of democracy within green political thought and the political institutions necessary to a green democracy. Each of these themes will be introduced below and related to the chapters in this volume.

THE DISCOURSE OF GREEN MOVEMENTS

In the 1990s greens are radicals as far as democracy is concerned; they want to extend and deepen it. But there are other traditions of political ecology and these have not always been democratic. Anna Bramwell (1989) has emphasised the importance of what she calls the Nordic tradition of ecology. There is a major ideological gulf between today's greens and the reactionary ecologists of the inter-war years. Yet, fears have also been expressed about the anti-liberal potential of contemporary greens by their political opponents. The call by greens to adopt particular kinds of lifestyle has been seen as a narrow form of Calvinism. Andrew McHallam regards greens as 'The New Authoritarians' (1991), because he believes that their solutions can be achieved only by a state that is prepared to take over large areas of economic activity. If greens represent a threat to capitalism, then for those who believe that economic liberty and political liberty are indivisible, greens are a threat to true liberal democracy. Here, however, the criticism is outdated, since few greens now propose a non-market alternative to capitalism, and even fewer support planning as an alternative since it is seen as too bureaucratic and centralised. Instead, green political and economic alternatives cut across traditions of both left and right in giving priority to decentralisation.

Green arguments for decentralisation are of two kinds: those based on arguments from ecology and those based on arguments from democracy. From an ecological standpoint greens view decentralisation as essential because it is less wasteful of resources, giving priority to local production and consumption rather than the production and transport of goods for a global market. But some greens also argue that political institutions need to be reorganised more fundamentally to allow human beings to get back in touch with the land. These 'bio-regionalists' argue that we need to 'reinhabit' (Berg 1978) the land, as a precondition of understanding our own role in the natural world. Learning from nature rather than trying to dominate and suppress nature might also mean learning to live in communities determined by natural boundaries. The size of such bio-regions would be determined by the area needed to sustain a stable community with minimal disruption of its ecological balance. Hence bio-regions in desert environments would cover a larger area than those in rich farmlands. Reorganising human settlement in this way would mean living within the constraints set by the natural world. It would also clearly entail major political changes, challenging the power of the nation-state – one of the central products of modernity – and reversing the globalisation of the post-war era. There are therefore good reasons to be cautious about making the green case dependent on such a radical shift and most green parties and movements have taken inspiration from such ideas but argued for less far-reaching forms of political reorganisation.

Through bio-regionalism and other, less radical, proposals greens have made the need for stronger politics of community central to their discourse. Michael Kenny (Chapter 1) sees both strengths and weaknesses in this. On the one hand, he says that greens tend to use community without paying sufficient attention to its multiple meanings. On the other hand, greens can 'enrich and deepen' our understanding of community by showing how 'we are embedded not only in human "constitutive communities" but also within much larger biotic ones'. One of the weaknesses of the green conception of community is that it is too solidaristic and makes no allowance for the 'difference' of minorities who might be threatened by the dominant group. Kenny says that green arguments for the importance of a sense of place are quite compatible with the kind of multi-dimensional understanding of community advanced by Iris Marion Young and Seyla Benhabib. In the latters' arguments individuals are seen as both rational beings and concrete others with histories and identities embedded in overlapping and cross-cutting communities. Acknowledging individuals as 'concrete others' could provide a foundation for an ethic of justice based on a situated notion of care which might embrace non-human as well as human interests. Kenny says that 'if greens face the impossibility of privileging one communitarian identity – the ecological – over others in a rigid way' then they will be better placed to negotiate the sociological realities of modernity. Furthermore, the principle of alterity which suggests that our identity is formed by and depends on engagement with others who are different from ourselves presents a contrasting possibility to the dominant form of green communitarianism. It suggests that our sense of self 'may involve not only greater embeddedness in [our] constitutive communities but occasional or frequent escape from them into the "other".'

As was noted, not all the arguments for extending democracy made by greens depend on an ecological starting point. Greens have been among

4

the most radical of advocates of participatory democracy in the 1980s and 1990s. In their organisation green parties and many grassroots green groups have tried to counter what they see as the dominance of political organisations by bureaucracies and leaders. The latter are seen as unresponsive to new ideas and unwilling to share their power with the grassroots of the party or movement. This means that existing political organisations are no longer able to act as effective channels of representation in society and this contributes to their failure to deal effectively with the crises facing humanity and the natural world (Kitschelt 1989; Poguntke 1993).

Historically and sociologically the ideas on democracy of most of the western European green parties developed from the models provided by the New Left in the late 1960s and from the practices of the new social movements in the 1970s and 1980s. The challenge to the bureaucratic character of modern government, and the call for self-management were unifying elements of the discourse of the New Left. In their praxis women's movements tried to overcome the barriers which had made personal experiences secondary to the struggle to reach the end of liberation; and anti-nuclear and peace movements took up the theme that the means of change must be consistent with the ends sought in making nonviolence central to their action.

Brian Doherty (Chapter 2) explores this latter theme of the relationship between means and ends in his analysis of the position of green parties on nonviolence. Green parties in Europe have given greater priority to making nonviolence an end of green politics than green theorists and this is because of the influence of non-ecological movements on the green parties.

The strategic problems posed by making nonviolence an end of green strategy are most obvious in the case of a green government. Doherty argues that because green parties pursue several competing ends they are right not to refuse the chance to exercise power, even if this means taking responsibility for exercising the use of force. Moreover, making this choice does not mean giving up on nonviolence. As long as green policies are directed towards reducing the use of violence and challenging the view that violence is inevitable, green parties are being both morally consistent and strategically realistic. A second problem for political theory arises from the greens' highly conditional sense of political obligation. For greens, civil disobedience is a potentially legitimate expression of active citizenship. Only when it becomes violent are the rights of other citizens threatened and this cuts across traditional debates about civil disobedience in a novel way. In practice, however, this optimism about a protesting democracy has been tempered by the decline of protest activity in the new social movements since the mid-1980s. In similar vein, the initial hopes of green parties, that by creating a new type of party they could help to usher in a more participatory democracy, have been tempered by the experience of intra-party conflicts.

The greens' advocacy of participatory democracy extends well beyond the reorganisation of parties. If they have been forced to accept certain compromises as far as party organisation and strategy is concerned, perhaps they should place more emphasis on forms of democratisation outside the political sphere? One such form of democratisation that has been central to the green project has been the reorganisation of work. Greens argue that the hierarchical organisation of the workplace concentrates too much economic and bureaucratic power in the hands of too few. They argue in favour of placing more emphasis on the informal economy, for a secure basic income independent of work (to provide individuals with more autonomy in their work) and for a redistribution of available work (to overcome the dangers of a polarisation between a skilled labour aristocracy and an insecure, marginalised and low-paid labour poor).

One means for achieving this, repeatedly advanced by greens, has been the workers' co-operative. Neil Carter (Chapter 3) argues that greens generally assert the value of co-operatives without making an adequate argument in their favour. Greens hope that co-operatives will enhance local democracy and lead to a more egalitarian organisation of work. They also believe that co-operatives will be more environmentally benign than the existing capitalist firms. But, as Carter shows, the actual experience of co-operatives often contradicts such hopes. For instance, rather than en-couraging wider political participation outside work, co-operatives seem to have either no effect on participation, or even to encourage more privatised behaviour. Moreover, many co-operatives are hierarchically organised and have less equality of skill and income than their proponents would suggest. Theories of degeneration, such as those advanced by Roberto Michels and Beatrice and Sidney Webb, show that the greens need to consider more than just the question of formal ownership and control of the workplace. Informal processes such as the role of founder members and leaders, the organisation of the workplace and the pressures of the wider capitalist economy may also play a role. Here, the greens' experience of the internal and external pressures on the party organisation parallels the case made by Carter regarding co-operatives.

Concerning the environmental responsiveness of co-operatives, Carter sees some good reasons for believing that local ownership of co-operatives will mean that they are more responsive to their local environments. But, if job interests clash with environmental ones it is not clear that environ-mental needs will necessarily be given priority, and this would be even less the case if environmental damage was likely to fall outside the local area. Carter argues that many of the 'heroic assumptions about the capacity of the co-operative organisational form to produce certain values, attitudes and behaviour amongst its members' do not stand up. There are still some good reasons for supporting co-operatives but they will not of themselves achieve all the goals that greens demand of them.

GREEN POLITICS AND DEMOCRATIC THEORY

If the greens' commitment to participatory democracy depends con-
siderably on the ideas and experiences of other new social movements it
might be questioned whether there is anything specifically ecological about
the green view of democracy. Indeed, to consider green political thought
and democracy as related may seem odd. If the core of green political theory
concerns the political issues that arise from arguing that nature has some
intrinsic value it is hard to see what this has to do with democracy. After all,
despite the multiple meanings given to democracy in the twentieth century
the most consistent meaning of democracy has been 'rule by the people',
(Arblaster 1994: 9). In whatever way 'the people' is defined, it does not
include non-human species or the natural world. If nature cannot be part
of the people then nature cannot rule in a democracy. Yet, the questions
raised by greens do pose two very specific challenges to this position.

First, the nature of ecological problems suggests the need to consider a
redefinition of the form of the democratic community. The impact of
pollution may affect those living well beyond the place where it was created
which suggests the need to think about democratisation at a transnational
level. Furthermore, the impact of contemporary ecological degradation
may be most keenly felt by those living in the future at a time well beyond
the point when the degradation was caused. This suggests the need to think
about how obligations to future generations might be related to democracy.

A second, more radical, possibility suggested by greens concerns the
expansion of the moral community. If we ask 'Are human beings part of
nature?' and the answer is yes, and if, moreover, the boundaries between
humanity and the natural world are blurred and uncertain, then it is harder
to be categorical about restricting democracy to rule by the people. The
main controversy is not over whether nature should have votes. Rather, it
centres on the degree to which, if it is accepted that nature has intrinsic
value, this influences the kind of democracy envisaged. On one side are
those who argue that democracy can be defined in terms of specific rights
and procedures necessary to achieve the aim of responsive rule. On the
other are those who believe that democracy depends on particular positive
values, such as justice and autonomy and that the definition of these
principles regarding nature will influence the form that democracy takes.

Arguments critical of the view that greens are necessarily committed to a
particular kind of ecological democracy have been made by Robert Goodin
(1992) and Michael Saward (1993). Goodin argues that there is a distinction
that greens fail to acknowledge in their theory between a theory of value
(about the natural world) and a theory of agency (about how to act
politically). The core of green ideology, and its coherence, lies in the
argument that the natural world has intrinsic value. This has practical
consequences and demands that we defend the self-reproducing character

7

of the natural world against the kind of damage that humans are currently visiting upon it. Other green arguments, for instance, in favour of radical decentralisation, nonviolence, or for radically different lifestyles, are not necessary in order to defend the integrity of the natural world. Worse still, they may actually hamper the chances of doing what is necessary. In arguing that means must be consistent with ends, greens confuse too many different things. Participatory democracy may be desirable in itself, but it is separate from the issue of valuing and defending the natural world. And, if support for participatory democracy and other elements of the green theory of agency alienate potential supporters they should not be allowed to take priority over saving the natural world. Goodin's argument finds an echo in arguments within green parties over the appropriate scope of green ideology. In France, Antoine Waechter, erstwhile *de facto* leader of the French greens, has split from the main party and rejected its commitment to social and organisational radicalism. A similar impatience led to the criticism of the British Green Party by two of its best known figures, Sara Parkin and Jonathon Porritt, who were tired of the insistence by party activists that they remain consistent with the full range of green radicalism, a position that they saw as damaging the party's priority of saving the world from ecological disaster.

Michael Saward (Chapter 4) has argued previously that there are no good reasons for accepting prevailing green assumptions about the compatibility of democracy and ecology (Saward 1993). He has pointed to the problems with justifying political structures in the way that bio-regionalists do, by drawing selectively on examples from the natural world. He has also raised questions about whether the green claims for the value of small-scale communities are really justified. Rather than strengthening democracy he sees the confusion of ecological and democratic goals as posing the danger that when they are in conflict, democracy might be sacrificed to ecological imperatives. Greens' highly instrumental attachment to democracy leaves them open to the danger that their arguments will produce authoritarian solutions.

This argument is developed further in Saward's contribution to this book. He maintains the stress on a view of democracy as a self-sufficient idea which is threatened by attempts to mix it with other, possibly worthy, but extraneous propositions. Saward offers an essentially empirical definition of democracy; democracy is justified as the best means to take account of the essential fallibility of human knowledge. Since no individual can demonstrate any claim to superior knowledge perpetually, political author-ity should be limited. From this follows an assumption that no one person has better insight into the citizenry's right course of action than another. Assuming such equality means that only decisions that correspond with the expressed preferences of the majority of citizens can be justified. Democ-racies require the familiar forms of defence against the rule of the majority being used against the rights of minorities. Other rights to forms of welfare are also recognised as necessary to make democracy meaningful. If the right to adequate health care is one such right it can be argued empirically that this embraces some environmental threats to health. Thus the right to an undegraded environment can be supported as a consequence of the right to adequate health care.

This is the most that can be done regarding building environmental considerations into democratic procedures. Other issues such as according intrinsic value to nature cannot be part of a constitution designed to defend democracy. Saward argues that with the exception of a right to action aimed at dealing with preventable risks to health, democracy remains separate from environmental imperatives, although democracy will not necessarily always be more important than them. If Saward is right then there is no necessary link between the most general ecological arguments of greens and democracy. His argument is contested, however, in the other chapters in this section.

Mike Mills (Chapter 5) argues that for greens expanding the moral community to include nature takes priority over other ethical concerns. His focus is on whether expanding the moral community means expanding the political community. Accepting that Saward is correct in stressing the danger that the green concern with outcomes could pose a threat to the procedures of democracy, Mills argues that this problem can be overcome only by including nature in the processes of democracy. This means that the processes of democracy should reflect consideration of the rights and interests of the non-human world. If nature could be represented in certain forms (even if by humans acting on its behalf) this would mean that the moral community and the political community would become more con-gruent. Mills does not aim to show that ecocentrism is merely compatible with democracy, but rather that it can become compatible with democracy only if ecocentric concerns are made part of the process of democracy, without entailing specific policy ends. Thus, reformulating the demo-cratic process to represent the interests of the natural world will not guarantee that specific policies will be adopted, but it should mean that non-human interests will be considered alongside human ones.

John Barry (Chapter 6) takes a more human-centred line; he argues that sustainability must be understood as a normative concept since it embodies a particular moral attitude to future generations of human beings. Implicit in Barry's position is the view that the interests of the non-human world can be secured by defending sustainability on the grounds of our moral responsibility to future generations. It follows that sustainability is primarily a political-ethical rather than a technical concept since many of the questions that it raises demand normative answers. For instance, how far in the future should we look and whose interests count for most when there are conflicting interests? If this is so, it allows greens to make some traditional arguments for democracy – for instance, as the best means for dealing with problems that require judgements about competing interests and the uncertainties of the future.

Barry's conception of democracy is essentially discursive. For him, democracy is not simply about how to articulate a given set of preferences expressed by citizens; a position which sets him at odds with Saward. And for greens the process of transforming preferences is a means of creating a specific kind of citizenship. Moreover, Barry argues that the imperatives of green politics point to the need for a form of citizenship based on a strong conception of civic virtue, embracing duties that go beyond the formally political realm.

Andrew Dobson (Chapter 7) also includes a commitment to a form of discursive democracy. He provides an overview of the central positions on the status of democracy in green political theory and drawing from these he makes a strong argument that democracy is connected to green theory in more than a purely instrumental way. The first problem he addresses is that of relying on sustainability as the precondition for a green democracy. Dobson says 'The problem with working at this level of generality, though, is that it is possible to use [sustainability] to endorse virtually any process of decision making. It is as true of authoritarians as it is of democrats that they need an ecologically viable society within which to operate.' However, if democracy can be justified discursively because it is the most open form of decision making, it can also be argued to be the form of decision making most likely to produce the right sort of answers as far as nature is concerned. This is because it allows for more open expression and representation of conflicting perspectives on the nature of the ecological crisis and the most appropriate means for dealing with it. If greens are right about nature then democracy gives the best chance of such ideas emerging, although it cannot guarantee that they will be those that greens want.

Yet, this leaves only instrumental reasons for greens to favour democracy. If greens are as concerned with means, or process, as with achieving the right outcomes, or ends, they will want to find a defence of democracy as right in itself. Taking up Robyn Eckersley's argument in her chapter, Dobson says that the autonomy of humans is necessary to democracy and the autonomy of other species is necessary to the green critique of the human domination of the natural world. But the rights specified by Eckersley, such as the right to freedom from harmful ecological actions, can be seen as applicable to any system of decision making and not just to democracy.

Dobson says that autonomy can provide the basis for a theory of justice which has a naturalistic basis in that it includes needs that humans share with other species, but it also needs to be balanced by a recognition of the material preconditions for democracy. Combining the two preconditions,

10

sustainability and autonomy, shows how ecology and democracy are linked for greens and that greens are right to be concerned with both outcomes and processes.

THE INSTITUTIONS OF A GREEN DEMOCRACY

If ecology poses some new questions regarding the nature of representation and the boundaries of democracy, it also reinforces the relevance of some more traditional ones. One of these concerns the problem of legitimacy. The justification of the view that the ecological crisis may pose a threat to democracy has mostly depended on the likelihood that ecological problems will undermine political stability and that this will lead to an erosion of the legitimacy of liberal democracy. Perhaps the most plausible reason is the fact that the scale of ecological problems might be beyond the scope of national governments to deal with. As governments prove ineffective, for instance in preventing rising sea levels or feeding their populations adequately, they could lose legitimacy in the eyes of their people. Yet, real though these problems are, they are problems of the effectiveness of nation-states rather than necessarily problems of democracy. Indeed, those states in the Third World that would suffer most from the effects of such instability are least likely to be liberal democracies. Yet, the arguments of 'survivalists' are a reminder that it is possible to use the ecological crisis to support anti-democratic arguments. Survivalists argue that the coming change is so severe that only a concentration of power will be effective enough to achieve a solution.

Apocalyptic thinking of this kind has played an important part in the green movement, especially in its formation. Leading figures within green movements, such as Herbert Gruhl in the early days of the German greens and Edward Goldsmith in the British greens, have combined doom-laden predictions with a call for urgent and effective action by a strong government. Impatience with moderates because 'Time is Short' was also a motive for the actions of those like Dave Foreman, who founded the direct action organisation Earth First! in the USA. The misanthropic comments of some within Earth First!, such as the view that Aids and famines were useful means of controlling over-population, soon became infamous. They did not represent either Earth First! in general, or a view that is widespread among greens. However, they do show how apocalyptic thinking can lead to a focus only on what is to be done, rather than how it is to be done.

If warnings about an ecological apocalypse pose the danger that green arguments will lead to an anti-democratic outcome, then it is especially important to consider how greens can be effective as democrats. The chapters in Part III provide various answers to this question, but all share a concern with the institutional basis for an effective democratic ecological politics.

Peter Christoff (Chapter 8) looks at the prospects for building new forms of citizenship that are capable of responding to the challenges of globalisation, including the transnational character of ecological issues. He points out that the relationship between citizen and nation-state is already one of considerable tension; for, whilst the nation-state remains the main site of its expression (since formal citizenship must be attached to an identifiable and legally bounded political community), citizenship no longer seems to be exclusively tied to any one nation-state. He says that the democratic content of the concept of citizenship is increasingly being dissociated from its formal expression in a post-national political environment. Christoff then investigates how we might institutionalise stronger democracy so that it is equipped to deal with complex ecological decisions and argues that it is of vital importance to include and enfranchise all those with an identifiable vital interest in the outcome. This also means that existing humans must assume responsibility for future generations and other species and 'represent' their interests and potential choices according to the duties of environmental stewardship. Ecological citizenship can be defined by its attempt to extend social welfare discourse to recognise 'universal' principles relating to environmental rights and to incorporate these in law, culture and politics.

Whereas Christoff's focus is beyond the nation-state, Marius de Geus (Chapter 10) investigates the question of why many discussions of the environmental question conclude that increased state interference in society is necessary. He rejects statist solutions of this kind, but is equally critical of radical green arguments such as those of Murray Bookchin, chief theorist of 'social ecology', that renounce the state and market economy altogether. He argues that there is a feasible alternative.

In examining the existing models of ecological change de Geus comes to the conclusion that the model of piecemeal engineering based upon modest reforms and change is ineffective. But, on the other hand, the radical utopian model that seeks far-reaching changes and a fundamental transformation of society will also produce a range of unexpected new problems and unintended consequences. He argues instead for middle range reforms, what he calls 'ecological restructuring'. This is a model of change that can skirt the shortcomings of both 'piecemeal' and 'utopian' engineering. De Geus then discusses the basic principles for the ecological restructuring of society and argues for a green market economy in combination with a freedom-oriented and ultra-flexible state that is capable of countering environmental problems on exactly the scale that they occur. This 'ecostate' will have to concentrate primarily on creating situations and conditions that will make it attractive for citizens to make environmentally friendly choices. The central question this poses for green politics is not whether the liberal democratic state must be done away with, but how it can be adapted to become more democratic and in such a way that environmental policies can be implemented effectively.

Wouter Achterberg (Chapter 9) also deals with the difficulty of creating a climate in which ecological reforms can be undertaken. He argues that the political challenges posed by sustainability are underestimated, especially now that sustainability has become a term in widespread use and with varied meanings. He charts the history of such usages since the 1970s, but argues that the central presupposition of sustainability has remained unchanged: the need for substantial social changes to deal with the problems posed by the ecological crisis. One of the central problems is developing the kinds of community solidarity that could achieve measures such as the global distribution of wealth. This is where the institutional changes suggested by proponents of associative democracy could help. Existing forms of liberal democracy give priority to the protection of individual interests and property rights, but they lack strong forms of associational life. Expanding the role of civic associations within democratic decision making could help to overcome this problem. For greens, a disadvantage of associative democracy is that it could develop only gradually. But it also has the advantage of being a change that can convincingly be seen as positive, when the answers to larger problems are not yet clear. Achterberg does not argue that associative democracy is a necessary part of a green conception of democracy, but he does believe that it will make achieving sustainability easier by providing the institutional form most likely to build global and intergenerational solidarities.

Robyn Eckersley (Chapter 11) is also concerned with reforms to liberal democracy, but her focus is on expanding the discourse of rights to include the natural world. She argues that liberal democracy under-represents ecological concerns, first because it represents only existing citizens of territorially bounded communities, excluding as non-citizens those in the present and future who might be affected by decisions by a particular state. Second, because its own citizens depend for their own protection on poorly resourced environmental groups arguing for long-term interests against well-resourced groups able to appeal to specific short-term interests. One result of this is that environmental interests are treated in a utilitarian manner as sectional and open to bargaining and trade-offs, when really they are universal interests.

Eckersley argues that rights-based theories have advantages over utilitarian ones (including discursive democracy) because by specifying the limits of action by the state and individuals they provide a better defence for people and the natural world against the tyranny of a (human) majority. One problem with rights is that they are usually based on individuals' interests whereas greens are concerned with social and ecological wholes, but if the individual is part of a whole, autonomy can be seen as a mediating point between individual and collective interests. *Contra* Saward, Eckersley

13

argues that we cannot develop a theory of democracy without enlisting some kind of theory of autonomy and justice. The main disagreement between greens and liberals is not over the meaning or form of democracy, but instead over the meaning and scope of autonomy and justice.

For greens concerned with rights the central problem with environmental rights is whether they create duties that can be enforced practically. In cases of conflicts with other rights a choice would have to be made, but defining environmental concerns in terms of rights has the advantage of providing a stronger benchmark of principle which would make it more difficult to trade off such rights lightly. Eckersley does not present environmental rights as a panacea for the green movement on the problem of democracy, but accepting that in the new mood of 'political realism' the environment is likely to have to work within the constraints of liberal democratic institutions, they are presented as a vehicle for critique and practical reform.

A GREEN DEMOCRACY?

The chapters in this book reveal the richness of the dilemmas that arise from the collision between democracy and green thought. On the critical side those who write on the discourse of radical greens have shown that greens still have considerable work to do in fleshing out the weaker elements in their democratic arguments. In particular the lack of an adequate green theory of power is an implicit problem recognised in the chapters by Kenny, Doherty and Carter. In the contributions by Saward, Mills, Barry, Dobson and Eckersley there is an argument not simply about the compatibility of green concerns and democratic ones, but also about what democracy is. On the latter question there are, of course, multiple traditions. In this book at least three partially distinct approaches are identifiable – discursive (Barry and Dobson), associational (Achterberg) and liberal democracy (Saward). But beyond this, a central controversy remains the extent to which a green democracy will be a post-liberal democracy; working with the forms of liberal democracy, but expanding them to include the natural world as the chapters by Eckersley and Mills suggest.

Among those who defend the view that there is a basic compatibility between green ideology and democracy a number of different arguments are identifiable. Mills and Eckersley both argue that liberal democracy is in principle ecologically biased and that rights discourse is fluid and extendiable and can be developed into new institutions. There are also arguments that suggest that green ideas are new because they introduce new preconditions – both ecological and social – for democracy (see the chapters by Dobson and Barry). On the other hand it is recognised that sustainability is too general a precondition to guide us to specifically democratic means of resolving the ecological crisis.

14

The context in which green arguments must be made is also an important theme in several chapters. For instance, Achterberg, Barry and Kenny stress the view that only democratically reached agreements will stick. Others argue that for democracy to work in the context of the ecological crisis new institutions will be needed, though not revolutionary political changes (Christoff and de Geus). The obstacles and limits placed on projects for radical change by the nature of capitalism and the existing political institutions are themes for de Geus, Carter, Christoff and Achterberg.

This book does not cover all the issues connecting green politics and democratic theory, for instance the internal organisation of green parties and the specific character of the threats to political stability posed by the ecological crisis are not dealt with, but these have already been debated elsewhere in some depth (Poguntke 1993; Walker 1988). In contrast, questions of democratic theory have had less attention, hitherto. The themes that recur throughout the book – Is liberal democracy ecologically biased? Is there a green theory of justice that shapes the green view of democracy? How might states be designed that meet green criteria? – have been explored here for the first time. If these issues remain disputed and unresolved in this collection, this is itself testimony to the new possibilities for democratic theory brought face to face with nature in a new political form.

REFERENCES

Arblaster, A. (1994) *Democracy*, Milton Keynes: Open University Press.

Berg, P. (ed.) (1978) *Reinhabiting a Separate Country: A Bioregional Anthology of Northern California*, San Francisco: Planet Drum Foundation.

Bramwell, A. (1989) *Ecology in the Twentieth Century*, London: Yale University Press.

Dalton, R. (1994) *The Green Rainbow*, London: Yale University Press.

Dobson, A. (1990) *Green Political Thought*, London: Unwin Hyman.

Goodin, R. (1992) *Green Political Theory*, Cambridge: Polity.

Heilbroner, R. L. (1974) *An Enquiry into the Human Prospect* (1991), New York: Norton.

Kitschelt, H. (1989) *The Logic of Party Formation*, Durham, NC: Duke University Press.

McHallam, A. (1991) *The New Authoritarians*, London: Institute for European and Defence Studies.

Ophuls, W. (1977) *Ecology and the Politics of Scarcity*, New York: Freeman.

Poguntke, T. (1993) 'Goodbye to Movement Politics?', *Environmental Politics* 2, 3: 379–404.

Saward, M. (1993) 'Green Democracy', in A. Dobson, and P. Lucardie (eds) *The Politics of Nature*, London: Routledge.

Walker, K. (1988) 'The State of Environmental Management', *Political Studies* 37, 1: 25–38.

Part I

THE
DISCOURSE
OF
GREEN MOVEMENTS

1

PARADOXES OF COMMUNITY

Michael Kenny

The concept of community is one of the most widely used, but least analysed, terms in green political discourse. Whilst community is interpreted and applied in a variety of ways by greens, it can be depicted in a more universal, or ideal-typical, manner in terms of the role it plays within ecological discourse and the types of problems which are connected with its usage. Theoretical tensions arise from the normative claims attached to community and from the tendency to confuse different kinds of arguments when community is invoked.

Community is frequently seen as a core value within the ecologically sound society which greens hope to create. As Michael Saward puts it, 'commonly, the hope and the belief is that truly ecological societies will be small, decentralized communities with decision-making procedures based on "direct" rather than "representative" democracy' (1993: 63). In addition, community is repeatedly presented by some ecologists as a political means toward this goal (Dobson 1990: 199). For a minority in the green movement, the construction of ecologically sustainable communes constitutes the most meaningful political strategy that greens can pursue (Bahro 1986). Small-scale communities, according to this perspective, will provide a social form more conducive to the values of ecology than other forms. This argument is echoed by commentators who regard the ends–means interpenetration of ecological communitarianism as a source of intellectual strength: 'the principal advantage of community strategies for change is that they anticipate the advertised Green future, particularly its decentralized communitarian aspects' (Dobson 1990: 149).

Unfortunately, the claim that community sits neatly within the value-set of political ecology, and is thus a necessary precondition of a society founded on ecological principles, is weaker than it first appears. Ecological communitarians rarely consider possible tensions between community and the core principles of ecology, or how these different imperatives might be 'traded' against each other. What, for example, would prevent the principles of ecology requiring that a particular society abandon a communitarian ethos because of the 'higher' demands of ecological security?

One of the most popular justifications for the place of community within the value-set of ecology provides little help here: the claim that values appropriate to ecology can be derived from nature does not provide a solid epistemological foundation for naturalistic political arguments, as Saward demonstrates (1993). Despite these problems, many greens – not just deep or dark ones – refer to a naturalistic ideal of community and suggest that it would be ecologically and socially advantageous if we lived in tightly knit, solidaristic communities akin to those which characterised pre-industrial society. This impression is reinforced by the prevalence of organic metaphors in the varieties of green political thought. The communal life of the sustainable future is presumed to be one where the individual's fate will depend on a close symbiotic relationship with a clearly defined social (or ecological) *telos.*

When greens cite community as one of the normative preconditions for sustainability, however, it is not clear that they can justify this claim. In fact, community can be only contingently related to ecology. This point is especially pertinent in the context of debates about how sustainability might be connected to democracy. Contrary to the views of many political ecologists, community is not necessarily linked to either; nor can it guarantee a relationship between them.

Confusion is also generated by the interweaving of normative and empirical arguments typical of ecological communitarianism. Greens, like other radicals, use community to advance a number of critical observations about the weaknesses of contemporary society – especially the trend towards the alienation of the individual in modern industrial society – without separating out the different senses of this concept. Three interpretations are routinely confused: a nostalgic historical reading of community as a principle which underpinned social relations in the past; a sociological assertion that the bonds of community are under threat from the market; and a normative view that the ethics of community ought to determine the political and economic shape of contemporary society. For greens, community carries extra implications. It encourages the imaginative blurring of the boundaries between human and other members of the larger biotic community and expresses the distinctive commitment many greens feel for a 'politics of place' – a sense that the natural environment in which people live has been under-represented in conventional political ideologies and traditions.

Community is therefore firmly established in the green political lexicon, though its different senses are routinely confused and conflated. Its rather vague metaphorical status encourages greens to evade difficult questions about its normative implications, some of which are traced below. As we shall see, its current usage not only confuses different kinds of arguments but also carries some highly undemocratic implications. The difficulties connected with ecological communitarianism need careful consideration.

In the process of rethinking the relationship between communitarianism and ecology, greens would benefit from attention to the insights offered by some leading (non-ecological) communitarian thinkers, as well as from insights drawn from the ongoing debates about the concepts of difference and alterity.

Before we assess these non-ecological ideas, however, we need to understand the connections between conventional green usages of community and some of the weaknesses which commentators have observed in green political arguments more generally.

PROBLEMS OF COMMUNITY IN GREEN DISCOURSE

Community may well constitute the 'locus' of some of the paradoxes which characterise green politics. This argument runs counter to the arguments of those critics who view the ends–means interpenetration of ecological communitarianism as a strength: community, it seems to me, is more likely to exacerbate than resolve the weaknesses of green political thought. The most important problems to have surfaced in the literature on this subject include: first, the tension between the libertarian and authoritarian sides of ecologism (Lewis 1992); second, the conflict between homogeneity and diversity within the green political imagination (Dobson 1990: 121–2); third, the fundamentalist hostility towards the world of conventional politics which ecologism often encourages (Jones 1993); and fourth, the ambivalence towards democracy which characterises ecologism (Saward 1993). Taking these criticisms in turn, each can be connected to the implications of green usages of community.

First, community for many greens combines a libertarian emphasis upon decentralisation, self-government and the absence of external restraint – particularly the state – with a belief that these communities will uphold an ecological version of the 'good life'. When combined with a strong sense of the ecological good, green communitarianism engenders some controversial policy preferences. These are implicitly justified by a conception of the 'ecological general will' within particular communities. This leads greens to neglect the dangers of superimposing the values of ecology on to a *gemeinschaft* model of community and to reproduce some of the most troubling aspects of 'general will' theory – the lack of emphasis on minorities and inattention to individual rights (Crick 1962).

Andrew Dobson's discussion of the support for strong immigration policies which some greens have enunciated is a striking example of the indifference to minority rights which ecological communitarianism encourages (1990: 82; 96–7). Support for immigration controls is one policy outcome of the commitment to population reduction – and the latter is stressed by some commentators as a litmus test for 'true' greens (Eckersley 1992: 157–60). Whilst many greens would not support such measures (most famously, the German greens) this defence of minority rights could be submerged beneath the *gemeinschaft* logic of ecological communitarianism. This trades on tight-knit and organic images of communal life which seem at odds with the ethnic and religious diversity of multi-cultural and multi-community modern societies. As Dobson shows, the green commitment to people living 'in place', in stable, well-defined and self-reliant communities, generates suspicion about external influences, alien presences and the cosmopolitan and destabilising aspects of *gesellschaft*. This explains the hostility enunciated by eco-utopians such as Rudolf Bahro to the idea of excessive trade and external travel in the sustainable communities of the future. Similarly, some commentators suspect that 'deviants' or criminals in the sustainable society would receive unduly severe punishment (Lewis 1992).

Of course, greens believe that these problems are more likely to characterise modern industrial society where fleeting and unsatisfying 'wants' – epitomised and artificially stimulated by the growth of an advertising nexus – engender a culture of greed and individual acquisition. This assumption, however, ignores the coercive possibilities arising from the connection between ecological goals and communitarian politics. Members of minority or 'deviant' groups have little reason to be reassured by these ideas. Like other 'strong' communitarians, greens prefer the cohesion and solidarity of community to liberal conceptions of individual rights. But the community which lacks a language of rights and denies access to a higher legal authority, beyond the community, runs the risk of becoming, in Gorz's words, 'a prison' (Frankel 1987: 59). Whilst some greens are aware of these tensions and foresee some reconciliation between community and individual rights (Harvey 1993: 21–2), it is interesting to note the authoritarian connotations which opponents often attach to environmentalist ideas (Dobson 1993: 234–5). This seems perplexing to greens, yet is, to some degree, the consequence of the ideological and symbolic resonances of small-scale communitarian politics.

Second, the sustainable world conjured up by ecologism can appear one-dimensional, dull and monolithic. Greens seem to confuse their critique of choice in a modern industrial context – which, they argue, often arises from artificial and wasteful wants – with the notion of individuality itself. An important debate has emerged out of the crisis facing the left in western Europe since the 1980s, concerned with the wide range of social, political and cultural variables which shape individual identity in modern society (Giddens 1991). Yet, in contrast, ecological communitarianism suggests that the processes of 'overdetermination' can be transcended by a new, dominant identity – the ecological. In practice greens accept that these other identities will not wither away in the sustainable future and will play a key role in constituting the vitality and plurality of community life. Ultimately, though, they remain subordinate to the 'general ecological will'

22

of the community. This puts greens at odds with a range of other critical and radical theoretical currents, including feminism and the arguments of radical democrats. Consequently, it is hard to envisage ecologists connecting their strong political goals with the prevailing desire for social and cultural diversity and pluralism – a problem which socialism has also encountered (Rustin 1985).

Third, a number of commentators have remarked upon the absence of a sustained body of political theory within the green repertoire. Some of the most influential ecological philosophers have argued that greens must reject the structure, assumptions and framework of the conventional world of politics as inimical to any genuine emancipatory future (O'Riordan 1981). Only a fundamental reordering of this realm, it is argued, will bring about a more sustainable and socially solidaristic future. This fundamentalist response to the political world has left many greens out of touch with the arguments and practices of other radical movements which are committed to the wholesale democratisation and 'politicisation' of civil life (Frankel 1987: 230).

Thus, although greens benefit from the notion of the expansion of politics into everyday life which movements such as feminism have generated, in practice ecological communitarianism gives little emphasis to the idea of broadening and deepening political life. Unlike other radical currents, greens rarely prioritise the democratisation of civil life, preferring instead to imagine a world where competing interests and power relationships have disappeared (Frankel 1987: 230). Emphasis on community serves to conjure up a utopian future where present-day struggles and conflicts have no place, and downplays strategic assessment of the balance of forces arrayed against ecological emancipation. As a description of the complexity of current political economy and a strategic guide for political intervention, this metaphor remains singularly unhelpful. Its repeated usage in some green circles encourages the belief that power relationships can be transcended once humans and nature are operating harmoniously; the idea that networks of power operate throughout society, at all levels of community life, remains alien to many greens, though not because they possess a coherent alternative theory. Indeed, the absence of a distinctively ecological theory of power may constitute one of the central weaknesses of political ecology.

Significantly, despite their attention to the local and small scale, greens have also failed to explore the realm of micro-politics. Here individuals interact with each other and confront the boundaries of community life, processes which may result in the continual redefinition of individual interests and needs. The communitarianism of most greens is unable to incorporate this dimension of social life because it seeks to aggregate individual needs, suggesting that the community shapes its members' identities and defines the value-set engendered by the common good of

23

ecology. Beneath this level, however, ecological thinkers have said little about the political dimensions of the micro-relations of communal life, presenting this realm as one in which individual co-operation and eco-logical harmony obviate political questions (Naess 1989). This kind of communitarianism omits critical consideration of the process by which individual aspirations and interests are to be aggregated.

Fourth, as different commentators have observed, the relationship be-tween democracy and ecology is more problematic than the rhetoric of political ecology generally allows. Community is understood in some green thinking to constitute a vital intermediate link between these two goods, securing the connection between them (Bookchin 1982: 335–6). The argument here is that community is the form of human organisation most amenable to the delivery of sustainable policies and that, in theoretical terms, it is the form of human organisation most attuned to the imperatives of ecology. Consequently, greens have frequently tried to displace the difficult questions about the connections between democracy and ecology on to the apparently more promising terrain of communitarian arguments, supposing that these provide natural conduits to democratic practices. In fact, if community can be only contingently connected to ecological values, as I have argued above, then it cannot play the role of securing the necessary relationship between democracy and ecology. This is especially pertinent because ecological communitarianism carries some apparently undemocratic implications in terms of minority rights, pluralism and social differences.

Should greens, therefore, abandon community altogether in their polit-ical arguments? The answer to this question depends on whether com-munity can be reworked to generate a different set of political meanings and images, which may be more amenable to the requirements of demo-cratic principles.

NON-ECOLOGICAL COMMUNITARIANS

The problems associated with ecological communitarianism echo some of the central themes of the so-called liberal–communitarian debate. In fact, this is more accurately construed as an argument between liberal indi-vidualists and liberal communitarians, since much of it takes place within a shared epistemological framework and cannot be reduced to a simple binary division between two opposed sets of ideas (Schwarzenbach 1991). The work of some of the leading communitarian theorists – Alasdair MacIntyre, Michael Sandel, Charles Taylor and Michael Walzer – is full of insight into the nature and demands of community ties and identities. In this section I sketch several overlaps with green political thought and outline the possibilities which some of their ideas provide for the re-interpretation of this principle.

Much overlap exists between communitarian arguments and green ideas. Both currents believe 'that [classical] liberalism does not sufficiently take into account the importance of community for personal identity, moral and political thinking, and judgement about our well-being in the contemporary world' (Bell 1993: 4). Both reject three aspects of the liberal inheritance: its overly individualistic conception of the self (especially Rawls' notion that the self is antecedently individuated); the unfounded universalism of liberal ethical beliefs – particularly the idea that rationally conceived principles of justice can be exported to any society; and the suggestion that an individual self is constituted prior to his or her ends. For communitarians of all shades, individuals 'are . . . embodied agents "in the world", engaged in realizing a certain form of life' (Bell 1993: 43). According to Will Kymlicka, 'in a communitarian society . . . the common good is conceived of as a substantive conception of the good life which defines the community's "way of life"' (1990:· 206). In the case of putative green communities, this 'way of life' would be deeply ecological. Greens, it can be argued, enrich and deepen this notion, adding to the communitarian repertoire: we are embedded not only in human 'constitutive communities' but also within larger biotic ones. Our individual selves are deeply bound up with the geographical and ecological environment in which we develop our most important attachments. Greens suggest that the horizon which should always inform our life-choices as individuals is, in vital ways, ecological. Damaging the environment should therefore be as unnatural for communitarians as rejecting our deepest communal attachments. In this sense ecological communitarianism gives an extra dimension to the critique of liberal individualism, though communitarians have been slow to recognise the value of ecological ideas.

The parallel between liberal and ecological communitarianism makes greens equally vulnerable to some of the critical points registered by liberal individualist critics. In rejecting autonomy as the median of political life, the latter argue, communitarians risk lapsing into moral and political conservatism. This criticism echoes the problems we have already observed in ecological communitarianism. Other critics point to the difficulty in erecting a conception of justice which is not founded on some universal, and hence extra-communitarian, principles (Dworkin 1985). These have become established reference points in these debates. The major communitarian theorists have developed distinctive and diverging arguments on these questions. According to Charles Taylor (1989), for instance, our lives throw up choices between different communal attachments but we retain the capacity to reflect upon the merits and significance of these within the linguistic and intellectual traditions of our community life. Daniel Bell (1993: 39) echoes Alasdair MacIntyre in arguing that autonomy is central to communitarian concerns, because we remain capable of choosing between different traditions following a breakdown of communal

25

traditions. In both of these examples, though, the principle of autonomy is still not accepted as *a priori* or universally operative but is defined by communal traditions.

Several aspects of these arguments are especially pertinent for ecological communitarianism; so too is the development of a body of ideas in the field of communicative ethics which offers some interesting starting points for a radical reformulation of the concept of community within green thought. Whilst greens have been happy to inject a strongly communitarian logic into the relationship between human beings and nature, they have been less adept at examining the relationship between the individual and the (social) community. In particular, greens should avoid falling into the trap of assuming that all the logical alternatives in this area are exhausted by a simple division between individualism and communitarianism. If it is to justify its claim to be new, green politics needs to generate a new understanding of the relationship between these poles, rather than seek the victory of one over the other. In the wake of the problems embedded in ecological versions of community, some of the themes covered in these literatures are pertinent for greens.

DIFFERENCE AND THE SELF

One of the oldest criticisms of communitarian thinking concerns its tendency to rely upon an idealised, romantic or essentialist picture of the human self (Young 1990). Despite substantial variations here, critics point to the dependence of such visions on the goal of reintegrating the individual within the larger social totality sustained within a meaningful community. Ecological communitarianism frequently reproduces this claim, drawing upon the romantic project of recreating the 'whole' individual, presently torn apart by the conditions of modern life (Veldman 1994). Yet, the idea of a community embodying a single shared subjectivity has been challenged from a number of directions – most of all by feminists (Lacey and Fraser 1994). For these critics, this attribute of communitarian arguments has some damaging consequences, sustaining a political culture in which differences – of interest, perspective and identity – are seen as threatening. The idealised subject at the heart of communitarian thinking is all too often endowed with the features of dominant groups – defined by class, gender and race. According to Iris Young:

> The idea of community expresses a desire for the fusion of subjects with one another which in practice operates to exclude those with whom the group does not identify. The ideal of community denies and represses social difference, the fact that the polity cannot be thought of as a unity in which all participants share a common experience and common values.
>
> (Young 1990: 227)

Against the *gemeinschaft* metaphor at the heart of many communitarian arguments, with their strongly rural and arcadian overtones, she offers a radically different interpretation of community, celebrating instead the city ideal – 'a vision of social relations affirming group difference. As a normative idea, city life instantiates social relations of difference without exclusion' (Young 1990: 227). Following her rejection of *gemeinschaft* arguments, Young illustrates the possibility of avoiding the binary oppositions which frequently characterise the liberal–communitarian debate, urging communitarians to rethink the way in which they use the metaphor of community. In this she is typical of an increasing number of political and ethical theorists.

Whilst most communitarians, especially greens, place emphasis on 'shared subjectivity' or social solidarity – the realisation of the dream of 'unity through community' (Corlett 1989) – Seyla Benhabib (1982) points to a second, generally subordinated strand within communitarian thought: community as reciprocity or mutuality. This, as Young observes, involves 'the recognition by each individual of the individuality of all the others' (1990: 229). Both look to the development of an alternative communicative ethic founded on the insights of a number of modern theorists, and particularly the work of Jürgen Habermas. According to Young, we should be driven by the principle of 'the "concrete other"' to view each and every individual as a rational being with a concrete history, identity and affective-emotional constitution (1990: 231). She argues against the tendency of communitarians to abstract from our different individualities in search of our common inheritance or destiny within the community's *telos*. Instead, she conjures up a *polis* where the mutual recognition of and respect for individual differences are central. This would generate a social culture which prioritises 'responsibility, bonding and sharing', and where 'the corresponding moral feelings are those of love, care, sympathy, and solidarity, and the vision of community is one of needs and solidarity' (Young 1990: 231). This multi-dimensional and pluralistic community points to the possibility of a new metaphorical understanding of this concept as well as a new conception of human subjectivity.

This approach steers a course between strong communitarianism, on the one hand, and the 'ideal of impartiality' which underpins the central arguments of modern liberal epistemology and ethics, on the other. It suggests an alternative to the detached and asocial individual vaunted by the classical liberal tradition, lending weight to the argument that moral reason is a product of our complex communal identities. On this reading, we develop our moral perspectives as embedded, social beings and, for greens, as members of larger biotic communities. This perspective provides an interesting set of methodological possibilities for ecological ethics, some of which are traced below. Moreover, it offers an epistemological foundation for some of the most important arguments of political ecology,

supporting, for instance, the connection between place and ethical commitment central to green arguments.

Young's vision is pertinent for greens because this kind of communitarianism seeks to broaden the scope of conventional ethical arguments. It
offers the possibility of a conception of justice which is concerned with care
and responsibility and seeks to move beyond the strictly delineated moral
concerns of liberal theory. As different critics have suggested, if moral
arguments are to be extended beyond the human community to include
consideration of non-human interests, an ethic based on care and responsibility may prove more effective than one driven by tightly drawn notions
of rights and responsibilities. This brand of communitarianism also makes
the question of the most appropriate social and political arrangements a
matter for continuous rational debate, in which the public values of the
community will be openly questioned and re-evaluated.

Young's particular perspective, forged from a non-essentialist conception
of the self and a vision of humans as capable of communicative rationality,
is attuned to different aspects of the political ecological agenda. It fits neatly
with the communitarian logic of ecology, through which greens can deepen
our sense of the interaction of the different environmental and social
factors which have shaped the individual self. It is also compatible with the
arguments of John Dryzek (1987), who suggests that greens should not
reject reason altogether, but should construct an ecological rationality
which might transcend the dominant perspectives of industrial society.
Greens might, accordingly, deploy the Habermasian notion that 'subjectivity is a product of communicative interaction', and that 'moral rationality
should be understood as dialogic, the product of the interaction of a
plurality of subjects under conditions of equal power that do not suppress
the interests of any' (Dryzek 1987: 106). This is of particular relevance to
greens, concerned as they are to broaden the range of subjects involved in
this imaginary 'dialogue' beyond the human realm.

Young also sets out to overcome the recurrent concerns of critics of
communitarianism about the latter's potential for elitism, distrust of
minorities and 'thin' theory of democracy (Kymlicka 1990; Mulhall and
Swift 1992). Whether her ideas provide the basis for a communitarianism
which would necessarily be more democratic is a moot point. She says little
about the need to place boundaries on the scope of public discussion and
decision making. As Ross Harrison (1994) makes clear, however, democracy
requires the placing of limits on what can actually be decided in a
democracy. Can the rights of a particular minority be 'democratically'
suspended? This echoes one of the traditional liberal concerns about
communitarianism: how will individuals be protected from the general will
of the community? Communitarians following Young and Benhabib also
face the problem of balancing their celebration of difference against the
need to sustain a social and cultural fabric within community life. At what

point can the community limit or repress differences legitimately? It is hard to imagine a community which does not do this in some way or other. Moreover, strong communitarians ask whether a community can be meaningfully sustained if its central values have been pluralised so radically.

COMMUNITIES OF PLACE

Several critics have pointed to the problems attendant upon the celebration of face-to-face communal relations which recur in the utopian arguments of many greens. As Young points out, underlying the notion of face-to-face community lies the ideal of creating unmediated social relations which will automatically produce a more democratic politics. But the idea that such communities will sustain more 'authentic' and democratic internal relations avoids the political question of how to establish just relations among different decentralised communities and mistakenly assumes that it is possible to abolish the mediation of relations between persons (Young 1990: 233). However small the community, spatial and temporal differentiation means that human communication will always be mediated – by language, gesture and convention, for example. Likewise, small-scale communities have been presented by some ecologists as conducive to more benign and harmonious relations between humans and non-human nature. Again, this perspective underplays the depth and complexity of the mediations between humans and nature. In particular, the idea of abolishing all such mediations by returning to a small-scale, *gemeinschaft* living pattern cuts against the grain of modern society in so many ways that it is hard to imagine the profundity and depth of the cultural revolution which this shift would necessitate.

Emphasis upon the small scale also tends to obscure the question of the multiplicity of communal attachments which individuals currently feel and are bound to experience in any imaginable future. This insight is central to the visions of some of the leading communitarian theorists. The notion of multiple and overlapping constitutive communities developed by Taylor (1989), for example, highlights the contingency and complexity of individual identity in modern society within a communitarian framework. Greens seem to have scarcely begun to think through the implications of this kind of diversity in the future sustainable society.

Community might be reformulated from this angle to bolster the arguments of political ecology. Greens have a particularly strong sense of the importance of the spatial and territorial dimensions of human life. Their commitment to a politics of place should encourage them to recognise, and indeed celebrate, the different levels and kinds of community ties which individuals experience. In other words, the basis for a specifically green politics of identity lies in their recognition that one of the distinctive features of modern life is the interplay between these different communities of geography, interest and belief. In particular, greens should

29

mobilise the attachments which many feel to their immediate locale, neighbourhood or community, whilst allowing for individuals' need to transcend these in different ways and move meaningfully between their various commitments. They are also well placed to address the fracturing of older experiences of place and space which modern societies have produced. Ecology's feel for the juxtaposition of different spatial scales – articulating a simultaneous concern for the local and the global, for example – provides an important starting point for a politics which addresses the different pattern of spatial relations which place now signifies.

Some communitarians have been particularly sensitive to the existence of multiple, overlapping communities in contemporary social life. Political ecology, likewise, might generate a community-based politics which embraces this diversity and seeks to neutralise many of the destructive tensions and antagonisms which characterise relations between different communities of interest in modern industrial society. In the name of democracy, this may involve challenging the present interests of dominant and entrenched communities so that a broader range of groups and interests may be equally represented within the political process.

Modernity

The anti-urban ethos of small-scale communitarian thinking is reinforced amongst greens by a marked ambivalence about many aspects of modern industrial society, especially cities. Whilst for some, this makes pre-industrial models of social organisation attractive, others – usually 'lighter' greens – remain more ambivalent about aspects of modernity, hoping, for example, to harness its technological capacities, rather than envisaging its simple abolition. But community, as it is currently used, does not convey this dialectical position. Instead it tends to reinforce a simplistic nostalgia for a (mythical) arcadian past, whilst positing a simplistic dichotomy between an environmentally benign and socially harmonious future and the decay and destruction of the modern city experience. In fact, greens should consider models of community appropriate to modern conditions, for instance the polymorphous and open-ended networks constructed by users of new information technologies or the 'city ideal' celebrated by Young. The latter is founded on four principles – social differentiation without exclusion, variety, 'eroticism' and publicity. Clearly there is much room for debate here, not least about how these principles can be deduced from a metaphor, yet an important question underlies this kind of argument: how should greens understand and respond to modernity? As Benhabib suggests, one of the most important features of modern intellectual and political life is the heightening of our capacity to reflect upon the nature of our identities. Greens, I would argue, should also embrace the 'specifically modern achievement of being able to criticize, challenge and question the context of these constitutive identities' (Benhabib 1982: 74). Any emancipatory conception of community needs to incorporate, rather than refuse, this characteristic of modern social and cultural life.

Greens may have to face the impossibility of privileging one communitarian identity – the ecological – over others in a rigid and authoritarian way. Our selves are shaped by a matrix of particular identities and attachments – given by religion, education and locality, for instance – within which we negotiate and re-evaluate our selves and the common good. Moreover, in terms of democracy, such a project appears to satisfy some of the criteria for a democratic polity.

ALTERITY

An especially potent critique of communitarian arguments has been put forward by those concerned with the notion of alterity (otherness) – the idea that the identity of individuals is constituted through social, ideological and cultural difference (Barrett 1991). Theorists of alterity stress the boundaries (symbolic as well as physical) between communities, suggesting that these function as practices which construct and reproduce the identity of members of these communities (Cohen 1985). In other words, my sense of self depends upon engagement with the 'other', a process which involves both the reproduction and transgression of real and imaginary boundaries (Young 1990: 311–12). Whatever the merits or weaknesses of this perspective (its origins within linguistic theory make it unpalatable for some), it does highlight an important weakness of strong communitarian discourse: my sense of self-discovery may involve not only greater embeddedness in my constitutive communities but also occasional or frequent escape from them into the 'other'. This is the complete antithesis of the conclusion which many greens draw, based on their communitarianism. Given the homogeneity and smallness of the communities vaunted by some greens (Sale 1980), this point is all the more relevant.

Some communitarians have tried to incorporate the notion of alterity within their arguments. This approach seeks a more dialogic and differentiated public culture, and works against the closed, homogeneous and hierarchical implications of *gemeinschaft* communitarianism. For greens, attention to the principle of alterity might involve institutionalising a politics of difference, generating a more cosmopolitan approach than many currently favour. This might mean expansion of the opportunities for, rather than hostility to, trade and travel, for example.

THE HUMAN–NATURE BOUNDARY

A dialogic model of human rationality based on alterity, which 'attributes to individuals the ability and the willingness to take the standpoint of the

31

others involved in a controversy into account and reason from their point of view' (Young 1990: 74), generates some interesting possibilities in terms of our sense of 'community' with nature. Some longstanding difficulties recur in this context: if we are members of a community (or communities) with non-human beings, does this imply moral equality, or at least the grounds for an ethic which ascribes equality of consideration to all? The communicative ethics approach does not, of itself, provide new answers to this old question. In fact, Robyn Eckersley's perceptive critique of attempts to extend human models of rationality as the possible basis of a new environmentalist ethic is pertinent here (1992: 97–117). Still, this approach may prove useful in supporting the attempts by a number of theorists, and by greens in practice, to challenge the dominant version of justice within liberal democracies. This interpretation of communicative rationality allows for a broader range of values – care, responsibility and sharing, for example – which might inform a sense of ecological justice. The idea of extending this outlook so that non-human beings and interests are considered as members of the community enters the debate here.

At present, community helps greens express their ecological commitment to a different conception of human–nature relations, either through a belief in the 'holistic community of life' or through an attempt to blur the boundaries between nature and society by celebrating the virtues of communities built around place. Yet, as was suggested earlier, community is being invoked here as metaphor: it cannot provide the normative underpinning for the extension of ethical consideration which many greens seek. It is at this point that the arguments associated with environmentalist ethics have to be brought to bear. Community itself cannot deliver moral certainty here. Incorporating alterity within ecological communitarianism would mean adopting a far more fluid and dynamic conception of the borders between different communities, and the need for individuals to experience relations of difference on a continual and changing basis. Understood thus, community might play a key role in the green political imagination.

Certainly, if it can be shown that the values of responsibility, care and concern are generated by the 'conversational model' of human interaction, then the possibility arises for this model to be extended to human relations with non-human nature. This line of argument needs far more extensive evaluation. Despite their suggestive nature, Young's ideas are not wholly convincing here. Her claim to have articulated a political theory which secures a necessary connection between democracy and justice is unconvincing. Greens, she argues, like other radical social movements, implicitly strive towards an alternative definition of social justice, 'that seeks to reduce and eliminate domination and oppression. Democracy is both an element and a condition of social justice' (Young 1990: 66–7). This argument is weak in the light of the many criticisms levelled at the political agendas of these different movements. In terms of ecology, it severely underplays the tensions which might arise between the commitment to care for others (including non-human others), which might be expressed through paternalism for example, and the principles of democracy.

CONCLUSION

Greens need to reinterpret the principle of community for two reasons: first, in its current usage, community repeatedly confuses different kinds of arguments; second, because community is wrongly understood by many greens to be either a core normative element within, or a political pre-condition for, ecological sustainability. The arguments of critics such as Young and Benhabib, alongside the ideas of other leading communitarians, offer greens possibilities in terms of the reformulation of this principle. Undoubtedly, there are other ways in which community might be re-interpreted, yet the themes elaborated above bear on the most important and debilitating weaknesses in ecological communitarianism. Any reinter-pretation of community would have to deal with them in some way or other.

In fact, many greens have learnt in practice that democracy sits uneasily with ecology and that *gemeinschaft* communitarianism generates some unfortunate policy outcomes.[1] The important question here is whether community is necessarily inadequate, or might be reinterpreted to enable greens to generate both a sharper assessment of how the social and economic worlds currently operate, and a more flexible and multi-layered ethical alternative to present-day conditions.

One of the criteria for judging the efficacy of this principle in green political thought is its capacity to facilitate the development of a more hard-headed and cogent conception of the relationship between democratic principles and the imperatives of ecology. As we have seen, community cannot guarantee a necessary relationship between the two. Yet, interpreted differently, this principle remains pertinent to the reformulation of green political thought in the light of recent debates about democracy and ecology in four ways.

First, ecological communitarianism need not rely upon a 'Rousseauian' conception of the self, or a strong version of the general will. Instead it might develop a 'deep' recognition of individual and social difference and view the relationships between human individuals, social groups and non-human nature as the subject of ongoing, public debate.

Second, ecological communitarianism is especially sensitive to the role of space and place within our communal identities: any attempt to reconcile democracy with ecology needs to address the plurality of interests and outlooks generated by these multiple and overlapping allegiances – be-tween our sense of regional and national loyalty for instance. Exploring the dimensions of different community loyalties and thinking about how these

33

might be traded against each other is a vital element within any democratic politics.

Third, community need not be counter-opposed with modernity. Indeed, if greens wish to be democrats, addressing the plurality of identities and interests which modern society has generated, and deploying the 'self-reflexivity' particular to modernity may be imperative. The existence of alternative models and interpretations of community points the way for a revitalised conception of this metaphor in green circles.

Fourth, the radical principle of alterity underpins some of the most pro-vocative developments within contemporary political and ethical thought, and, indeed, challenges the epistemological assumptions associated with many of the principles conventionally adduced to bolster the ideal of democracy. Whilst the relationship between alterity and democracy remains unclear, developing a deeper sense of our relationships with others – be they human individuals or the non-human biotic world – and viewing the boundaries between ourselves and others as far more permeable, may facilitate the development of a specifically ecological sense of justice. Given the importance of the relationship between justice and democracy in most accounts, the attempt to construct a putative green theory of justice – a project as yet in its infancy – may, indirectly, illuminate the troubled debate about democracy and green politics in stimulating and unexpected ways.

At the very least, greens need to become more sensitive to the meta-phorical status of community, which at present connects them to an authoritarian and unappealing social form in the minds of many, however vehemently they deny these connotations. Reformulating the principle of community is no easy task. Yet, if they avoid this challenge, green ideology will remain saddled with some harmful associations and greens will find it very hard to be democrats.

ACKNOWLEDGEMENTS

I would like to thank Brian Doherty, Andrew Dobson, James Meadowcroft and Martin Smith for their comments on an earlier draft of this chapter.

NOTE

1 The Green Group of MEPs within the European Union has spoken out against the dangers of racism and the need to defend the rights of minority groups (Green Group of the European Union 1992). Elsewhere greens have allied themselves with campaigns for political and constitutional reform, developing pluralist political arguments in these contexts. Significantly, the historical evolution of green activists' discourse has rarely figured in the more abstruse and high-level calculations of the critics of the ideas of political ecology, which tend to assume an unchanging set of ideas and commitments on the part of greens.

REFERENCES

Bahro, R. (1986) *Building the Green Movement*, London: Heretic.
Barrett, M. (1991) *The Politics of Truth: From Marx to Foucault*, Cambridge: Polity.
Bell, D. (1993) *Communitarianism and its Critics*, Oxford: Clarendon Press.
Benhabib, S. (1982) *Situating the Self: Gender, Community and Postmodernism in Contemporary Ethics*, Cambridge: Polity.
Bookchin, M. (1982) *The Ecology of Freedom*, Palo Alto, Calif.: Cheshire Books.
Cohen, A.P. (1985) *The Symbolic Construction of Community*, Chichester, London and New York: Ellis Harwood and Tavistock.
Corlett, W. (1989) *Community Without Unity: A Politics of Derridian Extravagance*, Durham, NC: Duke University Press.
Crick, B. (1962) *In Defence of Politics*, London: Weidenfeld & Nicolson.
Dobson, A. (1990) *Green Political Thought*, London: Unwin Hyman.
—— (1993) 'Ecologism', in R. Eatwell and A. Wright (eds) *Contemporary Political Ideologies*, London: Pinter.
Dryzek, J. (1987) *Rational Ecology*, Oxford: Blackwell.
Dworkin, R. (1985) *A Matter of Principle*, Cambridge, Mass.: Harvard University Press.
Eckersley, R. (1992) *Environmentalism and Political Theory: Toward an Ecocentric Approach*, London: UCL Press.
Frankel, B. (1987) *The Post-Industrial Utopians*, Oxford: Polity.
Giddens, A. (1991) *The Consequences of Modernity*, Cambridge: Polity.
Green Group of the European Union (1992) 'Text of the Official Response of the Green Group to Maastricht', *Green Leaves* 9.
Harrison, R. (1994) *Democracy*, London: Routledge.
Harvey, D. (1993) 'The Nature of Environment: Dialectics of Social and Environmental Change', *Socialist Register* 1–51.
Jones, K. (1993) *Beyond Optimism: A Buddhist Political Ecology*, Oxford: Jon Carpenter.
Kymlicka, W. (1990) *Contemporary Political Philosophy: An Introduction*, Oxford: Clarendon Press.
Lacey, N. and Fraser, E. (1994) 'Communitarianism', *Politics* 14, 2: 75–81.
Lewis, M. (1992) *Green Delusions*, Durham, NC: Duke University Press.
Mulhall, S. and Swift, A. (1992) *Liberals and Communitarians*, Oxford: Blackwell.
Naess, A. (1989) *Ecology, Community and Lifestyle*, Cambridge: Cambridge University Press.
O'Riordan, T. (1981) *Environmentalism*, London: Pion.
Pateman, C. (1989) *The Disorder of Women*, Cambridge: Polity.
Rustin, M. (1985) *For a Pluralist Socialism*, London: Verso.
Sale, K. (1980) *Human Scale*, London: Secker & Warburg.
Saward, M. (1993) 'Green Democracy?', in A. Dobson and P. Lucardie (eds) *The Politics of Nature: Explorations of Green Political Theory*, London: Routledge.
Schwarzenbach, S.A. (1991) 'Rawls, Hegel, and Communitarianism', *Political Theory* 19: 539–71.
Taylor, C. (1989) *Sources of the Self: The Making of Modern Identity*, Cambridge, Mass.: Harvard University Press.
Veldman, M. (1994) *Fantasy, the Bomb and the Greening of Britain: Romantic Protest 1945–1980*, Cambridge: Cambridge University Press.
Young, I.M. (1990) *Justice and the Politics of Difference*, Princeton, NJ: Princeton University Press.

2

GREEN PARTIES, NONVIOLENCE AND POLITICAL OBLIGATION

Brian Doherty

The problems in justifying democracy and defending the use of violence are not wholly equivalent but they are related questions. As Hannah Arendt pointed out, if power is defined in ideal terms, as dependent on a public consensus, then violence must be its opposite (Arendt 1970: 56). States use violence when they lack power.[1] Yet, this ideal type definition is usually seen as too impractical to be useful. Arendt herself recognised that real governments do combine the use or threat of violence to impose policies and to maintain law and order with the attempt to draw legitimacy from popular consent. State violence is also often used against those who oppose a particular policy whilst accepting the general principles of liberal democratic government, a point difficult to square with Arendt's dualistic definition. And yet, few would disagree that reducing violence is important to the quality of democracy. The reason the discussion goes no further is that it is assumed that the main political answers are institutional ones. Violence is endemic, therefore the most that governments can hope to do is to maintain the institutions that minimise the extent of violence and at best, through social reforms, seek to reduce the structural causes of violence.

Greens are sceptical about this. They believe that violence is reproduced in cultures, practices and structures that can be challenged. Reducing violence is an end in itself of green praxis, and so for them, it is a necessary part of their democratic project. Thus, the usual distinction between domestic and international violence is blurred for them by their critique of the related cultural justifications of, for instance, militarism and male domestic violence. In this they are clearly drawing on the arguments made by earlier anti-militarists and by feminists. This apparent lack of novelty is one reason why nonviolence has not been central in debates on green political theory: it is difficult to find an ecocentric justification for nonviolence. It is true that greens have seen their peace policy as related to their ecological policy, as when the German greens said: 'A lifestyle and method of production which relies on an endless supply of raw materials and uses those materials lavishly, also furnishes the motive for the violent appropriation of raw materials from other countries' (Die Grünen 1981: 7) but although warfare could be understood as an ecological threat the human-centred justifications for anti-militarism have been most prominent in green parties' arguments.[2]

Where nonviolence has been discussed by theorists of green politics, as for instance, by Robert Goodin, it is acknowledged that greens use the principle in a consistent way to relate their means to the end of nonviolence, but this is trumped by the stress in a green theory of value on avoiding the consequences of damage to nature that might result from refusing to use violence (Goodin 1992: 138). Goodin recognises that there are good pragmatic arguments for following the principle of nonviolence, and he recognises that it is a desirable end, why then should it not also be a part of a green theory of the good? The problem lies in two areas: greens themselves see it as both part of their theory of the good, and part of a theory of the right means, and as will be apparent below, this does not help them in cases of conflicting priorities between ends, nor in formulating strategies to reach those ends. In part this is the old problem of means and ends, but the moral problems in means/ends debates are not necessarily the same as the strategic ones. As a collective agent, pursuing diverse ends, green parties in particular have to grapple with the problem of how to interpret green moral commitments in a way that allows for an effective strategy to realise them. Second, for contingent reasons, to do with their origins in the new social movements and New Left, greens, at least in the form of the western European green parties, seek several ends which cannot be reduced to an ecologically based interpretation of the green theory of the good. Nonviolence is therefore understandably passed over by those concerned with green political theory because it appears as a constraint on green action which does not follow from an ecologically based theory of value. But in this chapter it will be argued that nonviolence can still be seen as both innovative and an end in itself that can govern green strategy without requiring an absolute choice between it and other green ends, such as the achievement of sustainability.

Thus the main discussion in this chapter focuses on the strategic questions that arise from making nonviolence an end of green ideology. Apart from its own role in green ideology, nonviolence can also illustrate the problems of developing a strategy that is appropriate for green parties that pursue several ends of equivalent status simultaneously. First, however, the origins of the greens' support for nonviolence are explained through a discussion of their experiences in the 1970s and early 1980s. This is important because it helps to explain why problematic totalistic interpretations of violence and nonviolence emerged alongside a view of a politics of nonviolence that was more open to strategic judgements. A second question is raised by the attitude of the greens towards political protest. The greens seem to reject the traditional liberal contractual arguments for political obligation, and yet they do accept that parliamentary democracy has some legitimacy. What are the reasons underlying this highly conditional sense of political obligation and what role does their commitment to nonviolence play in these arguments?

WHY NONVIOLENCE?

For Die Grünen it was one of the four founding pillars of their first programme, and despite having qualified other principles they have retained a very radical position on nonviolence.[3] But the Germans are not distinct from other European green parties on this question. Even the French greens developed a strong commitment to nonviolence, despite the absence of a strong independent peace movement in France during the 1980s (Les Verts 1987).

The commitment to nonviolence is surprising, in part because many of the 1960s and 1970s protests, which provided many recruits for green parties, had a different view of violence. The student movements and protesters against the Vietnam war viewed the question of violence against the police in tactical terms and differed substantially from earlier disarmament movements in their willingness to engage in direct conflict with the police. Their own view of themselves as the metropolitan branch of a worldwide guerrilla movement against imperialism also helped to make violence seem justifiable (Stansill and Mairowitz 1971: 123–7; 134–51). In parts of the alternative milieu of the 1970s violence was also justified from an expressive point of view, and in this case its defenders were most often groups of anarchists arguing for a Sorelian version of the liberation of instincts:

> The youth protests have rediscovered the body. They feel that it is not there for indolent self-reflection or for self-destruction but for expressive public display, for fighting, for trying out one's powers in order to experience things. This discovery is one of the main reasons for the use and support of violence. . . . A young demonstrator says: 'You don't know this liberating feeling when the windows of a boutique selling furs or of a bank shatter.' This is no senseless brawl, but rather the effort to change the room for manoeuvre in a world that is bureaucratically covered in glass and concrete.
>
> (Papadakis 1984: 33)

Thus in some groups that fed into the German greens (but also the French and Italian green parties) an abstract rejection of the system was a possible but not an inevitable route to a violent politics. The green movements largely retained this absolutist rejection of the system in the early 1980s but they also developed a more positive commitment to nonviolence. What lay behind this change? The first reason was the experience of violence at anti-nuclear demonstrations in the 1970s. In 1977 Creys-Malville in France and Grohnde and Brokdorf in Germany were turning points in this regard. In both countries some groups in the anti-nuclear movement continued to fight the police thereafter but there was a more explicit commitment to nonviolence from the mainstream of the movement. There had already been lively debates on violence (Bennahmias and Roche 1992: 45; Chafer 1982: 207; Rüdig 1990; Nelkin and Pollak 1982: 196–7) but the scale of police action meant that there was a new concern with non-provocative styles of demonstration. Here, however, nonviolence was being adopted by some for tactical reasons and was not generally an end in itself for the movement.

A second contributory factor was the critique of male celebrations of violence by the women's movements. Feminists had criticised the macho character of the romantic vision of the guerrilla fighter that had inspired 1960s radicals. More generally, they argued that violence against women was a reflection of a cultural endorsement of violence by men that was most fully realised in the military machine (Strange 1983). This argument did not always depend on an essentialist view of violence as exclusively male, but it did identify violence itself as a problem connected to patriarchy. Only by rejecting violence as a means of change altogether could the cultural acceptance of violence that justified its widespread use by men and by the state be overcome.

The peace movement was the third reason why the greens came to support nonviolence as an end in itself. The 1980s peace movements have been described as distinct from the 1960s movements in that they were motivated more by fear than by pure morality (Rootes 1989). It was the rhetoric of the superpowers and the specific dangers of mutual mis-perception or attempts to engage in limited nuclear wars in Europe that motivated most participants. But one result of this less moralistic position was a greater concentration on strategic questions. The 1980s peace movements argued effectively with the military on questions of strategy and helped to demystify policies that had remained undebated because they were seen as the preserve of a specific expertise. The green parties adopted the strategic arguments of the peace movements against nuclear deterrence and along with the most radical wing of the peace movement also developed a critique of militarism itself. The role of the peace movements was vital in embedding green support for nonviolence, but the experience in anti-nuclear protests had already convinced greens of the 'tactical' reasons for nonviolence, and the women's movement had restated in an innovative form the argument that nonviolence needed to be part of the means of change itself. The peace movement employed these tactics and used these arguments and was probably the most important reason that they became more generalised. The role of the peace movement as an influence on a green party is most clearly evident in Britain where there was no major

39

protest movement against nuclear energy and no significant input from the women's movement into the then Ecology Party in the 1970s. Nor was there any extensive debate about nonviolence in the Ecology Party prior to the 1980s. In other countries, however, there were often already movements in existence that defended nonviolence as important in itself. The Dutch Pacifistisch–Socialistische Partij (PSP) was perhaps the most important of these (Lucardie 1980), though the Scandinavian New Left parties were also influenced by philosophic ideas of nonviolence (Logue 1982).

STRUCTURAL VIOLENCE

One legacy of the 1970s movements that carried over to the green parties was analysis of society based on a logic of totality. The existing system was defined as a total unity; each element conforming to a functional logic. This was evident in particular in the use of the concept of structural violence: greens questioned the legitimacy of the state itself because it was seen as a violent institution. As Spretnak and Capra noted in their interviews with German greens, 'Many Greens mentioned Max Weber's observation that the state is the seat of legitimized violence' (1985: 48). But greens also speak of violence in even broader terms as characteristic of the whole social order. The British Green Party's *Manifesto for a Sustainable Society* seems to suggest as much in saying:

> Violence underpins our social fabric and international relations depend on the use or threat of force. Our whole world can be defined as already at war. Nuclear weapons are the tip of an iceberg in a world built and sustained on the principles of violence, exploitation and domination. To rid ourselves of all weapons of mass destruction we have to transform the material and cultural foundations of society. Lasting peace is impossible in the context of a patriarchal social and political system based on domination, a denial of feelings and an unquestioning obedience to authority. An economic system that exploits people and the entire planet, that fosters excessive competition, aggression and consumerism, cannot be the basis of a peaceful world.
>
> (Green Party 1989: DF109)

As this statement implies, simply ending the use of force by the state will not be enough in itself to challenge the deeper causes of violence. However, it is also unclear from the above passage whether violence results from an unjust social order or whether that injustice is itself a form of violence. This kind of ambiguity is likely to cause problems for the greens in defending other aspects of their critique of violence. The advantage of a broad interpretation of violence is that it can seem to justify green support for improved aid for the Third World, or for greater attention to challenging male violence. This seems to be the case, for instance, in the comment by Capra and Spretnak that 'an economy that is ecologically balanced and socially just will naturally be nonviolent' (1984: 89). But if violence is merged with its causes it does undermine the moral clarity of the critique of the use of organised violence by the state. Suffering in the form of death, disease and impoverishment that results from structural injustices may in some situations be objectively greater than suffering from war or civil strife, but it is not necessary to define these results as a form of violence in order to show that greater harm has resulted.[4]

The concept of structural violence is therefore unclear and contentious. In its original usage (Fanon 1968) it was intended to describe the effects of colonialism on the colonised. Its usage presupposes that the analysis of oppression should not be restricted to the direct use of force but should also include the results of colonialism: economic exploitation and loss of cultural identity. The most obvious problem with seeing particular social structures as necessarily violent is that the intention and responsibility of individuals concerning the threat of physical harm to others becomes blurred by competing judgements about the immorality of social structures. It might be argued that this reflects a more realistic theory of power than the implied individualistic morality of nonviolence, but as will be made clear below it is possible to develop nonviolence in a way that takes account of the constraints of power. It is not possible, though, to use structural violence to resolve the choice faced by an individual agent between violent and nonviolent opposition. One of the dangers of structural violence is therefore that it makes a nonviolent alternative so absolute that the temptation to return to violent means of achieving it seems stronger.

A slightly different interpretation of the Green Party's statement might be that the threat of violence helps to sustain other kinds of domination that are not in themselves necessarily violent. Challenging the implicit threat of violence as well as its actual manifestation may be the main object of the greens' critique. If, as Giddens (1986) argues, the use and threat of violence is an essential feature of the development and current form of the nation-state, then removal of that threat, at least from the state, could have far-reaching consequences for society as a whole. This seems to be a more defensible position, since although such a position would place violence in a social context by identifying violence as a cause of wider social problems, in principle violence would remain analytically separable from the consequences of its use.

For greens, however, the main problem has been how to define a nonviolent alternative vision of society while maintaining as broad-ranging a critique as possible of existing forms of domination, both violent and nonviolent. One line of division has been between those who argued for a mainly moral critique of violence and those who argue for reducing violence from a more pragmatic position. In the mid-1970s the Dutch PSP

41

was divided over how to define its pacifism. The most rigorous pacifists in the party defended the PSP's traditional position – that pacifism was based mainly on the moral goal of avoiding evil, but the majority supported the position that nonviolence should be seen as part of the broad aim of building socialism from below. Establishing a society based on principles of self-management would allow violence to be opposed more effectively. The traditional pacifists were defeated in their efforts to prevent a redefinition of the party's official position as 'the attempt to minimise violence on either practical or moral grounds' (Lucardie 1980: 115). But the question remains as to whether this combination provides a plausible basis for strategy.

STATE VIOLENCE

The issue of the monopoly of the legitimate use of violence by the state seems to expose the difficulty of combining a moral and a pragmatic condemnation of violence. For the greens, their commitment to non-violence seems by definition to require that they oppose the use of force by the state, and yet, rejecting the state's monopoly of force poses the question of how the greens would maintain public order. The debate on this issue has been most intense in Germany and this was probably a result of the strongly polarised relationship between the extra-parliamentary movements and the German state during the late 1960s and 1970s. The rejection of state policies and the critique of the bureaucratic character of the state itself led many to question whether they should accept that the state had any right to use force against its citizens. The resulting debate continued in the Green Party. The *Realos* generally argued that the greens should make a distinction between opposing particular policies as illegitimate and the legitimacy of the state itself, which they argued the greens should accept (Poguntke 1990: 33).

Otto Schily was the most outspoken of the *Realo* leaders in these debates. He said that 'The Greens must make it clear that they support this monopoly of force.... In the question of the state monopoly of force I am not prepared to compromise one inch' (Hülsberg 1988: 175). The opposing position voiced by the *Fundis* emphasised that the greens should not feel bound by any *a priori* political obligation to the current system and 'Acceptance of the state monopoly of force would lead to acceptance of the present system' (Hülsberg 1988: 175).

The official position of Die Grünen in 1994 remained fundamentally critical of the failings of liberal democracy and avoided an explicit, unequivocal, acceptance of the state's monopoly of force and it may be the case that a strategy of counter-power based on nonviolence does alter the terms of political obligation. This point will be taken up further below. However, an issue not resolved in the 1985 debate was the attitude that the party would take towards the use of force in exercising governmental power.

For Schily the position was clear: the greens had to accept the central liberal justification of the use of force by the state as necessary in order to regulate and arbitrate in conflicts, and so uphold the rights of individual citizens. Without a state and with 'the socialisation of force' there would be chaos (Hülsberg 1988: 175). But for most greens the use of force in order to impose government decisions poses real dilemmas. These were summed up by Roland Vogt as follows:

> What we have not yet accomplished is to say how we show ourselves to be nonviolent at the moment when we participate in governmental functions, because the state is itself an institution of violence. For example, how will a Green city council act against people who don't pay their rent, although they really could because they receive welfare or because they earn enough. . . . That is, there are still no thought-out concepts of how one can reconcile the demands of social responsibility with the demands of nonviolence.
>
> (quoted in Capra and Spretnak 1984: 43)

AN EVOLUTION TOWARDS REFORMISM

In practice, when greens have been in government, albeit only as minority partners in coalitions, they have not opposed the use of force by the police, but there have been incidents where green reluctance to use force has become an issue of conflict: conflicts with the SPD over the violent eviction of squatters led to the collapse of the Red–Green coalition in Berlin in 1989.

In the early years of their history green parties seem to have adopted a more utopian approach to the question of policing. For instance, in the 1977 municipal elections in Paris the green programme listed twenty proposals that were intended to transform Paris into an *Ecopolis*. These included the exodus of the French central government, which would be followed by the conversion of its ministries into buildings useful to the citizens and it was also argued that with the government gone there would be no need for the 'forces of repression' who would be replaced by locally elected 'Guardians of the Peace' (Gurin 1979: 158).

More typical of later green programmes are the juxtaposition, in Penny Kemp and Derek Wall's *Green Manifesto* of criticism of current police practices with an acceptance that 'Direct intervention by the police in violent and tense situations in today's far from green society may on occasion remain necessary. At the same time the police force risks becoming a political army. Policing should be made to operate within a framework of consensus rather than armed violence' (1990: 184). Similarly, as far as the army is concerned, although in the past parties such as the PSP have demanded immediate abolition of the military and greens still look forward to a system based on social defence, most now accept that a transition period would be necessary before the military could be disarmed. In the short-term greens argue for more democratic reforms within the army and for a stronger role for the UN in policing international conflicts (Kemp and Wall 1990: 143).

The tempering of fundamentalist attitudes to policing and to the military with a dose of political realism can be seen as the result of a learning process for the greens. They have not altered their moral opposition to violence, but the acknowledgement of the difficulty and uncertainties of transition has lead to a more pragmatic position that depends on strategy as well as morality. The practical result of green participation in government is more likely to be a reformist approach concentrating on reducing the use of force and curbing developments such as the militarisation of the police.

THE LIMITS OF FUNDAMENTALISM

Should this be seen as a betrayal of the ideals of nonviolence? From the point of view of a logic dependent on a totalistic negation of the existing system it would have to be seen as such. A totalistic critique helps to integrate the diverse strands of green thought and, if possible, to relate them to a single core idea in green theory. Thus Die Grünen attempted to relate their support for nonviolence to their ecological arguments as follows:

> The principle of respect and regard for all life – that is to say the protection of life and Nature – forms the basis of both our ecological aims and our aims regarding peace. The industrial system which prevails in European civilisation in which man is seen as exploiter both of other men and a natural environment regarded as hostile, has led society further and further up a blind alley. Technological progress and the organisation of labour follow a pattern of growth which is alien to man, and in which the development of forces of production are not subject to any conscious structuring. For decades the so-called 'modern' war machines, with their ever greater self-destruction have been the driving force and the major sector of this type of techno-logical 'progress'.
>
> (Die Grünen 1981: 6)

In similar vein ecofeminists have linked the devaluation of women and nature and shown how a male-dominated culture reinforces attitudes that encourage violence. However, while there are linkages between each of these areas, they are not necessarily all the product of a single cause. Nor, importantly, could they be tackled by a single institutional or cultural change. Another attempt to found nonviolence on ecological principles sees it as equivalent to treading lightly on the earth. In this case violence against nature could be seen in broad terms as including all

44

damage to nature. Here, however, the problem of what could count as non-interference with nature arises. If all human activity uses nature in some form, it must be hard to specify what counts as nonviolent activity. Violence can be clearly defined and remain open to moral judgement only if it is restricted to physical harm towards sentient beings. The problem with the totalistic logic of green fundamentalism is that by merging different objects of critique into a single cause, whether anthropocentrism or patriarchy, it makes it difficult to imagine how social problems could be overcome.

If we reject the idea that violence can be countered only at the level of the totality, and reject the idea of structural violence as morally dubious and unable to inform green strategy, what appears to remain is the Ghandian ideal of nonviolence, justified in terms of the individual conscience. This is the purest version of the view that means must be consistent with ends, and appears to offer the best defence against the relegation of nonviolence to a tactical level. In this view a strategy that allows for violence will not provide an effective transition to a society based on nonviolence. Petra Kelly argued that:

> The Greens must show how to avoid conflicts by regarding those who resort to violence not as enemies, but as people who must be liberated from their enslavement to violence. Practically every violent conflict or social change has proved that violence unleashes violence in return. Violent revolutions usually only mean a change of personnel at the top; the actual system of violence is only altered, never eliminated as a result.
>
> (Kelly 1984: 31)

This is within the Gandhian tradition of using nonviolence not simply as a tactic but also as a process of social change in itself and one that allows for greater communication with opponents. Green strategies for social and political change are informed by nonviolence, not so much as a negative 'absence' of violence, but as a value that justifies an approach based on the idea of counter-power. It also makes resistance to injustice an obligation, and thus is not purely passive, although it is still defined by the omission of violence from the possible repertoire of action:

> Non-violent opposition has nothing to do with passivity and nothing whatsoever to do with the demeaning experience of injustice and violence. In contrast to violent opposition, non-violent opposition is an expression of spiritual, physical and moral strength. This strength is shown most clearly by consciously and specifically *not doing* that which could be construed as participating in injustice. This could mean not obeying orders or not holding back in situations where injustice is being meted out to others.
>
> (Kelly 1984: 27)

45

The Gandhian view of nonviolent direct action is distinct from civil disobedience in that it goes beyond an appeal to the sense of justice of the rulers or public opinion (Rawls 1991) or an appeal to implement the formal rights necessary to democracy (Singer 1991). If the latter fail, in the usual apologies for civil disobedience the only choice left to the protester is between violence and acquiescence. Greens argue, however, that they are not obliged to obey the authority of a liberal democratic government. It is therefore legitimate to extend action beyond symbolic disobedience to a positive attempt to make government ineffective. This might be fine, as far as a strategy of opposition is concerned, but it does not help with the problem of how a green government would maintain order. The problem lies in the absolute form of the equation of means and ends. Kelly and other defenders of a pure equation between means and ends suggest that any compromise on violence will act to reinforce the system on which violence rests. Thus compromises are to be rejected on consequentialist as well as deontological grounds.[5]

The green analysis of the structural causes of violence suggests that violence is deeply embedded in society and culture. As Brian Martin (1984: 17) points out, this means that violence can be overcome only gradually and involves changes in a wide variety of spheres. Yet, in the view expressed by Kelly above, there is a conflict between the recognition of the institutional and cultural pressures sustaining violence and the view of nonviolence as the choice of fully autonomous individuals. Greens may remain committed themselves to nonviolence as both means and end, but by acknowledging that the structural sources sustaining violence are distinct from violence itself they can also be more realistic about how to achieve change. If the solution to the problem of violence is not seen as simply a matter of encouraging enough individuals to choose nonviolence, but also as re-quiring changes in culture and social structures, the greens can justify compromises of the kind that we have already mentioned in recognition of the need to make incremental progress. A position that refuses compro-mises therefore imposes too many constraints upon the greens' political praxis. In effect, it is an attempt to put into practice the distinction between politics and violence as opposites suggested by Arendt (1970). It also means that nonviolence would be forced into an unnecessary competition with other green ends: each time a green party joined a government and found itself having to run the police and army it would have to decide either to resign, giving up the chance to gain changes on other issues, or abandon the commitment to nonviolence.

One interesting example of how the interrelationship of green ends requires short-term trade-offs, but need not mean giving up the long-term aims, is evident in the response of one British green to the Gulf war. To Jenny Linsdell the invisibility of women in the media and their exclusion from the fighting served to reinforce the second-class citizenship of women.

Only by sharing responsibility could women reassert their status and despite being a pacifist she argued that this meant that any conscription and combatant roles for women and men should be equivalent. Only then could she have the choice to become a conscientious objector (Linsdell 1991: 3–4). Without that choice women could always be represented as 'the other' in need of male defence.

On the basis of what has been argued thus far we can say that the strategy of green parties regarding nonviolence can be judged, first, according to the extent to which it succeeds in providing an alternative to the view that violence is natural and inevitable; second to the extent that it expands the possibilities for individuals to live a life where the threat of violence is reduced; and third to the extent that they succeed in showing that its instrumental use is less rational than traditionally supposed. The creation of a nonviolent society, like the creation of democracy, is therefore more a process than an immediately realisable state. Following this strategy would also mean that greens would be forced to confront and engage more openly with the arguments of those who view violence as rational. Nonviolence in the fundamentalist form represents a solution primarily because it avoids the question of justification. It is presented as an autonomous choice with no guidance about how to achieve a transition away from violence. If greens accept instead that a nonviolent society is a persuasive end, they can justify their stance by showing how there are greater possibilities for effective nonviolent alternatives to the instrumental use of violence.

In fact, of course, greens and others have already done this to some extent. Much of their effort has gone into the debates about the conditions and conduct of modern warfare. Green parties have been able to argue that violence may be less effective than is assumed as the primary basis of defence policies. They argue instead for greater exploration of social defence. The crucial point being that green parties have recognised that they needed strategic as well as moral arguments against existing defence policy, and that they have accepted that the uncertainty concerning social defence on the part of others will require that social defence proves itself, gradually, rather than being open to immediate change. Again, the acceptance of this has not always been without conflict. The French greens speak of the need to 'experiment with forms of civil defence' in order to test the assumed superiority of existing military defence. But where the peace movement was stronger, hints of such compromise caused conflict. Thus in Die Grünen the defence policy drafted by their MP and ex-NATO General Gert Bastian in 1984 was heavily criticised for accepting the need for an interim stage (of non-offensive conventional defence) before a full social defence could be adopted. Critics such as Bahro saw any military defence as unacceptable (Langguth 1986: 91).

Green arguments about democracy can also lend weight to their criticism of the military. For instance, the arguments against the secrecy and bureaucracy necessary to sustain a military machine point to (some, but not all) costs for democracy of the assumed necessity of military security. On the other hand, arguments for effective social defence raise intriguing possibilities about the potential for citizens to organise to resist their own governments. If nonviolence is implied in green arguments about democratisation, it is important for greens to make it clear that both positions follow from adopting green principles and are related in green analysis.

NONVIOLENT PROTEST AND POLITICAL OBLIGATION

The role of protest has been central to the green debates about means and ends and the legitimate means of change within liberal democracies. Greens have not always been in full agreement over the scope and character of legitimate protest activity. Although all greens have been opposed to any use of violence against people there has been some disagreement over violence against property (Poguntke 1990: 33–4). Moreover, greens accept that violence at demonstrations can be provoked either by the police or by demonstrators and although the great majority of greens would still stress the importance of a nonviolent reaction to provocation, some fundamentalists in particular have been wary of condemning what they see as the use of violence in self-defence by other participants in demonstrations supported by the greens. This position may also depend on the ambiguity created by the concept of structural violence. If the structural characteristics of 'the system' are themselves defined as a form of violence then this appears to make violence against those who represent the system justifiable. As we saw above, this view had been widespread, although never unopposed, on the ultra-left in western Europe in the 1970s and its legacy continued to influence those green parties that included ex-adherents of ultra-left groups, especially in the disagreement about whether nonviolence was to be supported on tactical or on ideological grounds. The Marxist eco-socialists (now departed from the German greens) argued in the mid-1980s that by establishing nonviolence as one of its four constitutive pillars the party had adopted a moralistic approach that prevented it from developing an appropriate political strategy. As Jurgen Reents commented 'My critique of those who have turned nonviolence into an absolute inviolable ideology is that it leads to martyrdom, which makes me fear that one will remain morally clean in the end but politically without success.' He argued that although there is a moral integrity to the argument that violent action cannot lead to a nonviolent society that this cannot be 'used to support social resistance when it reaches its limits and the question arises shall we give up?' (quoted in Capra and Spretnak 1984: 46–7).

On the basis of the argument developed so far, Reents' position seems correct at first. Nonviolence should be the aim wherever possible, but not at the expense of all other aims. However, Reents in fact misinterprets the support for nonviolence as based only on a moral argument. The greens have also tried to justify their nonviolence from a strategic point of view, both regarding the arguments for social defence and also the state's use of force in policing. Furthermore, the position outlined by Reents rested on the weakest of the strands in green arguments for nonviolence: the ambiguous and dangerous category of structural violence. According to this view, being realistic about the structural basis of power meant seeing the social structure as violent. Adherents to this view remained unpersuaded, however, by the more defensible arguments for nonviolence as an end in itself of green ideology and supported nonviolence only as long as it was tactically necessary.

Thus one recurrent problem for the greens has been that nonviolent protest can be defended on either tactical or ideological grounds. Tactical justifications of nonviolence can include avoiding provoking an oppressive reaction from the forces of the state and also maintaining the image of the party as respectable and not in itself a challenge to the democratic system. In Die Grünen, both Marxist greens and *Realos* such as Otto Schily have defended nonviolence on these grounds. But whereas Schily viewed the principle of political obligation as decisive, Marxist greens such as Reents have argued that nonviolence is appropriate only in particular contexts. The problem with both these views is that they relegate the idea of nonviolence to a secondary status. It is no longer an ultimate end that must be taken into account in green strategy. The mainstream green view seems to be more consistent with the following statement:

> fundamental to a nonviolent anarchist approach is the continual erosion of state power through the growth of counter-structures alongside a continual struggle within institutions to dispute hierarchy and strengthen our collective consciousness.
>
> (Clark 1981: 21)

This, apart from the reference to anarchism, could well describe both a short-term green strategy for resisting oppression and a longer-term approach to political change. Green parties generally share the view that what they define as counter-power is essential to the creation of any long-term transformation of state and society.

What such an approach to protest reveals is the very limited sense of obligation to the state felt by green parties. Notwithstanding Schily's argument about political obligation, most greens, whether fundamentalists or realists, seem to have developed a very conditional sense of political obligation (Kelly 1984: 27). In seeing the state neither as the illegitimate committee of the whole bourgeoisie, nor as the sovereign arbiter of individual interests in a specific territorial community, the green parties seem to fall between two stools. Some greens have treated the state as wholly illegitimate, but, in practice, green parties have mainly supported the principles of representative democracy and have not therefore obeyed the law for purely tactical or prudential reasons. On the other hand, they stress the need to 'erode' power from the state and they appeal to a higher morality or to international law in 'resisting' the state.[6] Nor, in contrast for instance to Martin Luther King (1991), do they necessarily accept the right of the state to punish those who commit acts of civil disobedience.

From the standpoint of liberals who see civil disobedience as a threat to the liberal order the views held by many in the green parties would seem to pose serious dangers to political stability and public order. The thread that holds the green position together is the commitment to change through nonviolence. It is their opposition to the use of force that means that the rights of other citizens are not wholly undermined by the rather open attitude of the greens towards political obligation. Greens seem to be arguing that violence cannot provide a basis for political progress, and also that power based on nonviolent resistance can be an effective bulwark against violence. The most controversial consequence of their argument is the claim that the withdrawal of consent to the actions of the state does not necessarily challenge public order, as long as protest remains nonviolent.

In effect, the green parties' position could be justified on the grounds given by Carole Pateman (1985) in her critique of the liberal theory of political obligation. Briefly stated, her argument is that obligation is a red herring in liberal theory because it rests on an idea of consent that liberalism cannot sustain through the idea of a social contract. This is because it is implausible to impute consent to actors who have never actually consented in practice, and because liberal democracies cannot sustain social conditions in which meaningful judgements about consent can be made. Their restrictive definition of morally permissible civil disobedience shows the overriding fear of disorder on the part of liberals.[7] In fact, she argues, political obligation can be justified only on the basis of self-assumed obligation, which worries liberals as it means that political obligation has to be continually created by citizens themselves. Civil disobedience is therefore a potentially legitimate expression of active citizenship and not simply an appeal to the rules or to a shared sense of justice.

The first problem, though, with this view is that it would conflict with the communitarian nature of other green arguments about the state. If communal co-operation and the community as the essential social unit is central in the green vision of politics, then real harm might be done to the rights of others if individuals shirked their obligations to the community in the name of civil disobedience. Such obligations include the need to support those with few economic resources. The social ostracism of offenders, which is sometimes suggested as an alternative to the use of coercion in such cases, might not be sufficiently rapid or effective to guarantee the security of the poor. Greens would face a difficult choice in these circumstances between using force and appealing to communal values. Such choices might be an even more frequent problem if we accepted that the view of community upheld by greens is overly homogeneous and that real green communities are likely to be more diverse and overlapping than many greens seem to envisage. The more realistic the green view of power, the more gradualist their strategy has to become.

A further problem is that whilst the positive intention of nonviolent protest is fairly easy to appreciate, its actual consequences may be more difficult to manage. Protest activity is intended to provoke change and this usually entails conflict. It is thus very difficult to combine protest activity with the aim of ultimate reconciliation that Ghandi espoused (Carter 1992: 17–18). Greens have therefore tried to define their strategy as one that avoids the idea of a continual escalation of conflict. As Howard Clark puts it: 'Nonviolence doesn't try to avoid conflicts, but neither does it go along with a strategy of continually stepping up conflicts in order to provoke deeper and deeper polarisations' (Clark 1981: 19).

One method advocated by greens and peace movement activists for averting the inevitable escalation of protest into larger conflicts is to seek to communicate directly with the individual members of the state apparatus, or to challenge the officially sanctioned stereotypes of 'the enemy' (Die Grünen 1984: 4). So, nonviolence should involve seeing your opponents as fellow human beings and in some way separating them from their role, as for instance, police officer or soldier. But one problematic consequence of personalising the enemy seems to be a further abstraction of the idea of structural violence. If opponents who are in some ways responsible for the violence of the state are to be separated from their roles in that system, then the violence of 'the system' seems to have become even further removed from individual agency or responsibility.

Nevertheless, establishing some basis for communication with an opponent is clearly essential to a strategy which is the antithesis of the use of force to win conflicts. Greens also recognise that such restraint is unlikely to be felt by their opponents. As Clark puts it:

> No matter what individual capitalists may decide, however, any attempt at a fundamental and far-reaching distribution of power in society is bound to have the full force of the state and its repressive apparatus thrown against it at some point.
>
> (Clark 1981: 21)

Greens, therefore, have to take seriously the thought that their own nonviolent protest could create a violent response. This is particularly important given that political violence occurs most often in times of economic or political instability of the kind that the ecological crisis may make more frequent.

One of the benefits of the green attempt to legitimise protest activity is that it might challenge the political passivity of most citizens in liberal democracies, and this was a feature of green optimism about the potential of protest movements in the late 1970s and early 1980s. But although there is a clear link between participation in protest and the creation of a more vigorous public sphere, if public protest becomes established as superior to other aspects of counter-power then it could also lead to an elitist strategy. Nonviolent direct action of the kind practised by greens is certainly more inclusive and participatory than armed confrontation or mass mobilisation ordered by a party elite, but it still privileges the able-bodied and those with the most time and resources to devote to political action. Women with responsibilities as carers, elderly people and disabled people are therefore less likely to be able to participate in such protests. And since we know from the studies of political participation that very few people are prepared to contemplate even quite conventional forms of protest activity (Parry *et al.* 1992: 42–7; Barnes and Kaase 1979: 541) the greens' optimism about the scale of protests might be excessive – a result of their particular experiences in the alternative milieu.

The decline of the protest activity of the social movements in the mid-1980s and the evidence that structural inequalities still affect popular decisions over political participation (Parry *et al.* 1992: 84) means that the greens have to be realistic about the scope and endurance of a politics of mass protest. If a culture of protest is really essential to the creation of new public spheres, then the question has to be asked: what happens when protest activity subsides? Whilst feeling strongly about an issue and being confident that you have the right answer is a motivation for protest, given the unpredictability of protest activity greens should not see it as always the best strategic option.

CONCLUSION

There are, then, clearly strategic problems facing the green parties in their attempt to pursue the creation of a nonviolent society. As a result it might seem that nonviolence is such an abstract idea that it is bound to seem less urgent and less important than other green ends, such as achieving a sustainable society. One consequence of the view of it as an end in itself of green ideology is that it must at times compete with other green ends, such as the achievement of greater equality and sustainability. Greens can show relationships between these ends, but while some green action might be consistent with all these ends, others require decisions on trade-offs. Deciding that action on ecology is more urgent might be justifiable on empirical and strategic grounds, but nonviolence (as with other green ends) does make a difference to what kind of action might be envisaged. If they take nonviolence and other ends seriously, greens must take them into account in deciding how to deal with ecological risks. Thus nonviolence is an important counter to the kinds of ecological politics which might be vulnerable to technocratic arguments about how to achieve sustainability, precisely because it is independent of any ecological justification. And nonviolence can be defined in ways that make it a meaningful and practical end of green strategy. Nonviolence challenges the ideological assumption that violence is both inevitable and technically superior: it puts the onus of proof on opponents and justifies incremental policies governed by the aim of expanding the possibilities for individuals to choose nonviolence.

ACKNOWLEDGEMENTS

I am grateful to Michael Kenny, Marius de Geus and Julie Thompson for their comments on an earlier draft of this chapter.

NOTES

1 Arendt says, for instance: 'Violence appears when power is in jeopardy, but left to its own course it ends in power's disappearance. This implies that it is not correct to think of the opposite of non-violence as violence; to speak of non-violent power is actually redundant. Violence can destroy power; it is utterly incapable of creating it' (Arendt 1970: 56).
2 The Gulf war was treated by the green parties as a prime example of such a 'resource war' for control of oil.
3 In 1993 despite their supposed de-radicalisation they were still arguing for the scrapping of the Bundeswehr and for a world conference to cut conventional weapons (*Frankfurter Rundschau* 11 October 1993).
4 A clear example of this is the proposal for a Europe built on 'non-violent social structures' on the back cover of Kemp *et al.* (1992).
5 The more plausible claim here is the deontological one. If it is wrong to use violence, as greens are sure that it is, then this prevents them from accepting arguments that it is justified in certain circumstances. But if the argument is consequentialist the greens appear more vulnerable, since it is much more debatable whether a small amount of violence might on occasions help to avert worse violence without necessarily making it impossible to resume progress towards the end of a nonviolent society. However, even if they are more vulnerable, consequentialist arguments are still strategically more open.
6 For instance, Rudolf Bahro says, 'We regard civil disobedience as legitimate where the policies pursued affect life itself and the future' (Bahro 1986: 41).
7 Utilitarian arguments are based on prudential reasons for obedience rather than moral obligation.

REFERENCES

Arendt, H. (1970) *On Violence*, London: Allen Lane.
Bahro, R. (1986) *Building the Green Movement*, London: Heretic.
Barnes, S. and Kaase, M. (1979) *Political Action*, London: Sage.
Bennahmias, J. L and Roche, A. (1992) *Des verts de toutes les couleurs*, Paris: Albin Michel.
Capra, F. and Spretnak, C. (1984) *Green Politics*, London: Hutchinson.

Carter, A. (1992) *Peace Movements*, London: Longman.

Chafer, T. (1982) 'The Anti-Nuclear Movement and the Rise of Political Ecology', in P. Cerny (ed.) *Social Movements and Protest in France*, London: Pinter.

Clark, H. (1981) *Making Nonviolent Revolution*, Nottingham: Peace News Pamphlet.

Diani, M. (1990) 'The Italian Ecology Movement: Between Moderatism and Radicalism', in W. Rüdig (ed.) *Green Politics One*, Edinburgh: Edinburgh University Press.

Fanon, F. (1968) *The Wretched of the Earth*, New York: Grove Press.

Giddens, A. (1986) *The Nation State and Violence*, Cambridge: Polity.

Goodin, R. (1992) *Green Political Theory*, Cambridge: Polity.

Green Party (1989) *Manifesto for a Sustainable Society*, London: The Green Party.

Die Grünen (1981) *Peace Manifesto*, Offenbach Congress, 2–4 October.

—— (1984) *Think Globally – Act Locally! Statement of Die Grünen on the Forthcoming European Elections*, Bonn: Die Grünen.

Gurin, D. (1979) 'France: Making Ecology Political and Politics Ecological', *Contemporary Crises* 3, 2: 149–66.

Hülsberg, W. (1988) *The German Greens: A Social and Political Profile*, London: Verso.

Jones, L. (ed.) (1982) *Keeping the Peace*, London: Women's Press.

Kelly, P. (1984) *Fighting for Hope*, London: Chatto & Windus.

Kemp, P. and Wall, D. (1990) *A Green Manifesto for the 1990s*, Harmondsworth: Penguin.

Kemp, P., Wolf, F. O., Juquin, P., Antunes, C., Stengers, C. and Telkamper, W. (1992) *Europe's Green Alternative*, London: Greenprint.

King, Jr, M. L. (1991) 'Letter from Birmingham City Jail', in H. A. Bedau (ed.) *Civil Disobedience in Focus*, London: Routledge.

Langguth, G. (1986) *The Green Factor in German Politics*, Boulder, Colo.: Westview Press.

Linsdell, J. (1991) 'The Mother of Battles', *Green Line* 85: 3–4.

Logue, J. (1982) *Socialism and Abundance*, Minneapolis, Minn.: University of Minnesota Press.

Lucardie, P. (1980) 'The New Left in the Netherlands (1960–1977)', PhD Thesis, Queen's University, Kingston, Ontario.

Lukes, S. (1985) *Marxism and Morality*, Oxford: Oxford University Press.

Martin, B. (1984) *Uprooting War*, London: Freedom Press.

Nelkin, D. and Pollak, M. (1982) *The Atom Besieged*, Cambridge, Mass.: MIT Press.

Papadakis, E. (1984) *The Green Movement in West Germany*, London: Croom Helm.

Parry, G., Moyser, G. and Day, N. (1992) *Political Participation and Democracy in Britain*, Cambridge: Cambridge University Press.

Pateman, C. (1985) *The Problem of Political Obligation: A Critique of Liberal Theory*, Cambridge: Polity.

Poguntke, T. (1990) 'Party Activists versus Voters: Are the German Greens Losing Touch with the Electorate?', in W. Rüdig (ed.) *Green Politics One*, Edinburgh: Edinburgh University Press.

Rawls, J. (1991) 'Definition and Justification of Civil Disobedience', in H. A. Bedau (ed.) *Civil Disobedience in Focus*, London: Routledge.

Rootes, C. A. (1989) 'The Campaign for Nuclear Disarmament: From Moral Crusade to Mobilisation of Anxiety?', in C. Marsh and C. Fraser (eds) *Public Opinion and Nuclear Weapons*, London: Macmillan.

Rüdig, W. (1990) *Anti-Nuclear Movements*, London: Longman.

Singer, P. (1991) 'Disobedience as a Plea for Reconsideration', in H. A. Bedau (ed.) *Civil Disobedience in Focus*, London: Routledge.

Stansill, P. and Mairowitz, D. Z. (eds) (1971) *Bamn (By Any Means Necessary): Outlaw Manifestos and Ephemera, 1965–70*, Harmondsworth: Penguin.

Strange, P. (1983) *It'll Make a Man of You: A Feminist View of the Arms' Race*, Nottingham: Peace News Pamphlet.

Touraine, A., Hegedus, Z. and Wievorka, M. (1983) *Anti-Nuclear Protest: The Opposition to Nuclear Energy in France*, Cambridge: Cambridge University Press.

Les Verts (1987) 'Vivre Libres: Une Autre Défense Pour la Paix', Point de vue, Supplement à *Vert Contact*, 17.

3

WORKER CO-OPERATIVES AND GREEN POLITICAL THEORY

Neil Carter

Most varieties of green political thought – ecosocialism, ecoanarchism, ecofeminism, bio-regionalism *inter alia* – display a fondness for the worker co-operative. Outlines of a 'greener' world, whether in polemical tracts or restrained academic tomes, frequently expound the virtues of the co-operative and its central role in protecting the environment. Green party programmes promise to encourage the growth of co-operatives. The majority of green thinkers envisage a future society in which the ideal form of workplace organisation (alongside the self-sufficient commune) would be that of a co-operative: a democratic workplace characterised by small-scale production, equity, community, and non-exploitation of workers, consumers and, crucially, nature.

The case for co-operatives in green political thought is, however, usually asserted rather than made. Green writers have generally failed to engage with the extensive theoretical and empirical literature about co-operatives. Yet even a cursory examination of this literature would show that many of the claims made on behalf of co-operatives are contentious. In particular, the claim that co-operatives will display greater benevolence towards the environment than capitalist firms is not as straightforward as much green writing seems to imply. This chapter draws together the various strands of the green case for co-operatives under two core hypotheses: first, that a co-operative is characterised by small-scale production, democratic and egalitarian organisational structures, greater individual self-development and better working conditions than a capitalist firm; second, a co-operative will be more benevolent towards the environment than a capitalist firm. Drawing on the theoretical and empirical literature on co-operatives it is shown that there are many problems with these hypotheses and that they will be valid only in certain circumstances. It is argued that greens need to adopt more sophisticated theories of organisational control and ecological consciousness.

First, it is necessary to define precisely what is meant by the term 'co-operative'. There are many kinds of 'co-operatives': farming, fishing, housing, consumer and worker co-operatives are all familiar forms. Although most types of co-operatives would undoubtedly flourish in a greener society, this chapter is concerned with the worker (or producer) co-operative. The worker co-operative is, for present purposes, most usefully defined as 'an organisation which is owned and controlled by those working in it'. Thus a co-operative should be an autonomous organisation with formal provision for direct employee participation in decision making at all levels of the organisation on a one member, one vote principle. Members own the organisational capital either collectively or through individual shares, and all members will have the right to a share in any profit (or surplus?) – though not necessarily on an equal basis.

THE GREEN CASE FOR THE CO-OPERATIVE

Green political thought is replete with favourable references to co-operatives. Sometimes co-operatives are simply included in a list of desirable or necessary reforms with little elaboration or explanation. More often they are deemed to merit a paragraph or two extolling some of the virtues of co-operative organisation. The more perceptive thinkers point to various difficulties associated with co-operative working. But few green writers attempt more than a superficial examination of the co-operative. To surmount this problem this section reconstructs, from a disparate range of texts and essays, the explicit green arguments for co-operatives.

First, greens argue that small units of production are inherently superior to large units because concentrated large-scale industrial production and the spatial separation of workplace and home with which it is associated (which multiplies resource consumption by transporting employees to work and the finished product to dispersed consumers) is massively damaging to the environment. Most greens share a vision of decentralised, small-scale communities in which the co-operative workplace is an integral part. The contemporary guru of small-scale production was Schumacher (1974), but the theme has dominated modern green writing since the publication of *A Blueprint for Survival* (Goldsmith 1972).

Second, the emphasis on small-scale production is closely associated with a preference for participatory, workplace democracy. The 1983 programme of the German greens declares that 'Large combines are to be broken down into surveyable units which can be run democratically by those working in them' (Die Grünen 1983: section II.3, p. 11). The co-operative is one of the various forms of 'democratic worker self-management' that subsequently would be established, as is made clear in the manifesto of the British Green Party: 'We support the formation and growth of co-operatives as a way of encouraging a democratic and non-hierarchical approach to work' (Green Party 1992: 70). Schumacher was attracted by co-operation, specifically praising the Scott Bader Commonwealth in which ownership of a successful chemical manufacturing company was transferred to a collectivity, or commonwealth (Schumacher 1974: 230–7). For Spretnak and Capra, in the 'self-managed co-operative enterprise ... those involved in production should decide themselves what is produced as well as how and where it will be produced' (1985: 98). Workplace democracy is of intrinsic value to greens because the removal of the hierarchies and divisions that characterise the conventional capitalist workplace is believed to enhance individual self-development and self-expression. In this respect support for workplace democracy is consistent with the arguments employed by, for example, Bahro (1986) and Bookchin (1982) in favour of the commune as the preferred form of social organisation in a greener society, and, more generally, with the widespread support for participatory democracy among greens (A. Carter 1993; Porritt 1984; Roszak 1979; Sale 1980; Spretnak and Capra 1985; Tokar 1987). For, as Goodin argues, the achievement of widespread democratic participation in society 'is arguably the central plank in the whole green theory of agency' (1992: 124). But greens also advocate participatory democracy as a means of reducing inequalities in the distribution of power in society. If individuals can have more say in the institutions of civil society it will be 'harder for the powers that be to resist popular demands' and more likely to produce, if not morally perfect outcomes, then at least morally better ones (Goodin 1992: 128).

Third, consequently, greens argue that co-operatives, by introducing greater equality in the workplace, will contribute to the broader objective of reducing imbalances in the distribution of power, wealth and income throughout society. Kemp and Wall assert that 'Greens believe firmly in the principle of economic democracy and support the argument that just as most adults have the right to vote, so we should also have the right to wield commensurate economic influence' (1990: 80). Daly and Cobb (1990) argue that the spread of worker ownership would undermine the power of industrial capital and help remove the disparities between wealthy owners and highly paid workers, and the much larger group of poorly paid workers, underemployed and unemployed people.

Fourth, greens also believe that co-operatives will improve the quality of life within the workplace. Roszak enthuses that in work collectives and producers' co-operatives:

> Whatever their form or origin, the spirit of these enterprises will be the same. Because they will be worker-owned and managed, they will offer the most advanced forms of authentic job enrichment; the fulfilment of people in their work, rather than the size of earnings or output, will be part of their basic standard of efficiency and success.
>
> (Roszak 1979: 238)

And in Callenbach's *Ecotopia*:

> The fact that the members of an enterprise actually own it jointly (each

with one vote) puts certain inherent limits on what these enterprises do . . . the enterprises tend to be just as concerned with conditions of work as they are with profits, and in many instances members seem willing to accept lower profit and wage levels in exchange for a comfortable pace of work or a way of organizing work which offers better relations among the people doing it.

(Callenbach 1978: 93)

This quality of life argument can be interpreted as extending the concept of environment to include greening the workplace.

Porritt is just one writer who develops this argument in another way to suggest that the individual co-operative will therefore be more concerned about the local community:

A co-operative is much more likely to be sensitive to the needs of the community in which its members live. The profit motive is linked to a broader collective concern: concern on the one hand that the working members are adequately cared for, and on the other that the co-operative is playing a constructive part in the wider community.

(Porritt 1984: 139–40)

It is not much of a jump from this to assert that co-operatives will therefore be more benign towards the local environment. Thus Porritt argues that the creation of community savings banks to promote co-operatives would mean that:

The initiative for regenerating the economy would be coming from local people with local knowledge, and the whole community would become involved in the creation of real, long-term wealth, rather than the spurious 'wealth' of advertisement-induced mass consumption.

(Porritt 1984: 141)

However, green writers offer few detailed arguments in support of this important claim.

The green case for co-operatives can be broken down into two parts. First, that co-operatives should produce the following features to a greater degree than current capitalist ownership: small-scale production, participatory democracy, greater equality at work and in society, and a better quality of life at work – all of which are core dimensions of a green political programme. Second, these features will also ensure that co-operatives display a more benign concern for the environment than capitalist organisations. Whilst the arguments assembled under the first plank are similar to those forwarded by many other proponents of co-operatives, the claim that they are better for the environment is a distinctive, though not unique, feature of the ecological thesis.[1]

In evaluating the green case for co-operatives, it is useful to make three further distinctions. First, do co-operatives eliminate all environmental problems or do they simply generate fewer problems than capitalist firms? Second, are all co-operatives or most co-operatives better for the environment than capitalist firms? Third, what difference does it make for a co-operative to operate in an economy dominated by co-operatives as opposed to a capitalist economy? Greens do not normally make these distinctions; it is argued here that they should.

DO CO-OPERATIVES BRING CHANGE?

This section evaluates the various green claims for co-operatives against both theoretical and empirical arguments. In both respects, green writers seem to be largely unaware of the extensive academic literature on co-operatives. For the co-operative is not a new idea; its roots can be traced back at least as far as the Levellers in the seventeenth century. In the nineteenth century it was widely lauded as an alternative to the dominant capitalist organisational form. More recently, western industrialised economies witnessed a rapid growth in the number of co-operatives during the 1970s and 1980s (Bate and Carter 1986). Academic interest focused in particular on one much-publicised contemporary success story: Mondragon, a thriving federation of co-operatives in the Basque region of Spain. In the following discussion frequent reference is made to Mondragon as a successful and oft-cited model.[2]

The first claim, that co-operatives will engage in small-scale production, is probably the least persuasive. This is essentially an argument for small-scale production irrespective of the organisational form. But there is nothing unique to the co-operative form that necessitates small-scale production. Of course, many co-operatives are small, but several co-operatives in Mondragon and in Italy and France have well over a thousand members: greens simply assert that they will be small. A more persuasive case can be made by drawing on various economic arguments about co-operatives. In a market economy co-operatives may face a hiring problem: they will grow only if extra staff increase the productivity of existing members, whereas capitalist firms will hire so long as the net marginal return remains positive. But if co-operatives choose to remain small – as many undoubtedly do – then there is no hiring 'problem', unless larger-scale production is needed in order to survive in a competitive market. Even this difficulty will be less acute in a changing world where technological advances increasingly result in enterprises having a small workforce whilst undertaking large-scale production – the ideal of post-industrial thinkers such as Toffler and Gorz (Frankel 1987). However, co-operatives are also likely to remain relatively smaller than technologically identical capitalist firms because, as Miller (1989) points out, they 'will be unwilling to invest as heavily as capitalist enterprises, and will therefore be unable to compete in an open market whenever investment is needed to maintain techno-logical advance' (1989: 90). These economic arguments might suggest a rather more moderate green defence of co-operatives in a market economy as employing fewer workers and engaging in smaller scale production than capitalist firms. But it is not clear how this would be better for the environment, particularly if overall production levels in the economy were maintained by other firms – capitalist or co-operative – taking up the opportunities forsaken by less entrepreneurial co-operatives.

A quite different argument about size states that the democratic mechan-isms of a co-operative may not operate so effectively in a large organisation. Indeed, after a strike at the largest Mondragon co-operative, ULGOR, it was decided to limit the size of co-operatives to a maximum of 500 workers. Similarly it is not difficult to envisage a situation in which larger organ-isations break up their operations into offices or plants each with no more than, say, 500 workers and run on co-operative lines. At the other extreme, having studied several grassroots collectives that sprang up in the USA during the 1960s and 1970s, Mansbridge (1980) argues that democracy can work effectively only in a relatively small group – although Rothschild and Whitt (1986) can find no precise cut-off point beyond which democratic control yields to oligarchy. But this debate relates to the second claim, that a co-operative will be a participatory democracy and that this will have a beneficial impact on individual self-development.

Although each member has an equal share in ownership a co-operative may not necessarily adopt participatory structures and processes – as seems to be the assumption among green writers. Co-operative members may exercise their democratic right to forsake participatory mechanisms for the 'dual structure' of a representative democratic structure and a management system. There may be good reasons to do so. Some degree of delegation is clearly more appropriate for any co-operative larger than, say, twenty members, where collective processes become less practical. Alternatively, some members may be reluctant to assume responsibility for day-to-day decision making. After all, where participatory structures do exist, the intensity of face-to-face collective decision making frequently generates 'burn out' in members often resulting in their withdrawal from the co-operative (Rothschild and Whitt 1986).

Although many contemporary co-operatives do adopt pure participatory democratic structures, frequently some form of representative structure prevails as, for example, in the plywood co-operatives in the Pacific Northwest USA (Greenberg 1986), France (Batstone 1983), Italy (Thornley 1983) and in many British co-operatives (Cornforth et al. 1988; Mellor et al. 1988). In a Mondragon co-operative the General Assembly consisting of all the workers meets only once or twice a year. The Assembly elects from its membership a small Governing Council (the Junta) which then appoints a Management Council responsible for the day-to-day management of the co-operative. There is some controversy regarding the extent to which this kind of structure encourages active participation in the workforce. Clearly Mondragon workers possess far greater formal control over most forms of decision making than their counterparts in a capitalist firm. Nevertheless it has been argued that participation for the bulk of members amounts to:

> Little more than plebiscite-style elections once a year to approve or disapprove the current leadership team. It is little wonder, then, that most empirical studies show a marked absence of a participatory culture at Mondragon, few worker-members ever speak at the annual assembly, few are informed, and few have any contacts with management.
>
> (Greenberg 1986: 104)

Greenberg is rather ungenerous. In an extensive survey, Bradley and Gelb found that around a third of members perceive themselves as participating either directly or indirectly in making important decisions, compared to just 7 per cent in equivalent capitalist firms (Bradley and Gelb 1983: 54). Mondragon is no panacea, but it appears to be far better than in conventional firms. The Mondragon co-operatives have recognised the problem of marginalisation of workers as illustrated by their decision to limit the size of all new co-operatives to a maximum of 500 members and to set up a social council in each co-operative – in effect a network of work-based shop stewards – which can discuss directly with management any issues related to the immediate work environment. For similar reasons many co-operatives encourage the regular rotation of elected offices to draw a wider range of people into positions of responsibility.

It is therefore important to recognise the limitations that indirect forms of democracy impose on participation in a co-operative. There are specific pressures within the existing capitalist system which encourage the adoption of hierarchical structures, not least the simple discrimination that elected representatives or delegates encounter when dealing with financial institutions and other commercial organisations (Bate and Carter 1986). But even in a fully co-operative economy many of the factors that persuade co-operatives to adopt forms of representative democracy will still pertain.

One way for greens to resolve this problem would be simply to define it away by saying that without participatory democratic structures an organisation is not a co-operative. This is an unsatisfactory solution because it effectively sets a very small limit on the membership of a co-operative. It is also undesirable without conclusive proof that participatory democracy is better for individual self-development (and for the environment) than representative democracy. Consequently, it seems desirable to accept this weaker argument: that while individual self-development may be enhanced more effectively in a participatory democracy, it may still be encouraged in a co-operative with representative democracy to a greater degree than in a capitalist firm.

Whether any form of co-operative democracy succeeds in enhancing individual self-development is by no means as straightforward as greens seem to suggest.[3] When greens praise the beneficial effects of workplace democracy on the individual they are explicitly or implicitly influenced by the 'escalation' theory developed by Carole Pateman in *Participation and Democratic Theory* (1970). She argued that people learn to participate by participating. Pateman advocated worker self-management on the grounds that the impact of participating in decisions at work will escalate beyond the factory gate as individuals gain the confidence to participate in other institutions of civic society. In short, co-operatives should nurture democratic citizenship. Similarly, greens hope that workers can develop feelings of personal political efficacy through workplace participation which will encourage them to become active members of the local community.

However, although studies of political efficacy and participation among co-operative members do show evidence of escalating political consciousness arising from the experience of a democratic work organisation, no firm conclusions can be drawn from the surprisingly limited research existing on this subject (Elden 1981). Indeed, in the most extensive study of this question, Greenberg (1986) found that workers in US plywood co-operatives (admittedly not participatory democracies) were no more politically efficacious than workers in conventional companies; nor more likely to participate in political activity. More worrying for greens, members were actually *less* public spirited and community oriented than the norm; instead, self-interested, individualistic attitudes and values seemed to increase according to the length of time spent in the co-operative. Wajcman (1983) also found that the experience of working in the Fakenham women's co-operative left the political consciousness of the women at the societal level and, particularly, their orientations and attitudes to the sexual division of labour, largely untouched. On the other hand, although there is no evidence of Mondragon developing a specific political consciousness, there is a very close relationship between the co-operatives and the Basque community. In particular, the Caja Laboral Popular characterises this symbiosis: the savings of local people are placed in the bank to be reinvested in the co-operatives thereby creating local jobs. Elsewhere, when a 'defensive' co-operative emerges from a struggle against the closure of a factory, close links are often established with the local community (Bate and Carter 1986).

If there is any substance to the political escalation thesis, it seems likely that the social and economic environment in which a co-operative is located will influence the broader impact of participation. Thus in the capitalist USA where individualist values are nurtured there is little encouragement for the plywood workers to make links between their workplace and political experiences. But in the Basque country, ravaged by the civil war and subjected to discrimination by a hostile Franco, the Mondragon co-operatives sprang up in a close-knit, self-reliant culture where conditions were favourable to the development of close links between the co-operatives and the community. If co-operatives were located in the kind of green society outlined by deep ecologists, then members would probably be more likely to develop a political consciousness characterised by the dominant societal values of participation, democracy, equality, community and concern for the environment.

The egalitarian case is one that greens share with other proponents of co-operatives. It is an argument that can be broken down into two strands. Are the internal relationships within co-operatives egalitarian or, at least, more egalitarian than in capitalist firms? Can co-operatives help bring greater equality throughout society than exists within the existing capitalist system? The concept of equality also has several constituent parts. Is it equality of wealth and income? Or is it equality in power and influence? Is it equality between classes, genders or races? In this section, the issue of equality of income is addressed; we return to broader issues of control and influence later.

Worker-owners will possess an equal stake in the organisation and share ultimate control over decision making. They may, however, retain differentials in the reward system for there is no intrinsic reason why a co-operative should have equal pay. Many small collectivist co-operatives do insist on equal pay, but many others find it necessary to introduce differentials in order to attract suitable managerial or technical staff. In Mondragon, there was originally a maximum ratio of 3:1 between highest and lowest wages, which rose subsequently to 4.5:1 and, in 1987, to 6:1 (and 7:1 in the *Caja*) although the highest ratio exists only in exceptional circumstances and is not accepted by every co-operative (Morrison 1991: 72–3). This ratio is also used to distribute the members' share of the social capital (the surplus or profit) into individual accounts that accumulate until they are drawn out when the worker leaves the co-operative. At Scott Bader there is a similar range of wage differentials. In some small alternative co-operatives there is a policy of paying wages according to need, for example, extra pay for parents. Nevertheless, whilst inequalities of income may well remain – often by choice – the disparity of income within an individual co-operative will normally be less than within an equivalent capitalist firm.

The extent to which co-operatives can bring greater equality throughout society will obviously depend partly on what goes on within the workplace: in particular, the narrower the reward differentials, the less inequality. But this will count for little if co-operatives are operating alongside capitalist firms in a market economy. Some greens, along with market socialists (Miller 1989) and radical liberals (Dahl 1985), envisage worker co-operatives replacing the power of large private industrial and financial corporations, but the method of transition remains unclear. Even in an economy dominated by small participatory democratic co-operatives with equal pay inside the organisation, there could still be enormous disparities of income, wealth and power *between* co-operatives. Some businesses will be more commercially successful than others and will be able to offer higher monetary rewards. To assert with confidence that co-operatives will achieve greater equality it is necessary to know more about the economic system in which they will be operating.

Important reservations also need to be expressed about the capacity of co-operatives to alter the quality of life within the workplace. A different experience of work is not an inevitable outcome of worker ownership. A key issue here is the question of alienation. For Blauner (1964), alienation has several dimensions – powerlessness, meaninglessness, isolation, self-estrangement – all of which are firmly rooted in the workplace. His belief that the key determinant of alienation is technology rather than ownership has some plausibility. After all, some work appears to be intrinsically repetitive, monotonous or unpleasant. If this is unalterable then the impact of worker ownership on the lived experience of the shopfloor worker will be minimal. As Eccles wryly commented about the shopfloor at the newly formed KME Kirkby co-operative, 'It is difficult to tell a man with a welding torch still in front of him that he's part of a new system' (Eccles 1981: 382). Gorz (1982) recognises this in his distinction between self-determination in the workplace and the elimination of alienating work. He believes that heteronomous (necessary and unpleasant) work and production cannot be abolished; simply minimised. Whether working in a democratic or an autocratic workplace, boring work is boring work (see also Frankel 1987: chs 1–2).

An objection to this argument could be that alienation is not primarily about boredom but about whether people are fulfilled in their work. In this view no work is intrinsically boring, let alone alienating – it depends on what meaning people ascribe to it. In a co-operative it may be that members feel a sense of ownership and involvement that is absent from the capitalist workplace such that even the most mundane of tasks is invested with purpose and meaning. At a philosophical level this objection is valid if it is accepted that ultimately it is the individual's definition of the situation that determines alienation. And, with a share in ownership and the potential for greater influence in the workplace than in a capitalist firm, the co-operative undoubtedly provides a different set of opportunities for individuals to redefine their situation in a more positive light. There is plenty of evidence that co-operatives are capable of generating higher commitment, greater motivation and more job satisfaction than capitalist firms.[4] But such attributes are by no means uniform and there are also many examples of co-operatives torn apart by conflict, or where morale is low, and the attitudes and behaviour of the workforce are very negative (Cornforth *et al.* 1988; Mellor *et al.* 1988; Rothschild and Whitt 1986).

One explanation for this mixed record is that the above arguments – both Blauner's stress on technology and the emphasis on the benefits that co-operative ownership may bring – are narrowly focused on what goes on within the workplace. By shifting attention to the issue of the control over the labour process, Braverman's (1974) seminal work relocated the study of workplace alienation within the broader capitalist system. Although Braverman's approach has encountered much criticism, his basic message remains important: what goes on inside the workplace will be profoundly influenced by events beyond the factory gate. It may be that the significance of co-operative ownership and the consequent opportunity for members to exercise choice over the organisation of work will be outweighed by external forces that shape the nature of the work process within the co-operative. A co-operative in a capitalist market will be under pressure to adopt existing work processes characterised by hierarchical control, division of labour and managerial prerogatives. At Mondragon a conventional hierarchical work organisation prevails and, although there is an interest in adopting more humane and enriching methods, the workers exercise very little control over their daily work experience (Bradley and Gelb 1983; Johnson and Whyte 1977). And, as noted, there are many small co-operatives effectively engaged in self-exploitation: working long hours for low wages in dreadful 'sweatshop' conditions. If the day-to-day work experience of co-operative members is no different from that of a capitalist firm, it is likely that their experience of work will be just as alienating. Indeed, if people form or join a co-operative with high expectations of enjoying the fruits of democratic ownership and control, but find that they can exercise very little choice over the form of their workplace, they may become even more alienated and disillusioned than before. This said, there may be something in the argument that it may be less alienating to have to do 'X' because otherwise your co-operative may collapse (and you have taken that decision democratically and in full knowledge of the situation), than to have to do 'X' simply because your boss tells you to do so. An example of such behaviour would be the case of self-employed people who frequently engage in what might be described as self-exploiting labour because they perceive themselves to be struggling against external constraints, not a boss.[5]

Before addressing the specific links between co-operatives and the environment, it is desirable to show how claims made regarding the first hypothesis can be refined by applying a more sophisticated model of control.

Forms of control

It should now be apparent that there are complex issues associated with worker co-operatives that are poorly acknowledged in green writing. One important debate that is central to the co-operative literature, yet has passed apparently unnoticed by greens, relates to what has become known as the 'degeneration thesis'. Sidney and Beatrice Webb (1914) argued that most co-operatives degenerate, or, in their words, 'democracies of producers' become in effect 'associations of capitalists'. Three forms of degeneration can be identified: 'constitutional', when some or all of the workforce are excluded from ownership and control of the organisation; 'goal', when the pursuit of profit supersedes any other aims the co-operative might have; 'organisational', when a small group of members obtain effective control and introduce a management hierarchy and division of labour (Cornforth *et al.* 1988: ch. 6). Degeneration results from both internal and external pressures. The most powerful of the internal sources are associated with Michels' (1949) 'iron law of oligarchy'. Briefly, he argued that direct democracy is inefficient and that elected leaders in democratic organisations will seek to become a ruling elite. The external pressures on a co-operative arise from the critical tension facing a democratic organisational form operating within a capitalist market which makes it difficult for co-operatives to break away from capitalist principles of organisation such as hierarchy, wage differentials and the minimisation of wage costs. Not surprisingly, the degeneration thesis has been the focus of much controversy within the co-operative literature.

The degeneration thesis suggests that there is a need for a more sophisticated model of organisational control which takes the study of co-operatives beyond the narrow focus on ownership and formal control structures that characterises most green writing. This model redirects attention to the informal processes of control such as the role of founder members and leaders, the organisation of the work process and the nature of the economy in which a co-operative is located.

All organisations have informal processes of control that circumvent or run in opposition to formal control structures and which individuals or groups can use to accrue greater power and influence. Some of these reflect broader societal inequalities based on class, race or gender; others are internal to the individual co-operative. Knowledge is, of course, an important source of power, and differential access to information or possession of technical competence may lead to unequal influence in decision making. In a co-operative the founder members, despite possessing equal formal powers, often exercise greater influence than newcomers because of the commitment and sense of purpose attached to being authors of the co-operative idea and by dint of their long-term knowledge of the organisation (Russell 1985).

Even if all organisational sources of power could be eradicated, there will always be individual differences:

Even in a collectivist organisation that might achieve universal competence, other sources of unequal influence would persist (e.g. commitment level, verbal fluency, social skills). The most a democratic

67

organisation can do is to remove the bureaucratic bases of authority: positional rank and expertise.

(Rothschild-Whitt 1979: 524)

A participatory democratic structure can reduce but not eradicate inequalities in the workplace – and that may be the best that we can hope for.

It is also important to recognise the role of external constraints on individual co-operatives. As small businesses, many co-operatives struggle to survive in the market. They are frequently locked into dependent subcontracting relationships with powerful corporations that allow individual co-operatives little autonomy over the organisation of the work process (Bate and Carter 1986; Mellor *et al.* 1988). Nevertheless the balance of evidence (and opinion) seems to be that whilst these constraints are significant they are also avoidable. For example, in a different economic environment opportunities for autonomy do exist. In the Emilia-Romagna region in central Italy interventionist socialist/communist regional governments have contributed to the emergence of a dense small-firm sector in which flexible specialisation has established a prosperous high-technology cottage industry (Sabel 1982). This sector includes a number of co-operatives boasting high wages, strong internal democracy and progressive work practices. What goes on inside a co-operative largely depends on the way in which individual co-operatives negotiate their relationship with the economic environment. But if co-operatives are to exert a radical impact on the workplace (and society) it will require broad structural reform of the capitalist economy.

ARE CO-OPERATIVES ENVIRONMENTALLY BENIGN?

The second hypothesis suggests that co-operatives will be more benign towards the environment than conventional capitalist firms. This claim seems to depend partly on the various organisational practices discussed in the previous section and partly on the close links that will exist between a co-operative and its local community. The outcome of both developments is that co-operatives will be more aware of, and more concerned about, the immediate environment – and also, presumably, the wider environment.

An evaluation of the first part of this claim is not helped by the poorly developed green case. For example, there are arguments suggesting why co-operatives should be less likely to use polluting technology or destroy natural resources that greens do not seem to have considered (Miller 1991). By sharing profits throughout the enterprise, economic stakes are lowered so that by comparison to a capitalist firm no individual has so much to lose by switching to greener technology. On the other hand, it could be argued that if everyone has something to lose it will be harder to produce change. Long ago the Webbs (1914) argued that co-operatives were unwilling to adapt to technological change because of the natural tendency of producers to defend their jobs and skills. If there is any truth in this claim it would suggest that co-operatives may be more conservative about adopting new, greener, technologies, although they may be equally conservative in adopting new environmentally damaging technologies. Moreover, as decision making should be more open in a co-operative than in a capitalist firm, which should bring more information into the public realm, it should be harder to pay lip-service to environmental legislation whilst secretly flouting it.

Yet, the green case as it is presented seems to depend on the belief that co-operative ownership will necessarily result in small-scale production – an assertion that has been shown to be largely unfounded. It is also assumed that democratic control will encourage environmental awareness on the grounds that members are unlikely to damage their local environment. This is a sound argument in so far as workers are unlikely knowingly to use technologies and materials that will directly harm the workforce. Whether this will extend to protecting the wider community is less certain.

There are a number of strands to the co-operative–community thesis. It is unclear whether greens anticipate the relationship between co-operative and community being such that production decisions are formally accountable and responsive to the wishes of local communities. Kemp and Wall state that 'Businesses ultimately need to be controlled co-operatively by the community' (1990: 81). But this would be inconsistent with their support for participatory democratic co-operatives in which productive decisions are taken by the workforce alone – and with the definition of a co-operative used in this chapter. Perhaps a more organic relationship is better, as with Daly and Cobb's (1990) belief that co-operatives will be strongly bound to the communities in which they are located. It seems reasonable to assume that co-operatives will be sensitive to the explicit interests of the local community. In a co-operative local people will be contributing to decision making; more actively in a participatory democracy, but also quite extensively in a representative democracy. It may be possible to have formal community representation in the decision-making process – although there would be problems of information disclosure if there were several co-operatives in an area in competition with each other. Being locally owned, a co-operative is less likely to uproot and move elsewhere. As at Mondragon, there are strong disincentives against leaving the co-operative due to an ownership structure that creates financial ties and generates high worker commitment to the organisation. Certainly, there is very low turnover in the Mondragon co-operatives, although Bradley and Gelb (1983) point out that this is characteristic of the entire Basque region rather than a result of the co-operative experience. But why should this close relationship with the community be better for the environment?

This larger claim is based on the argument that the democratic structure

69

of a co-operative will allow community interests to be represented, formally or informally. Unlike a capitalist organisation, a co-operative is less likely to adopt technologies that pollute the immediate (spatial and temporal) vicinity because they would directly harm some or all of its members (it is important here to distinguish between large corporations where productive processes are often made at a distance, and locally based capitalist firms which may display greater sensitivity to community interests – although still probably less than a co-operative). However, there is an implicit assumption in this argument that the community will place environmental interests above other material interests. But a local community might place job creation and protection above ecological considerations – as in the Cumbrian community in which the Sellafield nuclear plant is located. The expressed interests of workers and much of the local community have been identical: they supported the nuclear power station and lobbied in favour of opening the THORP nuclear waste reprocessing plant. If the interests of a community and a co-operative did diverge, would community concern about the environmental impact of an organisational policy be persuasive enough to change decisions made by workers seeking bigger profits or simply seeking to survive in the market? If the co-operative is dependent on a powerful corporation or operating on the margins of survival or collapse, it may have little choice over its actions. Rather than claim that co-operatives will necessarily place environmental considerations above those of job creation, it is more sensible to argue that a co-operative will balance such competing concerns in a way that better reflects the needs and interests of the local community – whereas capitalist firms will normally give greater weight to profit-related considerations.

Moreover, evidence of environmental concern amongst existing co-operatives is rather thin. Many of the grassroots co-operatives established in the wake of the counter-culture movement were specifically set up to market wholefoods, organic produce and vegetarianism. But amongst manufacturing co-operatives it is an under-researched question. At Mondragon, concern for the environment means that the planning process for new co-operatives or developments requires an environmental impact assessment which places it ahead of most – but not all – corporations. Yet even a sympathetic commentator has to admit that Mondragon has a 'mixed' environmental record with much still to do regarding industrial pollution abatement (Morrison 1991).

A further problem is that a community might be concerned and knowledgeable about damage to the local environment but it may not be worried by (or even aware of) damage further afield (or downstream, or downwind). Indeed, it could be argued that the green interest in encouraging individual self-development may work against the cultivation of a collective concern for those living further afield (or yet to be born). Unless individual self-development also encourages each individual always to bear the interests of others in mind, there is the potential for rational choice problems such as free riding to occur. Similarly, small communities often define themselves by reference to those outside, at a distance, and may be quite averse to considering wider questions, such as the possibility of environmental damage elsewhere.

It has been argued that what goes on inside a co-operative (and, by the same token, in a small community) will be greatly influenced by the kind of society in which it is located. Here it is important to note Eckersley's comment, offered as a critique of the ecoanarchist approach, that leaving decisions to the locals who are affected 'makes sense only when the locals possess an appropriate social and ecological consciousness' (1992: 173); or, at least, a consciousness that, even if imperfect, is superior to that of central authorities. Greens seem to suggest that the co-operative can play a role in the transition to a society with a more sophisticated ecological consciousness. Like other political creeds, greens make heroic assumptions about the capacity of the co-operative organisational form to produce certain values, attitudes and behaviour amongst its members, but we have seen how many of these claims do not stand up. In this context, it seems sensible to distinguish between the kinds of claims that co-operatives are less likely knowingly to use technologies that harm themselves or their local environment, and the quite different kind of argument that might say that a co-operative will also nurture an ecological consciousness within its workforce. To address this latter question, greens need to bring the members into the equation. By asking why people form a particular co-operative, what members want from their co-operatives, and how their attitudes and behaviour change as a result of working in a co-operative, greens might gain a richer understanding of the impact that workplace democracy may have on an ecological consciousness. As it is we can claim with confidence only that a participatory democratic workplace, with a more humane work environment and a close bonding with the local community, may combine to enhance the expression and implementation of existing ecological views. Whether co-operative ownership in itself will be the source of that changing consciousness is less certain.

CONCLUSION

The co-operative is not a new idea and greens are not the first to discover its apparent virtues – indeed, there is a remarkable political consensus supporting the co-operative (N. Carter 1986). Nor are greens alone in their partial and limited grasp of the complexities of this organisational form. The political consensus around the co-operative is significant because it suggests that the co-operative form has the versatility to reflect many diverse values. As a vessel into which almost any meaning can be poured and from which many different forms and meanings can emerge, the co-operative is

71

truly in the eye of the beholder. It is not surprising that this malleability has inspired considerable optimism about the capacity of co-operatives to invoke change: to the economy, to the community, to the workplace, to the worker and, recently, to the environment. But the nature of this change – what it is, how it comes about – is inadequately theorised in green writing.

It has been argued that a better understanding of co-operatives would emerge from a focus on two central features – control and consciousness – that characterise all the claims for change made by greens. A more sophisticated model of control would go beyond the narrow concern with co-operative ownership and formal control structures that characterises green writing by examining informal processes of control such as the role of founder members and leaders, the organisation of the work process and the nature of the economy in which a co-operative is located. The examination of ecological consciousness would place greater emphasis on the attitudes of individual members as well as the impact of broader social and economic transformation. It is also important to recognise the relationship between the two concepts. A participatory democracy that gives members sufficient control to create a more equal, less alienated workforce, utilising more convivial technology and in closer touch with the community, may not in itself be the catalyst of an ecological consciousness, but it should facilitate its development. Conversely, if workers bring an ecological consciousness into the workplace, they are more likely to insist that democratic mechanisms function effectively so that they can influence decision making on all issues that have an impact on the environment.

The use of these concepts shows that the green claim that worker co-operatives will be associated with a range of alternative organisational practices will occur only in certain circumstances. Co-operatives will normally be more democratic than capitalist firms, although the nature of that democracy – participatory or representative – will vary, and they will have greater equality of income. The co-operative form is itself unlikely to ensure small-scale production, although it may be relatively smaller than equivalent capitalist firms. The potential for individual self-development and a less alienating experience of work will be heavily dependent on the relationship that individual co-operatives can negotiate with the external world. On these issues, co-operatives would be more likely to deliver change in an economy with a large, thriving co-operative sector or, preferably, in a wholly co-operative economy. But even in a co-operative market economy, pressures of size and efficiency would still ensure the dominance of representative democracy, and competition between co-operatives would result in inequalities between co-operatives (only in an ecoanarchist non-market economy would this source of inequality be absent). Co-operatives do not eliminate environmental problems and the formation of even a wholly co-operative economy would not be sufficient to ensure a greener world. But there are good reasons why co-operatives can be less damaging to the environment than capitalist enterprises. The key factors are the democratic structure of the co-operative and the potential for close ties with the local community. Neither of these features will guarantee a more benign attitude to the environment than can be expected from a capitalist firm but, on balance, they make it more likely. Not all co-operatives will be better for the environment because some will place other priorities – jobs or profits – above environmental considerations; and some may place the interests of the local community above those of far-off communities. Even in a wholly co-operative economy with a widespread and sophisticated ecological consciousness, there would still be the need for some kind of central agent – presumably the state – to solve problems of co-ordination that would inevitably arise between different co-operatives and communities.

ACKNOWLEDGEMENTS

I would like to like Susan Mendus, David Miller, Andrew Pendleton and, particularly, Andrew Williams, as well as participants at the ECPR Workshop in Madrid, April 1994, for their comments on earlier drafts of this chapter.

NOTES

1 David Miller has suggested that co-operatives under market socialism would be less likely to adopt polluting technology or destroy natural resources (Miller 1991: 413).
2 The better studies of Mondragon include Bradley and Gelb (1983); Thomas and Logan (1982); Whyte and Whyte (1988). Many references to Mondragon veer towards the adulatory rather than analytical, for example, Robert Oakeshott (1978), and it appears that ecologists, such as Porritt (1984), have confined their reading to these uncritical accounts.
3 For a discussion of the precise meaning attributed to self-determination in the context of green theory, see Goodin (1992: 124–31).
4 See, for example, Bate and Carter (1986); Cornforth *et al.* (1988); Gunn (1984); Jackall and Levin (1984); Rothschild and Whitt (1986).
5 I am grateful to David Miller for this point.

REFERENCES

Bahro, R. (1986) *Building the Green Movement*, London: Heretic.
Bate, P. and Carter, N. (1986) 'The Future for Producer Co–operatives', *Industrial Relations Journal* 17, 1: 57–70.
Batstone, E. (1983) 'Organisation and Orientation: a Life-cycle Model of French Co-operatives', *Economic and Industrial Democracy* 4: 139–61.
Blauner, R. (1964) *Alienation and Freedom*, Chicago: University of Chicago Press.
Bookchin, M. (1982) *The Ecology of Freedom*, Palo Alto, Calif.: Cheshire Books.
Bradley, K. and Gelb, A. (1983) *Co-operation at Work: The Mondragon Experience*, London: Heinemann.

Braverman, H. (1974) *Labor and Monopoly Capital*, New York: Monthly Review Press.

Callenbach, E. (1978) *Ecotopia*, London: Pluto.

Carter, A. (1993) 'Towards a Green Political Theory', in A. Dobson and P. Lucardie (eds) *The Politics of Nature*, London: Routledge.

Carter, N. (1986) 'Co-operatives: the State of Play', *Political Quarterly* 57, 2: 182–7.

Cornforth, C., Thomas, A., Lewis, J. and Spear, R. (1988) *Worker Co-operatives*, London: Sage.

Dahl, R. (1985) *A Preface to Economic Democracy*, Cambridge: Polity.

Daly, H. and Cobb, J. (1990) *For the Common Good*, London: Greenprint.

Eccles, T. (1981) *Under New Management*, London: Pan.

Eckersley, R. (1992) *Environmentalism and Political Theory: Towards an Ecocentric Approach*, London: UCL Press.

Elden, J. (1981) 'Political Efficacy at Work: the Correlation between more Autonomous Forms of Workplace Organisation and a more Participatory Politics', *American Political Science Review* 75: 43–58.

Frankel, B. (1987) *The Post-Industrial Utopians*, Cambridge: Polity.

Goldsmith, E. (1972) *A Blueprint for Survival*, Harmondsworth: Penguin.

Goodin, R. (1992) *Green Political Theory*, Cambridge: Polity.

Gorz, A. (1982) *Farewell to the Working Class*, London: Pluto.

Green Party (1992) *Manifesto for a Sustainable Society*, London: The Green Party.

Greenberg, E. (1986) *Workplace Democracy*, Ithaca, NY: Cornell University Press.

Die Grünen (1983) *Programme of the German Green Party*, trans. Hans Fernbach, London: Heretic.

Gunn, C. (1984) *Workers' Self-Management in the United States*, Ithaca, NY: Cornell University Press.

Jackall, R. and Levin, H. (1984) *Worker Co-operatives in America*, Berkeley, Calif.: University of California Press.

Johnson, A. and Whyte, W. (1977) 'The Mondragon System of Worker Production Co-operatives', *Industrial and Labor Relations Review* 31: 18–30.

Kemp, P. and Wall, D. (1990) *A Green Manifesto for the 1990s*, Harmondsworth: Penguin.

Mansbridge, J. (1980) *Beyond Adversary Politics*, New York: Basic.

Mellor, M., Hannah, J. and Stirling, J. (1988) *Worker Co-operatives in Theory and Practice*, Milton Keynes: Open University Press.

Michels, R. (1949) *Political Parties*, New York: Free Press.

Miller, D. (1989) *Market, State, and Community*, Oxford: Clarendon Press.

—— (1991) 'Market Socialism: A Vision', *Dissent* summer: 406–14.

Morrison, R. (1991) *We Build the Road As We Go*, Philadelphia, Pa: New Society.

Oakeshott, R. (1978) *The Case for Workers' Co-operatives*, London: Routledge & Kegan Paul.

Pateman, C. (1970) *Participation and Democratic Theory*, Cambridge: Cambridge University Press.

Porritt, J. (1984) *Seeing Green*, Oxford: Blackwell.

Roszak, T. (1979) *Person/Planet*, London: Victor Gollancz.

Rothschild, J. and Whitt, A. (1986) *The Co-operative Workplace*, Cambridge: Cambridge University Press.

Rothschild-Whitt, J. (1979) 'The Collectivist Organisation: an Alternative to Rational-bureaucratic Models', *American Sociological Review* 44: 509–27.

Russell, R. (1985) *Sharing Ownership in the Workplace*, Albany, NY: SUNY Press.

Sabel, C. (1982) *Work and Politics*, Cambridge: Cambridge University Press.

Sale, K. (1980) *Human Scale*, New York: Coward, Cann & Geoghegan.

Schumacher, E. (1974) *Small is Beautiful*, London: Sphere.

Spretnak, C. and Capra, F. (1985) *Green Politics*, London: Paladin.

Thomas, H. and Logan, C. (1982) *Mondragon: An Economic Analysis,* London: Allen & Unwin.

Thornley, J. (1983) 'Workers' Co-operatives and Trade Unions: the Italian Experience', *Economic and Industrial Democracy* 4: 321–44.

Tokar, B. (1987) *The Green Alternative,* San Pedro: R. & E. Miles.

Wajcman, J. (1983) *Women in Control,* Milton Keynes: Open University Press.

Webb, S. and Webb, B. (1914) 'Co-operative Production and Profit Sharing', *New Statesman* (special supplement) 14 February.

Whyte, W. and Whyte, K. (1988) *Making Mondragon,* Ithaca, NY: Cornell University Press.

Part II

GREEN POLITICS AND DEMOCRATIC THEORY

4

MUST DEMOCRATS BE ENVIRONMENTALISTS?

Michael Saward

Is there something about being a democrat that entails being an environmentalist? To what extent can democratic theory be pushed to green conclusions? If we are to deal with these questions, we must first jettison the view that 'there is no democratic theory – there are only democratic theories' (Dahl 1956: 1). I begin with the assumption that democracy is a three-dimensional and self-sufficient political concept. According to this assumption we can build up a single-best theory of democracy without recourse to liberals, socialists, anarchists and environmentalists. This theory shows us the inescapable core of what professed democrats ought to believe. If the theory works, we can explore with confidence the degree to which there is a logical compulsion on democrats to be environmentalists, and what kind of environmentalists they should be. In the early part of the chapter, I shall defend the view that democracy ought to be understood as a political system in which government responds fully to the felt wishes of citizens. The more responsive a government is, the more democratic it is. Although I regard this as the best way to define democracy, those who do not share my view can at least regard it as providing us with a strong test case of the links between democracy and environmentalism, since this definition leaves no room for governments to pursue substantive goals – such as environmental goals – unless a majority of citizens votes for them. From this unpromising base, I shall argue that there are democratic rights, and that there is a case for a democratic right not to be harmed in certain ways by certain environmental risks. The case for such a democratic right is not watertight. Various objections are canvassed and assessed in the final part of the chapter. No full closure of the subject is intended; the chapter is a conjecture on the power of arguments that democrats must be environmentalists.

The ingredients of democratic theory

No democratic theory can be adequate without minimally convincing arguments concerning: (1) the basic meaning of the term democracy;

79

(2) why democracy so defined is more desirable than non-democratic systems; (3) the decision rules appropriate to democracy; (4) the logical requirements of democracy; (5) the political units appropriate to democratic systems; and (6) the basis (if any) upon which trade-offs might properly be conducted between democracy and competing values. Space restrictions prevent a full treatment of these areas. However, as we shall see, the crucial points about environmentalism emerge within areas (4) and (6).

Why is democracy a good thing?

Of all the arguments that can be offered in favour of democracy, only one is near-decisive. Familiar types of justification that fall short of the mark include: 'basic principles' arguments, such as that democracy is good because it is consistent with the self-evident principle of equality; 'intrinsic benefits' arguments, such as that participation in politics is inherently worthy; and 'beneficial outcomes' arguments, such as that democracy produces greater liberty, or constrains conflict.

The first involves a style of argument that requires that a founding principle ought simply to be accepted at face value, without a supporting argument as to *why* it ought to be accepted (aside from the fact that it commonly *is*). The second asserts as always true what can only be established empirically from case to case. The third rapidly becomes lost in a fog of infinite regress, where the burden of justification is simply displaced onto yet another allegedly good thing.[1] For Sir Karl Popper, a myriad confirmations of a hypothesis could be rendered invalid by one, devastating, falsification. Analogously, these three types of argument amount to confirmations, whose status remains necessarily contingent and uncertain. A stronger justification can be derived from an effort to (so to speak) falsify anti-democratic arguments. Consider the basis of anti-democratic challenges. All principled arguments favouring perpetual government of the many by the few are arguments from superior knowledge (Thorson 1962: 135; Walzer 1983: 285; Shapiro 1994: 140). These arguments might be disguised in various ways; by virtue of their age, sex, race, class, virtue, military strength or whatever, these few have superior political knowledge such that they should rule the many.

Is such knowledge attainable? Even if it is, can we know when it has been attained? Commonly we do recognise many claims to superior knowledge, often in fields of technical or professional expertise. Doctors, lawyers, teachers and nuclear physicists are, normally, recipients of respect for superior knowledge within their fields. But knowledge of what is right in politics goes beyond such limited fields (though, depending on the issue, it may overlap with one or more of them). Certain politicians or administrators – even political philosophers – may have special insights into the effective and efficient running of government. That special expertise is, however, procedural; the ethical substance of state policies and actions is not something about which they can claim rightly an analogous superior knowledge. Knowledge of political rightness may encompass technical expertise from case to case, but always goes beyond this to embrace knowledge of values, and ultimately of what makes a good life. *That* is knowledge that no person, or group, can rightly claim to possess perpetually and with a higher degree of certainty than all others. In this way, justifications for non-democratic rule fall, and can be resurrected only by unsavoury doses of wilfully tailored ideology.

If generic anti-democratic arguments fail, we are left with democracy, where it is the view of rightness of the many, and not the few, that counts as the sole justifiable form of political system. Of the many further arguments that can be mustered in support of this view, two are especially significant. The first is the fallibilist argument. With its classic roots in the work of John Stuart Mill (1975) and Charles Sanders Peirce (1940), and more modern accounts in the works of Popper and his followers, fallibilism is the doctrine that 'our knowledge is never absolute but swims, as it were, in a continuum of uncertainty and of indeterminacy' (Peirce 1940: 356). In Thorson's words, 'the principle of fallibilism does not say that we can never know the truth, but rather that we are never justified in behaving as if we know it . . . we are never justified in refusing to consider the possibility that we might be wrong' (1962: 122). While on factual or procedural grounds we might dispute the fallibility of some absolute knowledge claims (those of the mathematician, perhaps) and other relative knowledge claims (those of the doctor, etc.), in the realm of values, or substance, or in the defining of the good life, any argument against fallibilism is surely both fatally flawed and politically pernicious.

The second argument is about interests. If the few can rightly be said to have a special insight into the substantive interests of the many, then the fallibilist argument is weakened and this style of justifying democracy weakened with it. Consider, however, what such a strong claim to know the best interests of others really entails. While we might concede that a political authority could have legitimate contingently superior knowledge of what is in the interests of a citizen with regard to one discrete political issue, the interests of that citizen at a given time reflect responses to a range of issues. Those issues will affect each other, often in complex ways, making an external judgement of our citizen's fuller interests tougher still. This is leaving aside different citizens – millions of them, perhaps – each with different responses and needs with respect to different issues. It also leaves aside changes in citizens' interests over time. The claim that a political authority can know the 'best interests' of citizens generally is a massive claim indeed, one that must be treated with great suspicion.[2]

The argument about interests pushes us towards an assumption that people must be regarded as the best judges of their own interests (when it comes to value judgements at least). This is not to argue that individuals are the best judges of their own interests (see Goodin 1990). Sometimes they will be, sometimes not. It is an argument for regarding people as the best judges of their own interests in the absence of a more secure ground upon which to make such judgements.

These arguments might be thought self-defeating. If claims to superior knowledge of political values are inevitably fallible, so far as we can know, and if a political authority's chances of knowing the better interests of citizens in any full sense are next to nil, then no prescriptions about politics are possible at all. In fact, they amount to a powerful argument for democracy, precisely because they reveal the hollowness of anti-democratic arguments, whatever form the latter take. Assuming that all political communities will need to make some binding collective decisions, the only reasonable path to choose is the democratic one, since the alternatives require unacceptable claims about knowledge of the community's political good. Clearly, other assumptions are at work in this argument. To address the question of ideal political arrangements for a community is implicitly to argue that each person is worthy of respect and consideration. The real work, however, is performed by the argument that instrumental knowledge is not substantive ethical knowledge.

Is it enough that the justification of democracy appears to be a kind of leftover, a last resort when all else is untenable? To return to the Popperian analogy, a hundred empirical confirmations of democracy's positive worth leave the extent, and comparative power, of its worth deeply uncertain. Further, they are all too easy, often conveying a smugness born of certainty that standard, self-evident, principles lead seamlessly to democracy (see, for example, Pennock 1989). As Barber (1984) has shown, sceptical justifications for democracy can take on a highly positive tone by stressing the liberating effects of overturning rarely questioned theoretical myths.

It will not have escaped notice that I have not yet defined democracy; an odd way to proceed, surely? The reason for placing the task of definition on hold lies in the fact that justification and definition are two parts of the one process. A proper definition will be one that is rooted in, and implied by, a convincing account of *why* perpetual rule of the many by the few has no secure basis. One does not 'justify democracy' as such; the point is to justify a certain definition of democracy.

The best definition of democracy that follows is: there should be necessary correspondence between acts of government and the equally weighted express wishes of citizens with respect to those acts. This is a modified version of the definition offered by May (1978), who also adopts the shorthand version of 'responsive rule'. Concentration on express wishes arises from the fallibilist principle applied to the sphere of substantive political knowledge. Inclusion of 'citizens' reflects the assumption of a given, bounded political community. 'Necessary correspondence' reflects

82

the fall-back acceptance of the best-judge principle. 'Acts of government' are all political and administrative actions or non-actions. The main element that appears to have been smuggled in is equality. Why should the wishes of citizens be weighted equally?

If, as I have argued, there is no secure ground upon which the wishes of the one or the few can rightly be imposed upon the rest in perpetuity, it follows that there should be equal consideration, and equal effective registration, of the wishes of all. This is not to say, for example, that some people's preferences are not more informed, or more refined, than others'. Rather, it follows from the principle of political fallibilism; given the ultimately unknowable status of the good life from one to another, and given the absence of a secure ground upon which to rank moral prefer-ences, the only reasonable course is to adopt an assumption of equality. The equality assumption is based on probabilities; it best captures the median position with respect to individuals' capacities to know the political path to the good life. To those who object that, given political fallibility, one individual can proclaim personal superiority and suitedness for dictatorial rule with no effective comeback from would-be subjects, my reply is: there is no rightful basis upon which the proto-dictator's claims can rest. This person would wrongly deprive others of the opportunity effectively to register equally valid preferences about political values, thus vastly reducing the number of valid perspectives reaching decision-making procedures.[3]

THE REQUIREMENTS OF DEMOCRACY

If this were as far as the story goes, then compatibility between green imperatives and democracy could be little more than contingent (Saward 1993c). If democratic rule is responsive rule, then (to put it bluntly) the majority should get what it wants. If it does not want (vote for) green outcomes, so be it. However, responsive rule does not mean unlimited rule, or 'tyranny of the majority'. Harrison (1993: 230) puts one of the key points clearly: 'If democracy is a good, then its proper exercise is a good. Hence those things necessary for its proper exercise can be secured against itself. So we may properly have democratic rights which may not properly be removed by the vote of the majority. . . . Such things should be entrenched as rights not subject to control by the majority' (see also Sunstein 1988). Harrison does not put the argument in its strongest legitimate form, however. The crucial point is that unless certain rights are recognised and guaranteed on an equal basis to citizens, democracy will be under threat. The rights that are to be guaranteed are those which follow deductively from the equality assumption and the responsive rule definition. In Dahl's (1989) language, these are primary, integral or internal rights; they do not exhaust the total set of legitimate possible rights, but they do exhaust those rights which citizens *must* have by virtue of democratic citizenship. I shall refer to them simply as democratic rights.

Taking all that has been said up to this point, we can deduce that there are fundamental democratic rights in each of the following areas: basic freedoms, such as freedom of speech or association or worship; participation, such as the equal right to vote and to stand for office; administration, such as freedom of information and adequate appeals and redress mechanisms; publicity, such as the right to be notified adequately of particular policy procedures and outcomes; and social provision, notably rights to adequate education and adequate health care. These are features necessary to the 'proper exercise' of democracy, and on that basis they give rise to rights that ought to be secured constitutionally.

All of this adds up to a democratic vision of a strongly participative, open and responsive polity. This is not merely a vision of ideal democracy; this is how democracy ought to be understood, since these features flow directly from the most compelling available justification of democracy. Greens or political ecologists who place faith in decentralisation, participative and/or direct democracy (for example, Sale 1985; Bookchin 1982; Porritt 1984; Carter 1993)[4] may feel that in an open, educative and responsive democratic system of the type I have outlined people will be more conscious of environmental problems and more willing and active in seeking solutions to them. If, for instance, as Barry has argued (see Chapter 6), 'sustainability' is a discursive notion, the details of which must be worked out in discussion and debate, then such a system would presumably be welcomed (see also Lauber 1978: 212ff).

The fact remains, however, that such a democracy may not promote green outcomes if we think in majoritarian terms. Greens do not, it seems, have a democratic leg to stand on. However, fortunately for greens the preceding analysis opens up an alternative line of argument no less friendly to the concept of democracy. In a proper democracy, majorities cannot rightly transgress rights that are intrinsic to democracy (Dahl 1989). Standardly, these rights are set out in constitutional documents and overseen by a constitutional court (or system of courts). Can at least some substantive environmental concerns be built into the very structure of democratic theory via a 'green democratic right'?

HEALTH CARE RIGHTS AND ENVIRONMENTAL RISKS

The case for including what are normally understood as social rights, such as those to an adequate education and health care, among the set of democratic rights, rests on the interdependence of civil, political and social provisions. The 'interdependence' argument suggests that so-called positive (social) and negative (civil and political) rights exist as different points on a continuum, rather than as rights that are fundamentally different in kind.

In their comments on Marshall's notion of the historical extension of rights from the civil to the political to the social, Kymlicka and Norman note that 'While this process can be seen as adding new rights, it can be seen as extending the earlier rights. Just as political rights are now seen as a way of guaranteeing civil rights, so social rights can be seen as providing the conditions for effective exercise of both civil and political rights' (1992: 11).

If democracy has value, then so does each of the conditions necessary for its persistence. Some key concerns that must be considered within the topic of adequate health care have a direct impact on a citizen's physical mobility. Citizens' physical mobility can play a central role in their capacity to associate, communicate, and to refine and register preferences.[5] At one level, this capacity may condition the degree to which citizens may forge informed preferences on policy matters; no part of the responsive rule conception of democracy *requires* that preferences be informed in order to count, but clearly that is a desirable state of affairs on any criterion.

The idea of a right to adequate health care on the interdependence argument seems straightforward enough. In fact, it contains many hidden assumptions and ambiguities. To explore the scope and character of some of the key aspects of the supposed health care right, especially those that may give rise to green democratic rights, we must make a number of careful distinctions. To begin, it seems more than reasonable to assume that health care is not only exhausted in curative care, but also centrally involves preventive care. It is in the area of preventive care that we may find grounds for positing a green democratic right to an undegraded environment.

Preventive care concerns a range of *risks* which, if realised in practice, stand a high probability of causing significant harm to a citizen or a group of citizens. Of course, risk is an elusive and contested category. For the moment, we can provide some focus by saying that positing a risk suggests that there is a greater or lesser probability that some specifiable harm may come to a person or people as a direct consequence of a definite, identifiable process or event.

Clearly, incurring a risk does not necessarily mean that one gains a right not to suffer a harm which may follow from an actualisation of that risk. Much depends on the nature of the risk in question. What features associated with a given risk could trigger a right not to suffer the associated harms? We can identify three criteria, 'conceptual hurdles' so to speak, to help us to pinpoint the appropriate features. The three questions to ask are:

1 Does the risk have an exogenous, or environmental, origin (in the sense that it was not voluntarily assumed)?
2 Is the risk reasonably preventable?
3 If actualised, would the risk diminish significantly citizens' physical mobility and/or become a factor of life-consuming concern?

Let us deal with each of these briefly. If a given risk does not have an exogenous, or environmental, cause, we cannot reasonably say that it could give rise to a green democratic right. Many classes of hereditary disease, for example, do not have such a cause. Leukaemia contracted as a result of a person's proximity to nuclear facilities is, however, another matter. If a given risk is not reasonably preventable then clearly we could not reasonably expect that anyone should feel (or suffer) an obligation to prevent it. Ought implies can. A risk of harm stemming from naturally occurring radioactivity may be a case in point. Asthma or emphysema arising from urban traffic pollution would, on the other hand, appear to stem from a reasonably preventable risk.

The third conceptual hurdle concerns the nature of the harm associated with a risk. Recall that when we are considering democratic rights, the key concern within a possible health care right centres on a citizen's physical mobility. Now, in a number of possible examples, to speak of 'physical mobility' severely understates the matter. Death from leukaemia induced by man-made radiation sources, or poisoning stemming from water pollution induced by industrial processes would be relatively extreme examples. Lesser harms may induce health problems the character of which comes to consume the time, resources and attention of the sufferer. In tandem with risks to physical mobility, life-consuming risks are included here because they can be expected to impair severely a sufferer's capacity to sort through, refine and register preferences on a range of related and unrelated political questions.

After the three conceptual hurdles, there is a fourth important distinction to be made. If a risk is evenly distributed across a given citizen population it would give rise to a subtly different right in comparison with a risk which is potentially to be suffered more by some than by others. Evenly distributed risks require us to focus primarily upon the severity of harms that may flow from an actualisation of the risk; an unevenly distributed risk leads us to focus also upon the unjust nature of the unequal distribution. In other words, there may be one class of green rights that arises from aggregative concerns about the total level of risk, and a further class which arises from concerns about the distribution of the risk. Maldistribution of relevant risks may occur according to region (or place), class, ethnicity, sex, or some combination thereof. Blowers and Leroy (1994), for example, write of how the politics of locating certain risky enterprises or processes can lead to, or reinforce, patterns of regional 'peripheralisation'. Austin and Schill conclude from their examination of the distributional consequences of pollution in the United States that:

> Poor black and brown people throughout this nation are bearing more than their fair share of the poisonous fruits of industrial production. They live cheek by jowl with waste dumps, incinerators, landfills, smelters, factories, chemical plants, and oil refineries whose

operations make them sick and kill them young. They are poisoned by the air they breathe, the water they drink, the fish they catch, the vegetables they grow, and, in the case of children, the very ground they play on.

(Austin and Schill 1991: 69)

In sum: incurring a risk of suffering harms which are exogenously caused, reasonably preventable, and which give rise to severe curtailments of physical mobility and/or which may become life-consuming, may trigger for the citizen-subject an otherwise latent green democratic right not to suffer the risk in question. This right would constitute one part of a possible broader democratic right to adequate health care. Since many well-known environmental hazards – from the depletion of the ozone layer and global warming to many more localised forms of pollution – may constitute the requisite risks, this is one leg of the strongest argument that democrats must be environmentalists.

The second key leg of this argument, directly dependent upon the first, stems from concern for the position of future generations of democratic citizens. Now of course the rights of future generations and the obligations of the present generation towards future generations are common and important themes in the literature on sustainability and the expansion of the moral community with an eye to ecological justice (or some such). The context in which the subject arises here is different. We are concerned strictly with capacities and rights of democratic citizens, not with broader questions about intergenerational justice as such. If we had confined ourselves to defining democracy and following through to examine its requirements, there would be little excuse for us to consider the position of future generations at all. This is so because we will not have bothered to justify defining democracy in one way or another. It will be recalled, however, that it was considered inadequate to attempt to define democracy independently of offering a convincing justification for it at the same time. Now, if democracy is justified, then its justifiability cannot be said to stop with present generations. If democracy is good for people now, it will be good for people in the future, since they will share in the same human attributes which lie at the base of democracy's justifiability. Thus, for the democrat a powerful concern for the aggregative and distributive nature of preventable harms with respect to future generations is unavoidable.

Standard arguments against considering some of the fundamental interests of future generations fall down in the face of the argument about democratic rights. The fact that future generations cannot enter into bargains with present generations is neither here nor there; the justifiability of democracy, and therefore the need to guarantee to citizens rights corresponding to democracy's logical requirements, sets aside the need for any such bargaining. The argument that we do not know what future generations will be like – what their tastes and preferences will be, for example – does not form a reasonable objection, since it is only reasonable for us to believe that democracy's fundamental worth will apply to future generations every bit as much and for the same reasons as it applies in the present.

Much more could be said on these topics. However, the argument has been taken far enough for some interim conclusions to be drawn. In order to exercise their basic rights and freedoms in the face of a certain class of preventable risks, citizens of democracy have, on the face of it, a claim to a green democratic right not to suffer certain consequences that would flow from the actualisation of such risks. To the extent that arguments for such a right are convincing, the tensions that exist between democracy and environmentalism are reduced (see Goodin 1992; Saward 1993c). Rather than being something *outside* the purview of democratic theory, core environmental concerns are part of it. Consistent democrats will want to prevent environmental harms to citizens, and will recognise a green democratic right to that effect. The idea that democracy is a means, and environmentalism an end, breaks down; environmental goals become an integral part of democratic means to democratic ends.

ASSESSING SOME OBJECTIONS

Whatever the strength of the case that democrats must be environmentalists, it is hardly foolproof. What are the major objections to it, and how convincing are they? I shall consider nine particular objections.

First, science is inexact. The prevailing state of knowledge about whether a given risk to health exists, and whether that risk would meet any or all of the three conditions discussed above is in many cases highly uncertain. Experts contradict experts on what constitutes relevant evidence and/or how evidence ought to be interpreted. Therefore, so the objection runs, it would be foolish to assign rights on the basis of uncertain risks and outcomes, for it may be the case that such rights turn out to have no foundation. Against this objection, we could cite the precautionary principle: if there is a strong *prima facie* case that a relevant risk exists, then we should act to guard against its deleterious effects. No absolute certainty about risks is attainable; reasonable evidence may be evidence enough in the face of imperatives stemming from democratic values.

Second, law is a blunt instrument in the face of uncertainty. Where law creates entitlements, it creates rights. If the arguments for it are strong enough, a green democratic right should be a basic constitutional right, but it is not like, for example, a negative right like freedom of speech, which more straightforwardly applies always and equally to all citizens. Health care rights, or at least the possible environmental subset of such rights, are positive rights which often have to be triggered differently (if at all) for different individuals, depending on the state of the risks they may incur.

One major obstacle to constitutionalising such rights is the common argument that only negative rights belong in constitutions. The first point I would wish to make here is that construing broadly 'civil' and 'political' rights as negative and broadly 'social' rights as positive is optional, a matter of rhetoric rather than substance. A green democratic right might be put thus: 'The state must not deprive citizens, or to allow them to be deprived, of an undegraded environment' ('an undegraded environment' could comfortably be replaced here by 'freedom of speech').[6] We can underline this point by noting that so-called negative rights do involve the state in positive actions, such as providing for a policing and courts system to give effect to speech and association provisions.

Third, even if it is reasonable to assign rights, this may have an un-democratic effect. Commenting on developments in the United States in recent decades, Lowi (1990) writes that

> where once the distribution of risk was a political question – whether in the hands of government or private institutions – these questions have been increasingly taken out of the political process ... [this constitutes] a means of delegitimizing politics itself, first by narrowing the universe of politics and second by creating expectations that cannot possibly be met.
>
> (Lowi 1990: 19)

Rights are adjudicated by courts, not parliaments, and judges are unelected. They will bring their subjective interpretations to bear on all constitutional provisions, and further, as Dryzek writes, 'legal systems are not insensitive to the distribution of power in the forms of social choice with which they co-exist' (1987: 143). To this objection, one can reply that it is wrong to assume that the role of judges is always to act as a brake on democracy. Whatever else they do, their central role is to protect fundamental democratic rights. Questions may be raised where constitutional courts are active beyond the range of democratic rights. But in that area at least, their role is integral to democracy. Only someone arguing from an unduly restricted, two-dimensional account of majoritarian democracy could deny the powerful democratic function of the judiciary.

Fourth, it might be objected that, in this discussion, health has been used 'as a surrogate for the environment' (Burger 1990). When greens, for example, speak of the environment, or when green parties define their principles and proposals, they go far beyond narrow considerations of health care (let alone a restricted area within such considerations). However, many of the most pressing environmental concerns come into the purview of the environmental sub-set of health care rights put forward here. No doubt there are environmental goals which fall outside health care concerns, and which are therefore justified by arguments outside the theory of democracy. I will say more on the latter point below.

Fifth, should we not make more of the role of democratic citizens? Why can we not assert the autonomy, stress the primary good of self-determination, etc., of democratic citizens? Surely that would mean that stronger, less equivocal and less derivative environmental rights could be asserted? Maybe so. However, my aim is to avoid rhetorical arguments, and to make as few basic assertions about human nature as possible. All such assertions are, at some point, 'essentially contestable'. To attach metaphysical significance to the role of democratic citizen would be to undermine the best available justification for the democratic system itself.[7]

Sixth, would not any democratic right to adequate health care place too many cash burdens on governments with too few resources at their disposal? If ought implies can, then

> the validity of the claim that individuals hold certain moral rights to welfare depends on its being possible for the state or some other agent to fulfil those rights. And given the problems of scarcity found in many countries, it is simply not possible for their governments to fulfil some of the most commonly appealed to welfare rights.
>
> (Jacobs 1993: 56)

In other words, if an environment largely free of preventable, exogenous, mobility-threatening risks is beyond the present financial means of a government, then it is simply wrong to say that citizens have a democratic right to such an environment.

This argument appears to have some force. However, it assumes secure knowledge of a given state's present financial capacity to deliver. The leaders of many poor countries with proportionately massive military budgets would no doubt like us to believe that to entrench in their countries certain social and environmental rights would be ridiculous, but this surely would be a question of narrow political priorities winning out over moral obligations. Further, by its nature a right is a right now and in the future; should even a genuine financial incapacity to meet the substance of a right now mean that social and environmental obligations should not be anticipated and planned for when state capacities change? If a government genuinely cannot afford to deliver on these social rights, then it may well be the case that acceptable discounting rules can be applied for a limited period.

Seventh, calculating 'acceptable' or 'tolerable' levels of risk standardly involves a balancing of risks and benefits. But in the case of modern 'mega-hazards', does not the calculability of risk break down altogether (see Beck 1992)? For example, the best-qualified experts are divided over the nature of the risks to people exposed to low-level radiation. Further, benefits are a matter for political assessment; what kind of society do we want to

90

have, with what standard of living achieved in what ways? Many would-be neutral, technical regulatory bodies charged with risk assessment have found themselves backing uncomfortably into this political territory (see Saward 1993a). There is considerable force in this objection, to which I return below.

Eighth, it might be objected that to include health care rights in the set of democratic rights opens the floodgates to the constitutionalisation of a much more extensive range of social, economic and environmental rights. For example, is it really the case that such health risks as those arising from genetic factors (excluded from the discussion) do not give rise to demo-cratic rights? I would concede that no clear cut-off point can be specified in a thoroughly non-arbitrary manner. This concession involves accepting that as we approach the (impossible) point of 'full democracy', we enter a grey area. If a full range of demanding social, economic and environmental rights were to be constitutionalised, it may well be the case that little would be left for determination by democratic majorities.

Finally, my account has been wholly anthropocentric, or human-centred. Ecocentrists will not be satisfied with the implicit assumption that only humans are eligible for democratic citizenship, and only their require-ments, capacities and interests are relevant in principle to democratic decisions (see the arguments of Mills and Eckersley, Chapters 5 and 11). Perhaps the fact that normally the *demos* has been understood as a human community stands in the way of a proper ecocentric extension of the *demos*? Just as unavoidable political fallibility is the basis of a principle of equality, so fallibility of our knowledge about animals (for example) might lead us to a principle of equal consideration for their interests as well as ours. Further, if animals (to pursue that example) act on preferences, why should they not form part of the community of those whose revealed preferences count in the future course of the community? From a different angle, if the conditions that make possible the registration of preferences generate rights within democratic discourse, then why not rights for animals, other life forms, and ecosystems, since respect and care for habitats (for instance) may ultimately be a condition for life itself?

Powerful arguments can be built on ecocentric foundations. Ultimately, however, many of the problems identified for the anthropocentric account would remain, and some new ones would be created, in a full-blown ecocentric account of democracy. We would still need to ask what type of society we want, and where the cut-off point for entrenchment of rights ought to be drawn. An extra problem would be created in the need to try to comprehend what might constitute (for example) an animal's expression of preference. In short, the major difficulties involved in reconciling environmentalism and an anthropocentric theory of democracy would not be overcome simply by radically broadening the *demos*.

THE INTERNAL AND EXTERNAL VALUES OF
DEMOCRACY

A considerable argument can be built to show that democrats must be environmentalists. Exploring that argument, however, has thrown up a number of theoretical and practical grey areas. Taken together, these problems suggest that the question cannot be dealt with entirely *within* democratic theory. Some values (and rights) are internal to democracy; others are external, good things that we might want to see realised apart from, or in addition to, democratic values.

Some of the problems identified in the discussion of a green democratic right can be dealt with only in terms of values external to democracy. The first of these is the adoption of the precautionary principle with regard to certain preventable environmental risks. Whether and when this principle is adopted is a matter of judgements about the vulnerability of the natural environment to various human interventions. Similarly, the kinds of values we might like to enter into judicial deliberations, the extent to which social and other benefits should enter into risk calculations, and the place to fix the cut-off point for constitutionalising rights, all touch directly upon this question: what sort of society do we want? If a free market society, then to what degree? What is the desirable balance between political stability and political dynamism? And, ultimately, should our political structures be shaped according to some basic ecocentric assumptions? These are fundamental questions which break through the boundaries of democratic theory.

It is standard for political philosophers to subsume other principles under the primary principle with which they are concerned; Rawls (1972) does it with justice, and Nozick (1974) with rights, for example. I make no such claims for my approach to democracy. There is an irreducible plurality of first-order political principles. Democracy is one of them. Democrats will prefer, other things being equal, to give priority to the requirements of democracy. But they cannot ignore entirely other principled accounts of value and right.

Many strong environmental imperatives will be among the values, goods and principles that are external to democracy's requirements. A strong ecocentric vision of 'green democracy', involving perhaps recognition of nature's intrinsic value, the moral standing of animals and other animate objects, and the desirability of near-stateless self-reliance in small decentralised, labour-intensive communities, can be constructed (no lack of such visions is available, of course). In more general terms, greens can in a variety of ways key into constraints – some of them more or less inevitable, though their precise character may be contested – on democratic outcomes. Sheer geographical embeddedness is the most obvious one. Democracies are always democracies somewhere; the constraints of location will be environmental constraints, and cultural constraints which greens at least can live with will often arise from this or that fact of a system's embeddedness. Sheer necessity arising from factors other than forms of embeddedness – such as actions imperative to survival – can form another hunting ground for greens. Whatever are the arguments, the key is to acknowledge openly the modifications, and especially dilutions, they contain for democracy considered as an independent value with independent justifications.

To the extent that green outcomes take precedence over strictly democratic outcomes, it ought to be recognised and acknowledged that democracy is being diluted. There is no necessary prescription that democracy must 'win' – or win fully – when principles conflict in practice, but at the very least the external values employed ought to be defended explicitly. I have argued that some important environmental concerns can be accommodated within democratic theory; the problem here is with such concerns that cannot be so accommodated. Ought we really to be frightened to suggest that we would ever want to be anything other than wholly democratic in our political logic and our political actions? If we are to gain a clear view of democracy – if we are to isolate its character and its value for us, separately from other considerations – then we must view in a clearheaded way how it will often be diluted in the desire to realise certain other key political principles.

CONCLUSION

It is common wisdom that 'democracy' has become a term of universal approval. Virtually all the world's political systems claim to be democratic. It is the basic ingredient in any political ideology which has pretensions to mass approval. Leaders, parties and commentators of all stripes profess it as an unimpeachable good. The common wisdom has, however, become a common lament of democratic theorists. If democracy can mean almost anything, then it stands in real danger of meaning nothing, its status reduced to little more than a rhetorical device.

But democracy does have a clear meaning. Its requirements, and the demands it makes on would-be democrats, can be set out in a straightforward fashion. I have argued that democracy should be understood as meaning responsive rule. On the face of this definition, there is little to comfort environmentalists. If governments, to be democratic, must respond to the felt wishes of a majority of citizens, then greens have little comeback if a majority does not want green outcomes. However, responsive rule is valuable; it can be justified by arguments ranging from equality and political fallibility to citizens' interests. If it is valuable, then it ought to persist. If it ought to persist, then rights and liberties essential to its persistence need to be protected from the will of a given democratic majority. I have argued that one such democratic right is a right to adequate health care, and that within this right lie a range of major environmental concerns. In particular, I have suggested that democratic citizens may have a right not to suffer certain harms from preventable environmental risks. If this is the case, then several green concerns, far from being in conflict with democratic ideals, are in fact integral to the democratic process. All of this flows from an anthropocentric, indeed in many ways traditional, conception of democracy. It does not preclude greens from constructing alternative, perhaps more radically ecocentric, models. What it suggests strongly, however, is that greens engaged on such a task must state clearly where they depart from democracy in order to realise a full range of environmental goals. It is not illegitimate to do that. Democracy is not the 'first virtue' of a society: there are other reasonable values people will promote, values which may clash with democracy in theory and in practice. The demand is for clarity – features of a political system that are designed to realise other than democratic goals must be justified fully and explicitly.

NOTES

1 See Holden (1974) and Saward (1994b) for a broad discussion of these types of justification.
2 For a more formal treatment of this argument, see Saward (1994a).
3 Some further comments on the responsive rule definition of democracy are appropriate. First, it focuses on outcomes rather than procedures, since having responsive outcomes implies having appropriate procedures (the inference does not work as strongly the other way around). Second, it implies that majority rule is superior to its alternatives. Third, it must apply to administrative and implementation arms of government, as well as representative institutions. Fourth, it implies nothing about what the appropriate political units of democracy are; the way a given unit is governed is important, not its size or scale, from the perspective of democratic theory. Fifth, it implies that direct forms of democracy (e.g. referendums) are superior – more democratic – than representative forms (see Saward 1993b), since they transfer citizens' express wishes more directly into policy outcomes.
4 See Dobson (1990) for an extended discussion of many of these points.
5 Seeing 'social' rights merely as a means to the exercise of civil and political rights may well rule out many important instances where people suffer a diminished quality of life but suffer no real loss of capacity to exercise other democratic rights. However, I do not deny that there may be a fuller set of social rights, derived from different foundations. I am focusing only on the question of whether certain rights flow directly from democratic foundations.
6 The precise wording of an environmental right will affect the opportunities open to citizens successfully to sue polluters. Muldoon's proposal for a statutory (as opposed to constitutional) environmental bill of rights for Canada involves 'the right of each person to a healthy environment' and 'the duty of governments to ensure this healthy environment in their role as the trustees of all public lands, waters and resources for the benefit of present and future generations' (Muldoon 1988: 35). Rights expressed in other ways can in effect become environmental rights. In 1994 the European Court of Human Rights 'ruled that damage to human health arising from environmental pollution can be construed

as an infringement of human rights'. In a case involving fumes from a waste treatment plant in Spain, the Court 'found that there had been a violation of Article 8 of the European Convention on Human Rights, covering the right to respect for private and family life and for the home' (*Environment Business* 1994).

7 Liberals are keener to derive fundamental rights from some notion of autonomous, self-determining individuals. Indeed, for some writers democracy needs liberalism to provide it with rights, since sceptical democrats can have little to say about fundamental rights (see McGregor 1988). McGregor is wrong, however, to think that guaranteed rights and democracy are odd bedfellows. Democrats can be sceptics – indeed, I have argued they ought to be sceptics – and still consistently propose democratic rights that are essential to democracy surviving and prospering. Further, despite the common rejection of liberalism by 'emancipatory' environmental political theorists (Eckersley 1992: 23–4), there may well be untapped potential in liberalism. Reminiscent of my argument here is Taylor's (1993: 279) comment that: 'Liberalism may not be the best theoretical approach to protecting the environment; it may indeed prove entirely inadequate to the task. However, since liberalism requires that all members of society be treated equally in some respect . . . it gives birth to obligations to protect the environment in the interests of those who are to be treated equally.'

REFERENCES

Anon (1994) 'Court Deems Pollution Infringes Human Rights', *Environment Business* 14 and 28 December.

Austin, R. and Schill, M. (1991) 'Black, Brown, Poor and Poisoned', *Kansas Journal of Law and Public Policy* 1, 1.

Barber, B. (1984) *Strong Democracy: Participatory Politics for a New Age*, Berkeley: University of California Press.

Barry, J. (1994) 'Green Political Theory and the State', in P. Dunleavy and J. Stanyer (eds) *Contemporary Political Studies 1994*, London: Political Studies Association of the United Kingdom.

Beck, U. (1992) 'From Industrial Society to Risk Society', in M. Featherstone (ed.) *Cultural Theory and Cultural Change*, London: Sage.

Blowers, A. and Leroy, P. (1994) 'Power, Politics and Environmental Inequality', *Environmental Politics* 3, 2.

Bookchin, M. (1982) *The Ecology of Freedom*, Palo Alto, Calif.: Cheshire Books.

Burger, Jr, E. J. (1990) 'Health as a Surrogate for the Environment', *Daedalus*, fall.

Carter, A. (1993) 'Towards a Green Political Theory', in A. Dobson and P. Lucardie (eds) *The Politics of Nature*, London: Routledge.

Dahl, R. A. (1956) *A Preface to Democratic Theory*, Chicago: University of Chicago Press.

—— (1989) *Democracy and its Critics*, New Haven, Conn.: Yale University Press.

Dobson, A. (1990) *Green Political Thought*, London: Unwin Hyman

Dryzek, J. (1987) *Rational Ecology*, Oxford: Blackwell.

—— (1990) *Discursive Democracy*, Cambridge: Cambridge University Press.

Eckersley, R. (1992) *Environmentalism and Political Theory: Toward an Ecocentric Approach*, London: UCL Press.

Elkin, S. L. and Soltan, K. E. (eds) (1993) *A New Constitutionalism*, Chicago: University of Chicago Press.

Goodin, R. E. (1990) 'Liberalism and the Best-Judge Principle', *Political Studies* 38, 2.

—— (1992) *Green Political Theory*, Cambridge: Polity.

Harrison, R. (1993) *Democracy*, London: Routledge.

Held, D. (1987) *Models of Democracy*, Cambridge: Polity.

Holden, B. (1974) *The Nature of Democracy*, London: Thomas Nelson.

Jacobs, L. A. (1993) *Rights and Deprivation*, Oxford: Clarendon Press.

Kymlicka, W. and Norman, W. J. (1992) 'The Social Charter Debate', *Network Analysis no. 2*, University of Ottawa.

Lauber, V. (1978) 'Ecology, Politics and Liberal Democracy', *Government and Opposition* 13, 2.

Lively, J. (1975) *Democracy*, Oxford: Blackwell.

Lowi, T.J. (1990) 'Risks and Rights in the History of American Governments', *Daedalus*, fall.

McGregor, J. (1988) 'Liberalism and Democracy', *Philosophy East and West* 38.

May, J. D. (1978) 'Defining Democracy', *Political Studies* 26, 1.

Mill, J. S. (1975) *Three Essays*, Oxford: Oxford University Press.

Muldoon, P. (1988) 'The Fight for an Environmental Bill of Rights', *Alternatives* 15.

Nozick, R. (1974) *Anarchy, State and Utopia*, Oxford: Blackwell.

Parekh, B. (1993) 'The Cultural Particularity of Liberal Democracy', in D. Held (ed.) *Prospects for Democracy*, Cambridge: Polity.

Peirce, C. S. (1940) *The Philosophy of Peirce: Selected Writings*, ed. J. Buchler, London: Routledge & Kegan Paul.

Pennock, J.R. (1989) 'The Justification of Democracy', in G. Brennan and L. E. Lomasky (eds) *Politics and Process*, Cambridge: Cambridge University Press.

Popper, K. (1983) *A Pocket Popper*, ed. D. Miller, London: Fontana.

Porritt, J. (1984) *Seeing Green*, Oxford: Blackwell.

Rawls, J. (1972) *A Theory of Justice*, Oxford: Oxford University Press.

Sale, K. (1985) *Dwellers in the Land*, San Francisco: Sierra Club.

Saward, M. (1993a) 'Advice, Legitimacy and Nuclear Safety in Britain', in A. Barker and B. Guy Peters (eds) *The Politics of Expert Advice*, Edinburgh: Edinburgh University Press.

—— (1993b) 'Direct Democracy Revisited', *Politics* 13, 2.

—— (1993c) 'Green Democracy?', in A. Dobson and P. Lucardie (eds) *The Politics of Nature*, London: Routledge.

—— (1994a) 'Democratic Theory and Indices of Democratisation', in D. Beetham (ed.) *Defining and Measuring Democracy*, London: Sage.

—— (1994b) 'Postmodernists, Pragmatists and the Justification of Democracy', *Economy and Society* 23, 2.

Shapiro, I. (1994) 'Three Ways to be a Democrat', *Political Theory* 22, 1.

Soltan, K. E. (1993) 'Generic Constitutionalism', in S. L. Elkin and K. E. Soltan (eds) *A New Constitutionalism*, Chicago: University of Chicago Press.

Sunstein, C. R. (1988) 'Constitutions and Democracies', in J. Elster and R. Slagstad (eds) *Constitutionalism and Democracy*, Cambridge: Cambridge University Press.

Taylor, R. (1993) 'The Environmental Implications of Liberalism', *Critical Review* 6, 2–3.

Thorson, T. L. (1962) *The Logic of Democracy*, New York: Holt, Rinehart & Winston.

Walzer, M. (1983) *Spheres of Justice*, Oxford: Blackwell.

5

GREEN DEMOCRACY
The search for an ethical solution
Mike Mills

Green democracy has, perhaps surprisingly, now become controversial. When such controversies appear the tendency is to search for principles or values that, when consistently applied, may properly guide our behaviour and our thoughts. This chapter is no exception and seeks to look for those principles within green political theory and environmental ethics itself. By looking, very briefly, at two branches of green political theory which do, indeed, compete in their use of democracy (ecoauthoritarianism and what I will call ecoradicalism), I will suggest that both suffer by failing adequately to consider two things. First, and most importantly, both advance policy prescriptions without purposefully expanding the moral community to which that policy should be addressed. My argument will be that however we characterise what greens believe or what they want to do, the question of the moral community – its expansion and the implications of its expansion – is logically prior to all others. Second, I will argue that green political theory (in both its ecoauthoritarian and its ecoradical sense) has been perhaps too concerned with outcome, and could risk being more concerned with process. I hope to make it clear that this will have a number of distinct advantages over taking a more consequentialist line. First it will help protect against autocracy; second, it is much easier to reconcile with a fundamentally green (ecocentric) ethic; and third, it is very useful in helping to promote the idea that democracy of various forms and at various levels is, indeed, absolutely central to green political theory.

ECOAUTHORITARIANISM AND ECORADICALISM

Ecoauthoritarianism

Whether it argues the perils of over-population (Hardin 1968) or of scarcity more generally (Ophuls 1977; Ophuls and Boyan 1992) the thrust of ecoauthoritarianism appears to remain the same. There are ecological imperatives which have to be addressed and the political organisation necessary to resolve them may not be particularly democratic. Primarily, this

97

disorientation towards democracy is a function of two things; first, a strongly Hobbesian conception of human nature which implies that individuals will not, of their own free will, make selfless, co-operative personal choices; and second, an apparently overwhelming orientation towards ends-based policies, structures and institutions, rather than means-based ones. In other words, ecoauthoritarians take a very consequentialist moral line in which stark and mutually exclusive choices exist based upon either avoiding the ecological crisis through authoritarian measures, or suffering it. In Hardin's case he argues for 'mutual coercion mutually agreed upon' (1968); in Ophuls' case he argues for some kind of competent aristocracy to distribute scarce resources. Yet, a generous interpretation of Ophuls' model of scarcity politics would lead us to conclude that although he sees democracy as constrained at higher levels – perhaps national or regional – he is very keen on democracy lower down because he sees that type of freedom (at the micro-level) as differentiating his eco-society from other authoritarian regimes. Although this does not rescue the theory as a whole it should sensitise us to the fact that different types of democracy can exist at different levels.

The major problem with taking this sort of line is the internal inconsistency of the arguments themselves. To my mind, any theory which accepts a Hobbesian version of human nature and then argues that political power should be wielded (by Hobbesians) without cursory political checks and balances (or the equivalent) is asking for trouble. In other words, the very arguments given by ecoauthoritarians to justify the circumvention of democracy will do quite as well in arguing the complete opposite – the greater the problem, the more severe the risk, the more pressing the imperative, the more necessary it becomes that democracy becomes extended, entrenched and practised. As Sagoff has argued:

> Democracy, as everyone knows, is susceptible to abuse and has all kinds of problems, but I know of no other mechanism for making policy decisions that has this ethical underpinning (citizens having the opportunity to present their views to legislators).
>
> (Sagoff 1988: 115)

The counter-argument to this given by Saward (directed against the ecoradicals, 1993) is that even if democracy is desirable (whether for intrinsic or instrumental reasons) it is simply incompatible with other green goals. Although I cannot resolve this question fully now, this point depends entirely on what these goals are. If green political theory is goal or ends oriented (as the ecoauthoritarians are) then this argument has some validity although it will depend on the extent to which we accept that democracy can exist within ecological constraints. However, it is not only possible, but also perfectly reasonable, to argue that green political theory should be more process oriented, in which case democracy becomes not only compatible with, but also essential to, green political theory.

Without labouring the critique, let me just make one more point, the full importance of which will also become more evident as we go on. For ecoauthoritarians the ecological crisis presents us with the need to manage the finite resources of the planet effectively to trust in political or technocratic decisions that will, presumably, secure and distribute goods and control the ecological effects of their consumption. I would argue, however, that our ability to manage on the scale envisaged by ecoauthoritarians must be limited. In this respect then, it may be better to ensure that whatever solution we find to the ecological crisis (and to the centrality of democracy to green political theory), it had better be a process-oriented one, that is, one which minimises the need for management on the basis of inadequate information.

Ecoradicalism

Ecoradicals, on the other hand, are a much messier proposition. My central point will simply be that ecoradicals (if we take ecoradicals to belong in part to green parties and radical green movements) could afford to be more concerned with political processes (as opposed to political ends) and this in turn would help to resolve problems of green democracy. I will not be able to resolve these arguments, however, until later on. Goodin (1992) suggests that while there is a great deal of policy prescription within green programmes (as you would expect) there is actually very little on institutional change and on political processes. He notes that 'it is ecological values that form the focus of the green programme' (1992: 183) and in this respect, green politics and political theory posits a largely holistic view of both problems and their solutions. In this, Goodin suggests that it is the non-discriminatory nature of green values and their push for diversity which lead them 'positively [to] embrace pluralism' (1992: 199) and 'cherish diversity in its social every bit as much as in its biological form' (1992: 199).

There is, apparently, some gap between principles (values) on the one hand and policies on the other because there does not seem to be much on the question of policy or political processes to join the two, even at a theoretical level. In the economic programme there is an onus on individuals to act, as Goodin notices (and as rallying calls like 'think globally, act locally' imply), and for policy and lifestyle to become one and the same thing in places. In economic relations, as in politics, the green message appears to be the same and appears, still, to imply the type of political (democratic) relations necessary for individuals to take control.

Dobson (1990, 1993) sees decentralisation as the central green prescription and sees the guiding principles of ecologism as subsumed under the broad headings of limits to growth (which implies interdependence,

99

finite resources, the paucity of technological solutions) and ecologism's commitment to non-anthropocentric principles and policies. As far as the principle goes, Dobson, quite rightly, says that: 'much of ecologism's momentum is controversially engaged in widening the community of rights holders to animals, trees, plants and even inanimate nature' (1993: 223). This provides us with our first tentative link between democracy on the one hand and philosophy on the other.

Ecoradicals, at a philosophical level, though, fall into a variety of camps. Eckersley, for example, distinguishes three varieties of ecocentrism – autopoietic intrinsic value; transpersonal (deep) ecology; and ecofeminist (1992: 60–74). Dobson's (1989) major distinction is between those who advocate the 'state of being' (deep ecology) approach to ethics and those who see nature as having intrinsic value. Both appear to agree that the transpersonal/deep ecology approach (which sees our perceptions, attitudes and behaviour toward the environment as changing with changes in consciousness, experience and intuition) is problematic as the basis of a political theory largely because it is itself non-axiological (Eckersley 1992; Dobson 1989). While Mathews (1988) is I believe, quite right in arguing, that a commitment to deep ecology is not a fatalistic, do-nothing choice, nevertheless, I will proceed on the basis that if green political theory is ethically informed, then it is primarily some version of intrinsic value rather than deep ecology that is likely to be most useful.[1]

The criticisms levelled at ecoradicals focus on the internal consistency of their ideas. One observation made by Saward (1993) concerns the relationship between direct democracy and other green goals such as intrinsic value and holism. Here, he makes the point, rightly, that it is difficult to work to imperatives on the one hand and have a fairly arbitrary decision-making process such as democracy on the other hand. The fact that the green movement does have a perception of a Good Life (Dobson 1990: 14) would seem to reinforce the point that the ecoradicals have a problem – how can you go for the Good Life when your democracy may not take you there? Given, in addition, that there clearly is a bottom line green commitment to political liberalism as seen in 'diversity' and 'direct democracy' for example, then Sagoff's point is relevant:

> Liberal political theory cannot commit a democracy beforehand to adopt any general rule or principle that answers the moral questions that confront it; if political theory could do this, it would become autocratic and inconsistent with democracy.
>
> (Sagoff 1988: 162)

Of course, we are not dealing with an exclusively liberal political theory, but green theory does have liberal political elements which make the principle the same in both theories. In fact liberal political theory does commit us to certain rules and principles which are thought to be, in some sense, prior to the democratic process itself. Mostly, these revolve around who or what might be considered as worthy of participation in such a process – who decides over these moral questions? Liberal political theory does, then, have something to say about the nature of the democratic process, it is simply reticent about policy outcomes. Indeed, although Paehlke (1988) has quite rightly argued that democracy can be enhanced by environmental policy, nevertheless, it is also true to say that the ecoradicals have few safeguards against the triumph of one laudable principle, say, sustainability, over another, decentralisation for example. Dobson observes that:

> It has been suggested that ecologism's commitment to principles such as liberty and democracy is compromised by apparently laying such great emphasis on the *ends* rather than the *means* of political association.
>
> (Dobson 1993: 234)

I will be arguing that both of these points are correct, and that they are related. In other words, philosophically, greens have been concerned to expand the community of rights holders (or something similar) and they have also been concerned with ends rather than means. A commitment to some form of liberalism may help in counteracting some forms of strongly prescriptive ideology but it is likely that democracy will suffer unless other safeguards are built in.

Of all the difficulties with the ecoradical's view of democracy, that is by far the most difficult to surmount. Yet in a broader philosophical sense, ecoradicals are far from as consequentialist as their programmes suggest; they lean quite strongly towards doing what is 'right', as much as they do towards what is ultimately 'good'. Certainly in terms of their views on the political system, we can see fairly clearly that their support for participatory democracy and decentralisation denotes a view of how people can develop, grow and take control which is independent of what outcomes that might entail.

Ecoauthoritarians and ecoradicals do display some of the same problems, but in different degrees. Primarily, we can see that both do not necessarily protect (or even advance) a position on democracy which is defensible against strongly asserted and pressing political, economic and social goals. While in the case of ecoauthoritarians I would argue that they are perhaps a little more democratic than we sometimes give them credit for, nevertheless, there is little room theoretically for a consistent commitment to democracy. Ecoradicals, on the other hand, do emphasise democracy but fail to reconcile it with broader imperatives. Such a reconciliation is possible if we change the emphasis of their thinking away from goals and direct it more towards political mechanisms.

Both approaches, to my mind at least, have not taken on board the consequences of their very starting point sufficiently. Before all else, for

101

both, comes the assertion that the ecological crisis is primarily a crisis of our ethical system. Although we may perceive our current problems as those of over-population, resource depletion, and food scarcity, these are first and foremost symptoms of an ethical crisis. Environmental philosophers have been criticised for not providing the types of guidelines to political action which political theorists prefer (see, for example, Dobson 1989) but it has to be said that there is plenty to be getting on with if an ethically based green political theory is what theorists are after.

THE EXPANSION OF THE MORAL COMMUNITY

If we consider what greens argue is distinctive about their ideology, their political theory and their practical concerns, it is invariably the case that these can be reduced to a concern to expand the moral community.[2] Eckersley (1992) argues that the fundamental characteristic of green political theory is the fact that it is ecocentric and this ecocentricity is logically prior to all other political considerations:

> A non-anthropocentric perspective is one that ensures that the interests of non-human species and ecological communities ... are not ignored in human decision making simply because they are not human or because they are not of instrumental value to humans.
> (Eckersley 1992: 57)

By accepting that humans are not the only ones with value or the only measure of value, we accept that our moral community expands because it is now necessary to accommodate others within our ethical choices. Eckersley, here, has made two interrelated points – one is that the non-human world should be given consideration and the second is that such consideration can be ensured only when a non-anthropocentric perspective is taken. This is a position I would support, indeed, my argument makes it essential that a non-anthropocentric approach is adopted – without this there is only a contingent expansion of the moral community, and if that happens, then democracy cannot be secured either. Goodin (1992) continues this line of argument when he says that it is 'naturalness' that greens value. If it is naturalness that has value, then presumably natural things should be given moral consideration. Dobson too (1990), as we saw earlier, took as a fundamental axiom of ecologism the idea that we should look toward a biocentric, or ecocentric (non-anthropocentric), basis for our political theory.

In terms of theory, we can see our ethical responsibilities shifting away from a largely human-centred approach to be ecocentric. These have been the primary terms of the debate and it is perhaps because of this that the political consequences of expanding the moral community – which I take to be a corollary of switching to an essentially ecocentric ethic – have not received the attention they might deserve. The 1992 General Election Manifesto of the British Green Party, for example, can illustrate this point quite well, not because there is no evidence of a shift, but rather because it surfaces in a rather *ad hoc* way and is not, to any large extent, directed at political variables.

From what we have said so far, we would expect to find the core axiology – that the Green Party was ecocentric and this entailed greater moral considerability of non-human species – represented somewhere within the manifesto itself, or at least an indication of such. And, indeed, it is perfectly possible to find such indications, but they tend to come in very specific forms. Largely, these are either in the forms of policy prescriptions (for example, rapidly phasing out factory farming or the greater protection of the soil) or in terms of changing the basis upon which future decisions will be made:

> [the Green Party] would revolutionize the system of national accounts by rigorously identifying real costs and real benefits in our industrial society. In so doing we would attribute equal value to the natural capital on which we depend (topsoil, water, clean air, fossil fuels etc.) as we do to the financial capital which greases the wheels of the world economy.
>
> (Green Party 1992: 11)

To the extent that decision making would change (in terms of values and outputs at least) then clearly this change is in line with a broadening of the moral community. However, green political theory might suggest that concomitant changes might also occur in the political system more broadly – for example, in the attribution of rights to non-humans on the basis of their having value. This type of analysis is not in the manifesto, the overtly political provisions are aimed largely, although not exclusively, at resolving problems of the British political system. Without wishing to labour the point, the critique of Saward (1993) and the warning of Sagoff (1988) still remain. If there is to be an essentially goal-oriented policy-making process (and one based on ecological imperatives) then the Green Party may have problems with democracy. The commitment that the manifesto shows to *ends* might need to be matched by a similar commitment to the reform of the *process* of politics in a non-anthropocentric way which would ensure that green goals did not take precedence over due process.[3]

A more consistent application of the holistic principle, and the greater incorporation of non-human interests into the political features of the state would make green positions defensible against the accusation that highly deterministic, imperative-driven, consequentialistic policy runs the risk of forsaking democracy. If we accept that value exists non-anthropocentrically, then it clearly is the case that what political movements (and philosophies) do should reflect this change and should find more things morally considerable. We can see in these programmes the obvious wish to expand the moral community but this is invariably associated with ends-based policies, rather than means-based processes.

So, greens propose the expansion of the moral community for very particular reasons (non-anthropocentric) and although such a position (which will be expanded below) does exist theoretically, in practice there are two problems. The first is that programmes are not necessarily informed by ecocentrism and holism and the second is that only certain formulations of this ethic will actually serve the dual function of both securing the democratic basis of green politics and the ethical basis that greens want. Importantly, greens appear to prefer, as you might expect, to argue their case in terms of policy ends, rather than in terms of the more deontological (axiological) premises of the policy process.

ACHIEVING THE EXPANSION OF THE MORAL COMMUNITY

The expansion of the moral community can be achieved in a number of different ways depending, to a great extent, upon how far we want to go and what arguments we are going to use along the way. I have already argued that the type of expansion associated with transpersonal/deep ecology is not one that I am going to pursue here but, rather, will follow Dobson and Eckersley in suggesting that it is difficult to formulate politically.[4] I am further restricted by the critique of green politics offered by Saward and the observations of Sagoff, both of which suggest that too great an emphasis on the ends of policy rather than the means will undermine the democratic basis of green politics. This inclines me to believe that it is best to avoid ethical arguments that are entirely consequentialist. Lastly, I have argued that I am concerned with an ecocentric ethic, one which finds value in the non-human world and leads to the expansion of the moral community.

In expanding the moral community the most obvious first step would be to include animals or sentient beings. For Regan (1984), it is the ability to be 'the experiencing subject of life' which denotes whether we get 'rights' or not. Once sentience is established Regan argues that all sentient beings are equal in having value and that it is only just that claims which these beings make upon us morally should be seen as valid (i.e. they have rights). For Regan then our moral community expands to incorporate sentient beings, although these rights do not have to be the same rights as those held by humans (because in some cases, such as the vote, it would be silly) and to establish a moral right is not the same as establishing a legal right (the classic case is that of keeping a promise).

So, the boundaries are pretty clear here, and Regan is looking very much to replicate for animals the existing ethic for humans. In this sense, it is not an 'environmental ethic' (Rolston 1987) because it does not look to the environment for the source of its value. Neither, then, is it holistic because Regan is concerned with individual sentient beings, not with species, nor with the systems which sustain the animals and to which the animals contribute. Consequently, we could not use this as the only basis from which to expand the moral community, primarily because it could not hope to resolve all of the ecological problems we might be interested in.

Another possibility is the 'reverence for life' literature which draws the line of moral considerability differently. Here the fundamental axiom, according to Goodpaster (1983), is not whether something is sentient but whether it has life or not: 'Nothing short of the condition of *being alive* seems to me to be a plausible and non-arbitrary criteria (for moral considerability)' (1983: 31). This distinguishes Goodpaster both from those who take a more holistic approach (and would value the systems of those who lived above the individuals themselves) and from animal rights/ liberation authors who do construct distinctions (which Goodpaster appears to believe are 'arbitrary') between living things, usually on the basis of sentience, the ability to suffer (Singer 1975) or having inherent value which it would be unjust to ignore (Regan 1984). Reverence for life theorists do not, therefore, distinguish between plants and animals as far as moral considerability goes, although this does not mean, of course, that each are as morally *significant.*

Those who are holistically minded have criticised the reverence for life approach as an ethical system because it takes a conventional view of ethics (that it should be concerned with discrete individuals) and extends it into the non-human world (Callicott 1983: 301) – in this respect the argument is very similar to those heard against animal rights. Presumably the complaint is that no psychological or perceptual change need accompany this ethical change. More important, though, is the argument that reverence for life is difficult if not impossible to live by because we would not be able to do anything any harm (Callicott 1983: 301). Interestingly, then, reverence for life (or life-principle) theorists provide an ethic which is ecocentric but which is not holistic. Again, perhaps, the predicament is that holism is making very particular demands of green theorists, and I will return to this below.

An environmental ethic which is going to be of any use is going to have to allow us to value systems as well as individuals – otherwise, as Sylvan (1984) pointed out, we may save the tree and spoil the forest. Equally though, we cannot risk having an ethic which does not protect individuals otherwise we are all dispensable in the scheme of things. Similarly, this ethic (which will allow us to expand our moral community) must find the source of worth or value of that which will be morally considerable, in nature, rather than in any instrumental value for people.

There are other approaches to the study of environmental ethics which can broaden our understanding of issues such as 'value'. Rolston (1975), for example, has argued very convincingly that it is possible to draw objective values from nature itself and this has made it possible for him to view ethics at a systemic level. However, he has also argued (1987) that we can find not only instrumental and intrinsic value, but systemic value as well in nature (this resides in the productive processes which generate intrinsic value). Consequently, it is possible to see both individuals and systems as the bearers or objects of value and our failure to appreciate this is simply a failure to discover it. If we take this line we are committing ourselves to a view of the moral community which, because it truly draws value from nature, includes the whole of nature. It does, therefore, have a very expansive view of our responsibilities.

A second holistic theorist is Baird Callicott (1983), who is often seen as someone who draws heavily on the work of Aldo Leopold and his land ethic (Johnson 1984: 353). He combines Leopold's views on biotic communities (that the 'good' of these communities is the 'ultimate measure of moral value', Baird Callicott, quoted in Moline 1986: 101) with Hume's ideas on the motivation of humans (passion, emotion, feeling or sentiment) and Darwin's concept of moral evolution to argue for social sympathy towards both members of communities, and society itself. It is the fact that these sentiments are excited by objects external to us which makes the ethic non-anthropocentric. Equally, Baird Callicott argues that this appreciation is not simply of the system but can be of the individuals as well, so it is not exclusively system oriented, or individualistic. He provides a very good basis for the belief that both systems and individuals deserve our moral consideration and should be members of our moral community. Interestingly, too, he rests his argument upon a defence of affection and sentiment which differentiates his theory from that of, say, Rolston.

Lastly, Attfield (1983) argues from an unorthodox 'holistic' perspective. He is more of the persuasion that in protecting the individual we imply some extended considerability to those things – habitats, systems or whatever – which support those individuals but he is very much against any extended holistic view. His argument is that we get no sense of obligation necessarily from establishing interdependence beyond 'strengthen[ing] the argument from human and animal interests for the preservation of the systems on which they depend' (Attfield 1983: 203). Here, we do have a non-anthropocentrism to the extent that animals are included in Attfield's moral community, but he has not attributed any intrinsic value to, for example, plants and rivers.

Although I do not really need to defend or promote one of these arguments over and above the others, I will make just one point. Green political theory, by virtue of it being 'green', emphasises holism, that is, it emphasises the value of the wholes of which individuals are a part, rather than the individuals themselves. In this respect, theories which are not properly holistic (Attfield's, for example) cannot be said to be green in any meaningful sense.[5]

PROCESS AND DEMOCRACY

Let me begin by briefly returning to the argument that greens should be seen as more process oriented than is the case at the moment.[6] Greens want to secure, for example, sustainability and through this the circumstances of future generations. It is perfectly reasonable to see this as a goal towards which any green polity should work. Following the arguments of Saward and Sagoff, making such an 'end' integral to the form of a green democracy would undermine democracy itself. Now if, as I argued earlier, greens are concerned with expanding the moral community, this need not be a problem – it has been perceived as such only because the implications of such an expansion have not been taken to their logical conclusion. If we ensure that those future generations, non-human species, and ecosystems are afforded the political consideration that we might expect for a member of the moral community then we do not have to prescribe as many of the policy outcomes in advance (i.e. we don't have to be as ends oriented). We simply have to construct our political institutions (which would include rules, structures, basic laws) in a way which guarantees that the political process will be 'considerate' of all those interests which are represented. If we take for example the four basic principles of the German greens (ecology, social responsibility, grassroots democracy and non-violence: Spretnak and Capra 1985) it is perfectly possible to see all of these as principles which are as much guides to the way the political system might operate, as they are ends which the system must achieve.

An anthropocentric polity, such as we have at the moment, displays certain characteristics which may give us clues as to how we may proceed to reconstruct democracy on the basis of green principles. Primary amongst these is that the polity is constructed for, by and of people – in other words there is some congruence between the nature of the political and the moral communities. This is not to say they are, or have to be, identical, but rather that there is a relationship between what, or who, is thought morally considerable, and what, or who, is politically represented. Presumably, then, a green polity would want to do the same thing – it would want to make the nature of its (expanded) moral community more congruent with the political community. To my mind, if we are following both the logic of the philosophical basis of green political theory and the idea that moral and political communities are similar, then we end up, broadly, with four central political areas which would need to be changed to accommodate the new moral community: standing, quality of democracy, decision making and political representation.

Standing

Under such arguments, which are largely based upon liberal conceptions of citizenship and the rule of law, it would be possible to allow various non-human entities (perhaps, a river, marsh, brook, beach, national monument, commons, tree, species)[7] to have action taken on their behalf against those who injure them. Although the 'liberalness' of this type of approach has been criticised because it reinforces current perceptions of individualism in law and in nature I would argue, first, that such redress *should* be available no matter what type of political theory we construct (because it would be arrogant to believe our theory to be so good that redress would never be necessary),[8] and, second, that it would be wrong to see this as an approach which could only reinforce individualistic stereotypes of our place in nature. Indeed, it is perfectly possible to argue that the idea of a whole 'system' being damaged and complaining about it could do a great deal to change cultural perceptions of ecosystems.

There is no reason why it would be only individual members of sentient species that would have standing – it is perfectly possible to have many non-individualistic aspects of ecosystems given legal and moral standing. It may be difficult to do this in a strictly 'holistic' way but on some (limited) versions of holism such an approach could be helpful if standing was not restricted to individual examples of species or ecosystems. I think the obvious qualification to make is not that liberal-legal solutions are un-necessary but, rather, that they are insufficient. Their problem, from a green point of view, is that all other aspects of the political, economic and social system remain unchanged and hence moral considerability, signific-ance and community membership becomes far too contingent upon purely legal processes.

We could make a similar case on the basis of attributing rights to the non-human world. These may be specific rights, say, to thrive, exist without threat of damage, and may exist independently of standing in other areas which may offer more general protection. If we are to take the idea of rights to their logical conclusion we could, for example, consider whether we might extend or redefine the notion of social rights (Marshall 1963), extending them from the civil and political to include the quality of life. Here, we might, for example, have to adjust either the legal or constitutional standing of non-humans or perhaps see their welfare in the same 'en-titlement' framework as we view our own. The possibilities for using such a system to change or promote consciousness is quite formidable. This sense of rights is distinct from Saward's use of rights in his contribution to this volume because here it is the rights of non-humans which are being considered independently of their benefit to humans. Saward is more interested in extending human or civil *rights* to include environmental considerations.

Quality of democracy

In existing (anthropocentric) political systems the ability of subjects to participate between elections is, in part at least, a measure of democracy. Equally, analysis which considers the role of the institutional arrangements of the state has increasingly suggested that how the state is organised can, and does, affect political outcomes (see, for example, Evans 1984; Hall 1986). For instance, as far as green politics is concerned, Kitschelt (1986) argued that the structures provided for political dissent did make a difference to the nature of participation in anti-nuclear movements.

The same judgements will be applicable to a green democracy. In other words we will have to consider whether such political systems represent a real expansion of the moral community. Precisely what is represented will, of course, depend upon the extent to which we expand our moral community. Nevertheless, it is possible to imagine that consultation exercises might be required to provide opportunities for human representatives of non-human interests to give an opinion; that licensing authorities for industrial plants may have similar constraints placed upon them; that the state may have a statutory responsibility to promote, fund and consult representatives of non-humans in the same way that some political parties are state funded; that regulatory agencies may be required to promote the interests of non-humans' entities and that the representative basis of these agencies should reflect this, and so on.

Decision making

I mentioned earlier that the British Green Party had promised to change the system of national accounting to accommodate the effects of economic policies on the environment and it is feasible to do this on the basis of discount rates and building in externalities which were not included before. It is, as Ophuls (1977) pointed out, still possible to try to maximise output within more ecologically tolerable limits, but equally, it is also possible to work well within our capacity and not push out to the limits of endurance. Given that we do have to operationalise our philosophical base then Goodin (1983) provides a very good starting place. Working from the assumption that we must now consider (if not apply moral significance to) non-humans then Goodin argues that rather than pursue a utility-maximising strategy, we should opt for decision-making criteria which are biased against irreversible decisions; in favour of protecting the vulnerable; in favour of sustainability; and against causing harm (1983: 16). We do not necessarily have to accept all Goodin's conclusions to see that such a formula could go a long way to satisfying the need we have to accommodate parts of the non-human world into our political community. In particular, the principle of 'avoiding harm' would now seem to be a central one given our commitment

109

to some notion of ecocentrism and the moral dispersion of value. This would also tend to accord with an orientation toward ecosystems which is more humble and one which was as concerned with doing the 'right' thing, as achieving a 'good' result. I do not say this is the only basis upon which decisions may be made within a green political theory, but it is one which, for all the problems it may cause, does illustrate the possibilities.[9]

Political representation

It has been my intention all along to use the issue of political representation as a means of circumventing arguments about green democracy. To be process oriented *and* to change the nature of political representation (in accordance with an expanded moral community) would mean we could expect green(ish) outcomes, without prescribing the ends of the policy process. We would simply be making a morally defensible case for changing the political process itself. Precisely how this may work out in practice is, I concede, a very difficult question. It is rather unlikely, for example, that individual species would, say, be represented in parliament – since this does seem to lead us into some peculiar possibilities.

Having said this, I think we could make a more plausible case for multi-member constituencies in which some of the representatives were expected to represent the interests of their non-human constituency members. Certainly there could be great benefits from a system like this at national or regional level where representatives are not always (or perhaps often) confronted with the ecological consequences of their actions. This would also fit with the idea that we should be concerned with systems (seen as areas or regions in this case) rather than individual species that might be threatened. It may eventually lead to political boundaries being drawn on ecological lines if, for example, ecological problems are seen as more pressing.

In fact, Kavka and Warren (1983) rehearse many of the arguments as far as the representation of future generations are concerned. They believe it is meaningful to argue that a being is representable if it has interests and if the representative takes instruction from the being, or, has a better than random judgement of their interests (1983: 25). Under these circumstances it should, on Kavka and Warren's formulation, be possible to represent a very diverse range of non-human interests within a green political system because their arguments appear to apply as much to non-humans as they do to future generations. Most arguments in favour of intrinsic value (or other holistic, ecocentric theories) do suppose some idea of the interests of those under consideration, so this is not in itself a problem. Once we have established that something has value or interests then it is representable. I do not propose to go into the questions of how an equitable representation might be achieved, but would say that if we are to make the moral and the political community similar then such an approach is valuable and we cannot dismiss this as an idea, particularly given that it would have a profound and positive effect on the nature of green democracy.

Kavka and Warren also consider, but then dismiss, the possibility that 'foreigners' might deserve representation. They argue against this on three grounds: that they are already represented better than other interests (e.g. through the UN); that it would affect sovereignty; and because it may raise moral questions about its effects on diplomacy and self-determination (1983: 33). I am less inclined to dismiss the possibility that those we do damage to might be entitled to a say in the decisions which affect them. In many ways this seems a much more plausible possibility than many others and is quite in line with green thinking on, for example, the transnational nature of pollution and the exploitative economic relations between the North and South. We could, for example, begin by inviting representatives from 'foreign' countries to act as observers at debates in national assemblies, or to participate without voting rights in the first instance.

This type of representational diversity is essential to green political theory and to the programmes of green groups and parties. It targets the democratic process as the mechanism which is, at present, failing to protect the vulnerable and the unrepresented. Process, then, is important. It is possible to build into political processes ethical criteria which are logically consistent with the type of moral community we might aspire to under green political theory.

The philosophical basis of such theory lends weight not only to the idea that we have obligations to species and the holistic nature of the ecosystem, but also to the idea that we have rightly to consider individuals and the propriety of the political processes we conduct. If we restore these latter two points within our theoretical schema (without ditching holism or eco-centrism) then democracy has a symbiotic relationship with ecocentrism. In other words, ecocentrism ensures that we do indeed establish a real diversity of political representation and it is this diversity which, in turn, ensures our democracy.

CONCLUSION

In many respects deep/transpersonal ecologists, ecofeminists and those who take a more spiritual line can fill in many of the gaps that are so apparent in a formulation like the one I have just given. It clearly is the case that certain aspects of moral considerability (for example, courtesy, magnanimity, self-sacrifice, humility, compassion) cannot be legislated – they are personal, cultural and spiritual aspects of ourselves (something with which Leopold would agree: Moline 1986: 106–7). I would not for a moment suggest that legal-formalism provides all, or even many, of the answers to the ecological, or the spiritual, crisis. Having said this, it must play some part and such a position is defensible on the basis of green philosophy and green political theory.

My argument has been that if we are only concerned with political outcomes, then green democracy may well be in trouble because such a concern undermines many of the necessary conditions for democracy. However, if we agree that the way we make decisions is a central part of green philosophy, then we begin to set rules by which we must conduct ourselves which, as long as they are not incompatible with democracy (and the important point is that they need not be), provide a solid basis for green decision making. I have also shown, in later sections, the types of theory which may be taken into account (ecocentrism, holism) and the opportunities which polities offer for the incorporation of such ideas (e.g. quality of democracy issues, legal standing, decision making, representation).

Does this mean that green political theory (or a future green government) is unconcerned with political outcomes? Clearly this cannot be the case because the ending of the ecological crisis and the achievement of a sustainable society is a green goal and a green good. We can get around this problem in two ways. First, by arguing for an indirect holism that emphasises tendencies within our orientation towards the 'biotic community'. Second, we can establish the significance of goals by arguing that political outcomes are important to green political theory to the extent that those outcomes may be adverse or unintended consequences of policy. This does not mean that certain ends have to be prescribed by green political theory, but rather, that it recognises the need to evaluate the decisions which are made to ensure there is some correspondence between what the decision makers intended and what actually happened.

Such a theory cannot ensure green outcomes, but it can ensure a green political process. Indeed, one of the anomalies of green political theory is that it need not guarantee green political outcomes – only a reconstruction of the political process. We can further these arguments by saying that this does provide some guidance to greens on how to behave politically, and how to decide what is politically beneficial to them. In general, anything which works to diversify the political community, to expand its moral constituency, to open up the number of political opportunity structures for that constituency's interests and which encourages tolerance and compassion in decision making will, to a greater or lesser extent, promote some aspect of green democracy. To paraphrase Leopold, anything which tends otherwise, is wrong.

NOTES

1 In fact I am not particularly interested in individual theories of intrinsic value, as my argument does not require me to choose between them, only to establish

that arguments of this kind are central and, if accepted, affect our views on green democracy.

2 By 'the expansion of the moral community' I simply mean the increase in the number of individuals, species or systems which become morally considerable. I do not expect, as some do (Moline 1986) that 'extending' the community means that the same ethic applies. I would say that the expansion of the community presupposes a change in the ethic.

3 Personally, I would not have much objection to surrendering some, or perhaps most, of my democratic rights to a loving and trustworthy green council which would pursue ends with which I agreed and which would benefit me and my family. It is quite on the cards that such sacrifices may be necessary at a practical level and we will have to risk the abuse of the democratic process. This does not mean, though, that, theoretically, we have to be happy at the prospect. Nor does it mean that a little more attention to the anthropocentric nature of the political process would go amiss.

4 I believe that the problems reside principally in translating the spiritual into the political with all the associated problems of accommodating things such as 'faith' and 'intuition' within a political framework. I have declined to do this, but believe that it is a job well worth trying nevertheless.

5 Holism is more complicated than it appears. Attfield is right to suggest it means more than simple interdependence (1983: 203). Moline (1986: 104–5) recounts that holism is a form of teleology in which what is best is judged in terms of its effects on the whole. He argues for a distinction between direct and indirect holism, in which the latter denotes a broad teleological concern with 'tendencies, practices, tastes, predilections, or rules' (105) but they apply distinctive principles or criterion in practice. In this way, we can defend Leopold's holism against the charge that he would be unconcerned about individuals.

6 By process oriented I mean a concern with the way the political system operates, the nature of political representation, the values which are embodied in the system, the opportunities there are for political participation and the constraints there are on political action (e.g. what the state may legitimately do).

7 These are all examples of real complaints that were filed in the USA.

8 Gandhi cautioned the west against thinking we could construct social systems which were so perfect that people no longer had to be good. Perhaps the same applies to green political theory?

9 Of course, Goodin was not arguing for an exclusively process-oriented solution and within his model there is guidance on both ends and means. My position is not that ends should not count, but rather, that axioms like avoiding harm can guide the minute to minute actions of decision makers and can produce desirable (green) results even if they do not prescribe a policy-specific end result.

REFERENCES

Attfield, R. (1983) 'Methods of Ecological Ethics', *Metaphilosophy* 14, 3 and 4: 195–208.

Callicott, J. Baird (1983) 'Non-Anthropocentric Value Theory and Environmental Ethics', *American Philosophical Quarterly* 21, 4: 299–309.

Dobson, A. (1989) 'Deep Ecology', *Cogito* spring.

—— (1990) *Green Political Thought*, London: HarperCollins.

—— (1993) 'Ecologism', in R. Eatwell and H. Wright (eds) *Contemporary Political Ideologies*, London: Pinter.

Eckersley, R. (1992) *Environmentalism and Political Theory: Toward an Ecocentric Approach*, London: UCL Press.

Evans, P. (ed.) (1984) *Bringing the State Back In*, Cambridge: Cambridge University Press.

Goodin, R. (1983) 'Ethical Principles for Environmental Protection', in R. Elliot and A. Gare (eds) *Environmental Philosophy*, Milton Keynes: Open University Press.

—— (1992) *Green Political Theory*, Oxford: Polity.

Goodpaster, K. (1983) 'On Being Morally Considerable', in D. Scherer and T. Attig (eds) *Ethics and the Environment*, Englewood Cliffs, NJ: Prentice Hall.

Green Party (1992) *New Directions: The Path to a Green Britain Now*, General Election Campaign Manifesto, London: The Green Party.

Hall, P. (1986) *Governing the Economy*, Oxford: Polity.

Hardin, G. (1968) 'The Tragedy of the Commons', *Science* 162: 1,243–8.

Johnson, E. (1984) 'Treating the Dirt: Environmental Ethics and Moral Theory', in T. Regan (ed.) *Earthbound*, Prospect Heights, NJ: Waveland Press.

Kavka, G. G. and Warren, V. (1983) 'Political Representation for Future Generations', in R. Elliot and A. Gare (eds) *Environmental Philosophy*, Milton Keynes: Open University Press.

Kemp, P. and Wall, D. (1990) *A Green Manifesto for the 1990s*, Harmondsworth: Penguin.

Kitschelt, H. (1986) 'Political Opportunity Structures and Political Protest: Anti-Nuclear Movements in Four Democracies', *British Journal of Political Science* 16, 1: 56–72.

McClade, J. M. (1991) 'The Seas and the Shoreline as Part of the European Biosphere', in S. Parkin (ed.) *Green Light on Europe*, London: Heretic.

Marshall, T. H. (1963) *Sociology at the Crossroads*, London: Heinemann.

Mathews, F. (1988) 'Conservation and Self-Realization: A Deep Ecology Perspective', *Environmental Ethics* 10, 4: 347 – 57.

Moline, J. N. (1986) 'Aldo Leopold and the Moral Community', *Environmental Ethics* 8, 2: 99–120.

Ophuls, W. (1977) *Ecology and the Politics of Scarcity*, New York: Freeman.

Ophuls, W. and Boyan, A. S. (1992) *Ecology and the Politics of Scarcity Revisited*, New York: Freeman.

Paehlke, R. (1988) 'Democracy, Bureaucracy, and Environmentalism' *Environmental Ethics* 10, 4: 291–309.

Parkin, S. (1989) *Green Parties: An International Guide*, London: Heretic.

Regan, T. (1984) *The Case for Animal Rights*, London: Routledge.

Rolston III, Holmes (1975) 'Is There an Ecological Ethic?', *Ethics* 85, 2: 93–109.

—— (1987) *Environmental Ethics*, Philadelphia, Pa: Temple University Press.

Sagoff, M. (1988) *The Economy of the Earth*, Cambridge: Cambridge University Press.

Saward, M. (1993) 'Green Democracy', in A. Dobson and P. Lucardie (eds) *The Politics of Nature*, London: Routledge.

Singer, P. (1975) *Animal Liberation*, New York: Random House.

—— (1993) *Practical Ethics*, Cambridge: Cambridge University Press.

Spretnak, C. and Capra, F. (1985) *Green Politics*, London: Paladin.

Sylvan, R. (1984) 'A Critique of Deep Ecology, Parts I and II', *Radical Philosophy* 40 and 41.

6

SUSTAINABILITY, POLITICAL JUDGEMENT AND CITIZENSHIP

Connecting green politics and democracy

John Barry

One could say that the use of the language of democracy in political debate is often for the same reasons a drunk uses a lamppost: for support rather than illumination. In much the same way as Achterberg (Chapter 9), following Kymlicka (1990), argues that any plausible political theory embodies a commitment to the view of individuals as deserving of equal respect and concern, in a similar fashion one can posit democracy as a value to be considered as an essential part of all acceptable political theories. In this respect, green politics is no different in its claim to be part of the 'democratic project'. However, beyond a shared commitment to democracy, political theories differ as to what they understand by democracy, the reasons why they advocate it, and how they envisage its institutionalisation. Thus, although all theories worthy of respect and serious consideration endorse the general concept of democracy, they disagree over the different possible conceptualisations of democracy. On both these points, the concept and conceptualisation of democracy, questions have been raised as to their necessary connection to green politics.

It is because of its status as an unqualified positive value or a self-evident 'good thing' that criticising a political theory as undemocratic, or claiming that it is only contingently committed to democracy, is a serious charge. Such charges have been brought against green politics by a number of authors, most notably Saward (1993), who argues that there is no necessary or logical reason why green politics should be democratic, and *a fortiori* why green politics ought to be understood as being radically democratic. Other interpretations of green politics indicate that by its very nature green politics to achieve its aims must be undemocratic and authoritarian (Passmore 1993: 478). This critique concerning the relationship between green politics and democracy is all the more damaging to green political theory precisely because it claims to be more democratic than contemporary liberal democracy. Greens often claim to be committed, for example, to participatory and direct forms of democratic decision making (Dobson 1990: 25–6; Eckersley 1992: 173–8; Goodin 1992: 124–7). How are we to understand and seek to resolve this apparent contradiction? Part of the problem highlighted by this critique relates to the under-theorised nature and status of 'sustainability' within green political discourse. The aim of this chapter is to argue that explicating the political-normative character of sustainability offers a way in which a non-contingent green adherence to democratic decision making can be grounded.

The essential indeterminateness and normative character of the concept of sustainability implies, I argue, that it needs to be understood as a discursively 'created' rather than an authoritatively 'given' product. The normative and factual dimensions of sustainability are what grounds the appeal to 'democratic will formation' with regard to its instantiation as a regulative social principle. Sustainability is thus both a matter of practical judgement, arising from its normative character, and a matter of know-ledge. Sustainability is thus more than finding ecologically rational methods of production and consumption; it also involves collective judgement on those patterns. It is not just a matter of examining the ecological means to determined ends; ultimately sustainability requires a political-normative judgement on the ends themselves. Sustainability is therefore a matter for communicative as well as instrumental rationality, but the former takes precedence over the latter. This normative character of sustainability as a public principle or social goal makes it conducive to democratic as opposed to non-democratic forms of 'will formation'. That is, we can link green politics and democracy by recognising first that as a normative concept sustainability is a political/ethical issue first and only derivatively a technical/economic one and, second, by demonstrating that this political articulation ought, for traditional democratic reasons and for reasons specific to the realisation of sustainability, to be democratic rather than non-democratic, such that democracy and ecological rationality are mutually reinforcing. Finally, we can show that the green understanding of democracy envisages the 'preservative transcendence' of aspects of liberal democracy, but that there are problems with the self-characterisation of green political theory as radically democratic in terms of seeking to replace representative institutions with direct forms.

This chapter starts from the observation that empirically there seems to be a positive relationship between democratic institutions and ecological protection. On the one hand, the more democratic a society is, the more likely it is that ecological sustainability will be enhanced, or could be enhanced. In some respects this is related to the way in which democracy as 'responsive rule' (Saward 1993: 65–6), or a communicative process (Dryzek 1990), is more effective in ensuring the relatively quick adjustment of economic–ecological processes in the face of ecological disruptions than authoritarian, non-democratic systems. On the other hand in their practical political activity environmental groups have been at the forefront of efforts to 'democratise' state institutions, particularly in relation to access to information, scientific data, public inquiries and more open forms of public policy making (Paehlke 1988). In a sense then although there may be a question as to the strict theoretical relationship between green political theory and democracy, in practice this tension seems more apparent than real. There is thus a sound basis upon which to establish the theoretical counterpart to this empirical connection.

It is the 'primacy of the political' that serves to underwrite the non-contingent place of democracy within ecologism. It is only if ecological sustainability is reduced to a technical injunction that other theories can claim to be 'green' or 'ecological', or that green politics and democracy become disconnected: such technical/economic interpretations ground environmental rather than ecological positions (Dobson 1990: 3). Following from this we can claim that a minimal position is to assert the compatibility of environmentalism with democracy, either in the sense of environmentalists being seen as another interest group whose aims can be included within the framework of traditional pluralist accommodation, or the 'environmental crisis' as an external factor to which existing democracies can easily adjust. However, what I want to establish in this chapter is a non-contingent relationship between green politics and democracy by arguing that from the green perspective enhanced democratic structures and practices are not merely desirable but in fact fundamentally necessary. That is, it is not just the case that democracy is weakly compatible with green politics, in little danger of being undermined (since greens are so democratic in practice), but, rather, that the achievement of sustainability makes democracy a core, non-negotiable, value of green political theory.

SOME DEFINITIONS

Sustainability and sustainable development

'Sustainability' here refers to the ensemble of social-nature relations in general, material and moral, which is to be distinguished from 'sustainable development', which refers more specifically to continuously productive economic–ecological exchanges, in terms of a non-deteriorating capital stock (both natural and human) (Pearce *et al.* 1993). Sustainability can be considered the set of which sustainable development is a sub-set, concerned with a much wider set of human relations than the aim to 'green' existing patterns of production, consumption and lifestyles.[1] Sustainability, unlike sustainable development, is concerned as much with the ends of our use of the environment as with the ecological means to economic development. In economic terms, sustainability is concerned with both human demand on the environment and ecological supply-side conditions. The reason for this distinction is that economistic notions of sustainable development may crowd out the more explicitly political-normative notion of sustainability and lead to more technical, less democratic forms of decision making. Briefly put, what is needed is to place the economics of sustainable development within the overall context of the 'ethics and politics of sustainability'.

Democracy

This chapter is not concerned with developing a particular green conception of democracy so much as with establishing some necessary connections between democracy and the realisation of sustainability as a social goal. As used here, democracy is understood to be first and foremost a communicative process, a political procedure between individuals and institutions, where the former decide collectively binding decisions which are then enforced by the latter. However, the model of democracy that is assumed to comport with green theory is a discursive/deliberative one of the type associated with a tradition in democratic theory which includes civic republicanism, Rousseau, contemporary theorists, such as Habermas (1987), who are concerned with the vital significance of the 'public sphere' to democratic politics, radical democrats such as Barber (1984), and ecologically minded democratic theorists such as Dryzek (1987, 1990). Other chapters in this volume (see Dobson and Achterberg) explore the details of this conception of democracy in more detail.

POLITICAL DISCOURSE AND SUSTAINABILITY

As a principle sustainability does not come with its own rules of implementation. In common with other normative principles, deliberation is required to apply it to particular circumstances. The collective analogue to this process of deliberation is public discourse and debate, that is democratic decision-making procedures. Making sustainability a co-ordinating social value and practice cannot be left up to 'specialists' since it is not simply a matter of expertise but, fundamentally, one of ethical consideration. In many ways its concerns are far too important to be left to scientists, never mind economists! The imperative to conjoin democracy and sustainability is not a contingent, *ad hoc* attempt to dress green principles in the legitimacy of democracy. The issues involved in the translation of sustainability from a political-ethical concept to a regulative social principle, expressed in law and policies, for example, require the deliberation as well as the consent and action of those whose lives will be affected by such a principle.

That sustainability is a normative concept should be obvious. It embodies a particular moral attitude to the future, expressing how much we care for and are willing to make sacrifices for our descendants and how, and to

118

what degree, non-humans figure in this process. Given the great power the present generation has over the welfare (and composition) of future generations, there is a consensus within green theory that with this capacity and knowledge of its likely effects comes a large degree of moral responsibility. Following on from this, the ethics of sustainability is partly concerned with how the current generation has duties (generally of a negative kind) to future generations. Arguments from sustainability usually propose wide-ranging changes in the present organisation of society, particularly the economy–ecology relationship, in the name of those yet to be born. The consequences of realising sustainability in social practices are so wide-spread, and the issues raised so important, that the elaboration of the 'common good' it refers to deserves democratic institutions that encourage the active participation of all concerned. But even if we agree on this general outline, and accept it as a principle that ought (in a moral as well as a prudential sense) to be socially instantiated, we have only begun the fleshing out process. For a start, as it stands it is far too abstract, being silent on many things. How far in the future must we look? One, three or fifty generations hence? What are we to pass on? What sacrifices are ruled out?

Such questions cannot be answered scientifically or metaphysically (that is objectively given), but because of their normative content they can only be articulated politically (that is intersubjectively created). And for traditional reasons we can say that this political process ought to be a democratic one. In one sense greens can ask why they should find new grounds for their adherence to democracy different from those advanced by socialists or liberals? The indeterminacies thrown up by sustainability require political adjudication, and given that the policies flowing from any conception of sustainability are likely to have a widespread social impact, leaving few citizens' lives untouched, it is uncontroversial to hold that they should have some say in the articulation and formulation of this social principle. That is to say the indeterminacy of the principle calls for citizen deliberation, while its translation into policies and laws call for their consent and equally important their active participation in realising it.

An objective account of sustainability, for example, can be seen as partly underwriting the ecoauthoritarian case, which involves sacrificing such values as democracy, liberty and equality, and is heavily dependent on political coercion in the name of ecological sustainability (Ophuls 1977; Heilbroner 1980). The problem with this conception is that it misconstrues the green case as concerned principally with the mere survival of our species for as long as possible on this planet. But as Roberts points out, 'Other animals may obey the simple dictum, "Above all, survive!" but the human animal tends to ask, "Survive *as what?*"' (1979: 10). If sustainability is conceived purely in terms of maintaining the ecological conditions for the infinite continuation of the human species, taking this as the primary green political value does open the possibility of a gap between democracy and

119

green politics. The utilitarian logic of such an interpretation of green politics does imply an instrumental rather than a principled acceptance of democracy.[2] But a purely utilitarian-coercive understanding of sustainability is unlikely to command consensus in public deliberation. If sustainability is viewed as combining democratic decision making (in terms of procedure) and intergenerational justice and moral concern for non-humans (in terms of substantive outcomes), it can act as the touchstone of green political theory. We could then reject conceptions of sustainability that are un-democratically arrived at (as in the ecoauthoritarian case) or imply unjust treatment of the future or unjustifiable use of non-humans.

It is the indeterminacy and uncertainty entailed by sustainability that means that it must be subject to political deliberation. Politics is an extension of ethics, and in the face of uncertainties it is the only defensible form our dependence on each other can take. The politics of sustainability is therefore a complex combination of democracy, normative claims and counter-claims, as well as questions of science and economics. In other words, it is concerned with the democratic articulation of questions of judgement, a public, political discourse of amateurs/citizens and only subsequently a (largely private) discourse of experts. By portraying it as a political question we avoid crude technocratic solutions, and by then portraying it as a particular type of political problem, that is democratic, we avoid the ecoauthoritarian scenario, which is often a sub-set of the technocratic approach.[3]

DISCURSIVE DESIGNS: FORMS OF DEMOCRACY

Having shown that the discourse of sustainability requires political articu-lation, and one that should be democratic given its impact on citizens, the particular form of democratic decision making and collective dialogue appropriate for sustainability needs to be examined. Here the concern is with assessing the common perception that green democratic theory must be some variation of direct democracy. With the state and citizen playing such a central role, representative forms of democracy are perhaps more central to green concerns than is usually thought.[4]

One of the arguments in favour of representative democracy is that unlike participatory or direct forms, the 'politicisation of everyday life' is not one of its goals. The disputes that occur within representative democracy are probably less intense than those that are likely to occur in the face-to-face context of Barber's 'strong democracy' (1984), or the small-scale, decentral-ised, self-sufficient communities that pepper the green political literature. In such a context it is often difficult to distinguish a fellow citizen's opinions from her as an individual, and while respect should always be shown to the individual independent of her particular views, under direct democratic conditions this important distinction may become blurred at least and perhaps ruptured. It is arguable that direct democracy works best where there is already a large degree of agreement between participants, and that representative forms are more suited to pluralist and heterogeneous collectivities.[5] The guiding logic should be *that the problems of democracy cannot be assumed to be solved simply by more democracy.* Accepting this idea implies that indirect forms of democratic participation can and should be included within arguments for, and the presentation of, 'green democracy'. Direct democracy must, as Saward (1993) reminds us, be distinguished from participatory democracy, and it seems more realistic to assert that green democracy implies that representative institutions will be supplemented by participatory democracy, rather than transcended by a direct democracy. That is, a green conception of participatory democracy is compatible with, and indeed politically will rely upon, extending and adapting traditional liberal democratic institutions (see De Geus and Saward in this volume).

However, there is an argument to be made to the effect that those more affected by a particular policy or decision ought to have more say than those who are only marginally affected. The premise of green democrats is the idea that all those affected should be considered as the relevant *demos* and that decision making should be made at the lowest level possible (Dobson 1990: 125; Porritt 1984: 165–8; Irvine and Ponton 1988: 78).[6] This implies that democratic decision making for some issues, that is, those of a transnational nature, transcends the nation-state, because the effects of its decisions transcend its jurisdiction. Here the advantages of representative forms of democracy are obvious, in this case the state can act as advocate for its affected citizens. On the other hand, in the interest of proportionality and equal consideration of interests, there are strong grounds for holding that those more affected by a decision ought to have more say than those who are not. This appeal to proportionality and fairness is at root one of justice rather than democracy-as-procedure. To give those not affected by a decision equal say as those for whom the consequences are potentially life threatening, for example, would be to treat the latter unequally. In other words the appropriate *demos* must be dependent upon and sensitive to the particular issue involved. Green democracy and considerations of justice may be said to be intertwined. Simply because a decision is democratically made is no guarantee of its moral worth. Understood in this way, the argument for the discursive understanding of sustainability is compatible with, and indeed will practically require, both representative and more direct forms of democratic participation.[7]

Another consideration is the importance of stability for any coherent political theory, especially democratic ones. According to Elster, 'All democracies, whether direct or indirect, have had some stabilizing devices to prevent all issues from being up for grabs by simple majority voting all the time' (1991: 130). Of such stabilising devices, a written constitution embodying the basic law of the land, setting out the political relationship between citizen and state and between citizens, is arguably of most interest and concern for green politics, especially in regard to freedom of information and access to policy-making procedures.

The significance of constitutional democracy is that it can include an 'ecological contract' between citizens and state, which sets out the nexus of rights and duties that constitute citizenship as a political and social relation. Apart from embodying the present generation's obligations to the future, a constitution could also be considered as expressing a society's considered and deliberated moral attitude to non-humans. That is, in so far as we can consider both non-humans and future human descendants 'moral subjects' (worthy of moral consideration but not morally responsible agents), a constitution can provide some legal protection for these vulnerables. There is nothing startling about this since such legal incorporations are common features of liberal democratic polities. We can think of this as involving constitutional provisions for the representation of the interests of non-humans as well as future citizens.

Here there may be scope for thinking that under deliberative or discursive conditions such an 'ecological contract' can be expected to express a concern with the 'ecological common good' and articulate 'generalisable' rather than 'particular' interests. As Dryzek notes, 'Clearly any policy that realizes general as opposed to particular interests is going to stand ecological concerns in good stead' (1987: 204). For him deliberative or discursive forms of democracy are more effective in developing ecologically rational forms of human–nature exchanges. Democratic institutions function analogously to ecosystems in that both are essentially concerned with transmitting 'information' (understood in the widest sense) acting as feedback mechanisms for the 'system' as a whole. Deliberative democracy should not, therefore, be interpreted as a demand for direct democracy, as opposed to more participatory democratic practice, where representative democratic institutions can be supplemented with more discursive institutional forms and of course greater citizen involvement in political and non-political spheres.

PREFERENCE TRANSFORMATION AND DEMOCRATIC CITIZENSHIP

One of the questions green politics addresses, and upon which its practical success depends, is expressed in Elster's statement that 'the central concern of politics should be the transformation of preferences rather than their aggregation' (1983: 35). Part of the reasoning behind this is that behavioural changes motivated by the internalisation of particular normative orientations is more effective and longer lasting than behavioural changes based on external or coercive imposition. In other words, changing one's lifestyle or pattern of consumption in the interests of sustainability is more effective if done out of a sense that one believes it is *right* to do so rather than because one is told to do so, or because it is simply expedient to do so. Sustainability policies then become less a *modus vivendi* or a prudential strategy, but more akin to an ecological version of a Rawlsian 'overlapping consensus'. But for this to work people must be genuinely committed to the moral rightness, rather than a begrudging acceptance, of, for want of a better word, the political 'sense' of sustainability. The rejection of utilitarian or economistic type reasoning, which relies on preference aggregation, is one of the hallmarks of democratic green politics, as the critique of the survivalist and utilitarian reasoning behind the ecoauthoritarian conception of sustainability demonstrated above. Preferences do not automatically command respect, but especially where they have other-regarding effects, they do require public justification. In other words, the reasons people give for their particular desires, ways of life, are important; the strength with which they hold these preferences is irrelevant to democratic decision making. To premise democracy on the idea that strength of belief ought to be recognised is to undermine the democratic principle of equality, as expressed in Bentham's classic formulation that 'each to count for one, and none for more than one'. The question of preference transformation involves judging preferences since actions, lifestyles, practices based on individual preference have, in our increasingly interdependent social and ecological world, wide-ranging effects on the lives of others.

The centrality of citizenship to sustainability comes from the belief that its achievement will require major institutional restructuring of contemporary western liberal democracies both internally and externally in their relationship to the rest of the world. However, institutional changes are not enough, and the contention is that such macro-level reorganisation needs to be supplemented with changes at the local and more importantly at the micro-level of individual citizens. Of particular significance here is the practice of citizenship and the role of active citizens. Citizenship is understood as a mediating practice which connects the individual and the institutional levels of society, as well as a common identity which links otherwise disparate individuals together as a collectivity with common interests. Citizenship is of course an integral part of any theory of democracy and the relationship between citizenship and the elaboration and realisation of sustainability is used to suggest a way of firmly establishing the democratic credentials of green politics.

The green claim to a principled as opposed to an instrumental adherence to democracy is that 'democratic will formation' permits the possibility that the preferences of individuals may be altered. Preference change is not a central aspect of sustainable development, given that the latter is largely concerned with finding 'supply-side' solutions to environmental problems, but it is a central consideration of sustainability. In this sense democratic citizenship may be understood as a form of social learning, the socialisation of 'ecological citizens' in response to ecological conditions and concerns.

Citizenship as an activity can be thought of as a means to, and a constitutive aspect of, the public elaboration of 'ecological rationality'. This is defined by Dryzek as 'the capacity of human and natural systems in combination to cope with problems' (1987: 11). In other words, the normative claims inherent within sustainability require public validation and debate, while the realisation of that collectively decided conception of sustainability requires citizen activism premised on the transformation rather than the mere articulation and aggregation of preferences.

In raising questions of intergenerational and international justice as well as moral claims on behalf of non-humans, sustainability captures the overarching direction of green politics. The immanent relationship between sustainability and democracy lies first in the prioritisation of the conjoint claims of both democracy and justice and second in seeing that citizen deliberation as well as consent and action are necessary for the realisation of green social aims. The role of the citizen is essential both on the 'input' and 'output' side. Democratic norms can be considered as the appropriate criteria for judging collective decision-making processes, while considerations of justice are often the most appropriate criteria for assessing the outcomes of such procedures.[8]

Apart from the intended or unintended effects of satisfying individual preferences, there are other difficulties with a politics that relies heavily on their aggregation. One is the contestable social ontology and view of the self that such a politics presupposes. In common with economistic reasoning, utilitarian-based politics is more concerned with states of affairs than with individuals (even though it is individualistic) who create or are the 'bearers' of those affairs. Another is the idea that preferences are fixed, simply given as the raw datum of politics. Preferences are important, but their articulation and justification ought to be seen as a crucial constitutive part of politics itself rather than being viewed as beyond (or before) politics. They are not 'given' but need to be justified and are thus open to change. The advantage of focusing on preferences is that it is generally easier to reach compromise where preferences as opposed to principles are at stake. That is, in so far as green democracy seeks to change preferences in a green direction rather than, for instance, opposing such basic moral principles as liberty, equality and autonomy, it is harder to criticise it on democratic grounds. The importance of questioning the exclusive attachment of some greens to radical forms of democracy lies in the central place occupied by preference formation and transformation within strong green arguments for democracy. Representative forms of democracy can act as filters for irrational and unreasonable desires, while also facilitating discussion and debate.

Aggregative strategies are also inferior to transformative strategies because in the provision of public goods, such as environmental protection, they are more likely to result in the 'tragedy of the commons' (Hardin 1968). Enhanced democratic institutions which stress citizen activity and deliberation on collective issues are more likely to avoid the prisoner's dilemma (Elster 1983) with regard to environmental problems. Communicative rationality makes it less likely that the collective result will be ecologically irrational. The ecoauthoritarians' formulation of the paradigmatic ecological problem in terms of the 'tragedy of the commons' can be criticised therefore for not making any allowance for purposeful communication between individual users of the commons. It simply assumes a prisoner's dilemma scenario with mutually disinterested and non-communicating 'rational individuals'. However, by introducing a communicative dimension, an intersubjective realm is created which permits the co-ordination of individual activity in such a way that the aggregate effect of individual behaviour is not, as in the tragedy scenario, both collectively and individually undesirable. Democracy understood as communication (Dryzek 1990) together with democratic citizenship as part of a social learning process provides some evidence that individuals can deliver enhanced environmental public goods and avoid or limit environmental public bads. This is partly because democracy allows preferences, expectations and behaviour to be altered as a result of debate and persuasion, binding individual behaviour to conform to publicly agreed norms. Democratic citizenship in short permits the possibility of the voluntary creation and maintenance of an ecologically rational social–nature interaction, informed by moral as well as scientific considerations. This is because it is communicative rather than instrumental rationality which characterises ecological rationality and the possible realisation of sustainability.

CITIZEN AND STATE

In comparison with anarchistic versions of green politics, the account presented here sees green politics as compatible with and indeed requiring a commitment to state or state-like institutions. The reason for this is that the state is a necessary (though not sufficient) condition for the elaboration of discourses of sustainability in the public sphere of modern liberal democracies. The state envisaged here is an 'enabling' one, one bound by the rule of law, with a constitution that embodies the outcome of citizen deliberation. So long as we acknowledge the inevitability of pluralism in modern societies and attach value to it, yet are also committed to democracy, the state is the obvious agent with the legitimacy and resources to make these social principles operable. A democratised, decentralised state and civil society would seem to fit best the demands of 'green democracy' and the achievement of sustainability.

However, the state is limited in what it can do. Even if we were to accept the legitimacy of the ecoauthoritarian solution, it is still the case that the state by itself cannot control or dictate all the necessary social, economic and political practices that sustainability will require. For example, in a

125

world of other states and a global market, the additional variable of ecosystems is simply another aspect of the external world that the individual state cannot control. This is where citizenship is important. Given that the state cannot do everything, there is an increased need for citizens, both individually and in association with others, to do their bit for the environment.

Traditional conceptions of citizenship define it in terms of rights, with citizenship understood as the right to have rights. This is a narrow understanding of what it means to be a citizen, a minimal view of citizenship typically associated with liberalism. With little or no demands on them apart from tax-paying and obeying the laws, the relationship between private citizens and the liberal state becomes distant and formal. This may have to do with the increasing pluralisation of society within contemporary liberal democracies, and the consequent and continuing 'emptying out' of any substantive content to citizenship. As such the emaciation of citizenship may be accounted for in terms of the fragmentary nature of such societies. However, Arblaster's observation that 'Perhaps it is only because the duties of citizenship have been reduced to a minimum ... that they [liberal democracies] survive as unitary states at all' (1987: 67) is telling. Citizenship as viewed by green democratic theory emphasises the duty of citizens to take responsibility for their actions and choices, and also an obligation to 'do one's bit' in the collective enterprise of achieving sustainability. There is thus a notion of 'civic virtue' within a green conception of citizenship. This implies that the duties of being a citizen go beyond the formal political realm, including, for example, such activities as recycling and energy conservation. In these cases there are roles for both the formal institutions of local and central government, the constitution, and the judiciary, as well as for more informal institutions of community, and the opinions of fellow citizens, which would help to prevent 'free-riding' by individuals and groups: that is to say a sustainable legal/state apparatus will also need to encourage a 'sustainability culture'. The role of the citizen and the practice of citizenship is constitutive of the latter by building an agreed 'sense of sustainability' on a notion of 'civic virtue', as well as performing the democratic function of a feedback loop between state and civil society.

Another role for the citizen is to take part in the general political debate around sustainability, that is to engage in the different facets of this debate where, according to Barber, '[The citizen's] task is to judge, evaluate and assess – to employ judgement rather than expertise' (1984: 289). Democracy in its various forms is a way of bringing expert and lay citizens together in a (hopefully) mutually enriching context.[9] But the final decision is left to all citizens, not the experts or the highly motivated. However, in the elaboration of sustainability a people may democratically decide on a policy of 'discounting the future', but this would violate the claims of the future to a just provision for their welfare. As Rawls notes, 'In the case of the individual, pure time preference is irrational. . . . In the case of society, pure time preference is unjust' (1972: 295). Where the outcomes are the main concern, their assessment cannot be on democratic criteria, since these apply to procedures rather than substantive outcomes. It is to justice that we must look for criteria for assessing outcomes. This is why greens need a theory of justice to complement their democratic credentials and ecological concerns.

CONCLUSION

The strategy of this chapter has been to argue for shifting the arena of debate about sustainability from science and economics to the political-ethical realm. And for reasons outlined this shift leads on to posit democratic as opposed to non-democratic forms of decision making. From this democratic conception then comes its translation into the legal or constitutional realm of society, becoming part of an 'ecological social contract' between the state and the (active) responsible citizen. So the process is from the moral to the political/democratic realm and then from the legislative to the legal/constitutional. In this constitutional provision and policy implementation the present expresses its duties of justice to future citizens, as well as allowing space for collective duties to non-humans.[10] But it is not simply the case that sustainability would be imposed from above by constitutional statutes, although this might be the case in situations of conflict between the demands of sustainability and other social values. Making the activism of citizens central gives the type of democratic processes being intimated here an interactive communicative dimension in which democracy is conceived of as a two-way process, a reciprocal flow of communication and information between institutions and citizens. With active citizen involvement at the deliberative stage the translation of agreed principle into policy will be less difficult since citizens will be morally, as well as legally, bound to that decision, since they are required to act according to principles they themselves have prescribed. This seems to indicate another way in which democracy and sustainability are linked. Under non-democratic conditions responsibility for the common good, including the ecological commons, cannot find an interactive, collective expression, in the sense that the state can always be blamed, thus relieving citizens of the onus to take responsibility. Under a non-democratic regime being denied rights would imply that duties lose their moral, although they may still retain their legal, or *de facto*, force. Yet, as argued earlier, it is action motivated by a sense of moral rightness rather than expediency or coercion that is essential to the politics of sustainability. Sustainability demands that citizens fulfil their duties, but this is premised on citizens' rights being protected, and democracy is the obvious candidate as the political system to articulate this, as it is centred on the balancing of rights and duties.

As such sustainability indicates that citizens are each others' keepers, and deliberative or discursive forms of participatory democracy provide the means through which this particularly modern form of interdependence can find expression.

The social goal of sustainability as opposed to either the technocratic/economistic discourse of 'sustainable development' or the utopian discourse of the 'sustainable society' is a defensible way for green politics to integrate its commitment to justice and democracy. Talking about the political sense of sustainability gets green politics away from the often fruitless preoccupation with developing 'greenprints' for the future society.

In the discourse of sustainability the interplay between expertise and judgement is clear. Its indeterminacy should be seen both as inevitable and indicating a necessary degree of flexibility that is an advantage rather than a deficiency. As a political–moral question sustainability is sufficiently wide-ranging that both human and non-human welfare can be accommodated and brought into fruitful relation with each other. In bringing together these different but intimately related areas, the politics of sustainability express the attempt to cope with the contingencies of 'being in the world', that is, being a 'citizen-in-society-in-environment'.

The discussion also highlights a particular feature of green political theory that is so obvious that its significance is often overlooked. In its concern for those who cannot speak, either because they are yet to be born (future generations), are incapable (non-humans), or are denied citizenship (affected foreigners), green politics can be characterised as the 'politics of advocacy'. That is, it attempts to bring into the political realm previously excluded others. Its concern is such that it seeks to represent these non-citizens, protecting their interests where possible, or limiting negative consequences.[11] This view implies that green theorists ought to look more favourably upon representative forms of democracy as well as extra-democratic institutions such as constitutions and the legal system, while acknowledging the potential ecological and democratic benefits of the state as the co-ordinator and bearer of the collective will. But perhaps the most significant import of this perspective is that the legal sphere is extremely important for green politics, and perhaps more important than previously thought.

What the discussion indicates is that by itself sustainability, the preservation and conservation of a viable environment fit for human and non-human welfare and fulfilment, is not only indeterminate in its definition and translation into policies, programmes and practices: from the perspective of green political theory as a whole, its status as 'the' green value is itself indeterminate. Simply put, placing a premium on sustainability does not, *ceteris paribus*, give us a reason *why* it ought to be a regulative social principle. What makes it something good is the value we place on that which is to be sustained. Sustainability *per se* is a value intensifier, but it is only if we value what is sustained, that we can answer the question *why* it ought to be sustained. The open-endedness of the principle implies that greens should not couch their positions in terms of sustainability without also indicating how it relates to commitments to democracy and justice. It is only by this process that green politics can be understood, as I believe it must, as a politics of the 'common good' as well as a politics of the 'ecological commons'.[12]

ACKNOWLEDGEMENTS

I would like to thank all those who participated in the ECPR workshop on Green Politics and Democracy in Madrid, April 1994, for their comments and criticism. In particular, I owe much to Chris Berry and Brian Doherty for their detailed comments on earlier drafts of this chapter.

NOTES

1 Pearce *et al.* dismiss the notion of sustainability as a policy aim because for them it implies a commitment to a no-growth economy with an implied coercive demand for radically altered lifestyles (1993: 4–5). Sustainable development, because it proposes that economic growth is compatible with less resource use, is for them a much more attractive policy goal. However, as used here, sustainability is distinguished from sustainable development for the purpose of highlighting the full range of normative issues expressed and surpressed in the politics and discourse of sustainability. What this distinction seeks to bring out is the non-technical, extra-economic dimensions of the debate, particularly those which relate to democracy.

2 A lurking utilitarian logic may partly explain Saward's doubts about the status of democracy within the green political canon. Defining democracy as 'responsive rule', as he does (1993: 68–9), could be interpreted as placing greater value upon the 'responsiveness' of rulers to the preferences of citizens, than upon *how* and more to the point *why* such responsiveness is actualised. If we are concerned about preference fulfilment we could argue that the real issue is not the type of government, but its scale/size. Osterfeld's conviction that 'Provided that exit is not barred, a large democracy would be less responsive, and therefore provide less utility to its citizens, than a local dictatorship' (1989: 155) could be said to be sensitive to the importance of 'responsiveness'. In other words, democracy as 'responsive rule' may imply an instrumental as opposed to principled valuation. Following on from this we may question Saward's view that 'there is a natural compatibility between liberalism and democracy which does not obtain between ecologism and democracy' (1993: 69). If, however, democracy is understood as giving those affected by a decision a say in its formulation and implementation, we could say that on this understanding ecologism may fare better than liberalism.

3 For an introduction to the relationship between technocratic approaches and authoritarian politics see O'Riordan (1981).

4 I do not wish to be interpreted as arguing that representative institutions are to be viewed as transitionary modes to more radical forms, although this is of course possible. I feel, and I give some indication later why, representative forms in a

pluralist society will always be necessary, and that in terms of politically raising the issue of the moral status of non-humans, representative institutions have their benefits.

5 One could say that direct democracy is more concerned with the expression of communal identity than as a non-coercive decision-making mechanism.

6 The decentralisation of the state may be an important feature in the formation of a coherent sustainability programme in that it frees central government to a large extent. It allows central government to 'plan' and co-ordinate, while leaving the details up to local communities, government and institutions.

7 Although beyond this chapter, there is reason to think that as well as different democratic institutions, there may be different democratic decision criteria that a comprehensive account of sustainability may merit. For example, it might be that simple majorities will not be acceptable for deciding a referendum on a national 'sustainability plan', where a two-thirds or three-quarters majority (or perhaps consensus) is more appropriate. See Tannsjo for further discussion (1992: 48).

8 Defined in this way sustainability could answer Goodin's (1992) conundrum concerning the non-derivability of outcomes from procedural constraints. The paradox he cites is that 'To advocate democracy is to advocate procedures, to advocate environmentalism is to advocate substantive outcomes: what guarantee can we have that the former procedures will yield the latter sorts of outcomes?' (1992: 168). This is where questions of justice which go beyond, but do not necessarily conflict with, 'procedural' democracy are important. Decision making, the results of which affect large numbers of people and/or are binding on them, cannot be assessed in terms of procedural requirements alone. From the point of view of green political theory taken as a whole, questions of democracy cannot be divorced from those of justice and wider moral considerations (Mills, Chapter 5). For this reason, 'extra democratic' institutions such as a constitution (Saward, Chapter 4) and a legal apparatus are important (or ought to be) for democratic greens (Eckersley, Chapter 11).

9 We could envisage a statutory duty on behalf of citizens to take part in various forums that a full elaboration of sustainability will require, along the lines perhaps of compulsory voting. This requirement is not a case of forcing people to be politically active, but can be thought of as a legitimate duty that can be expected from citizens. The minimum that may be expected of citizens may be to vote in referenda and local/national/transnational elections, and perhaps attend public inquiries.

10 The practice of sustainability, on enlightened anthropocentric grounds, will by and large have a positive impact in terms of the protection of non-humans, especially those critical to ecosystemic functions. Coupled with our ignorance of the complexity of such life-support systems we have a *prima facie* reason not to deplete the bio-diversity of the planet.

11 It is important to point out that the inclusion of non-humans is indirect while that of future generations is direct. That is whereas we include future generations in the elaboration of sustainability as members of the 'community of justice', the inclusion of non-humans is a matter of (some of) them being included as members of the 'moral community'. Thus even though both non-humans and future generations can be classed as 'moral subjects' as opposed to moral agents, how we treat human moral subjects will be different to non-human moral subjects. Whereas we can consider future generations as potential citizens, it does not make sense to talk of non-humans being potential citizens. This has the implication that to the extent that considerations of justice become important to green politics the more greens will have to address the inevitability

of weak anthropocentrism. However, arguing for the legal incorporation of non-humans, which expresses a community's collective moral valuation of non-humans, may be a more fruitful way of going about this, than attempting to include them directly as recipients of justice.

12 A comprehensive account of this would perhaps lead green politics to a quasi-Rousseauean concern with the democratic articulation of the 'general will', as opposed to the empirical 'will of all'. Given the emphasis of this chapter on 'public talk', discourse, persuasion and preference alteration this is hardly surprising.

REFERENCES

Arblaster, A. (1987) *Democracy*, Milton Keynes: Open University Press.

Barber, B. (1984) *Strong Democracy: Participatory Politics for a New Age*, Berkeley: University of California Press.

Dobson, A. (1990) *Green Political Thought*, London: Unwin Hyman.

Dryzek, J. (1987) *Rational Ecology*, Oxford: Blackwell.

—— (1990) *Discursive Democracy: Politics, Policy and Political Science*, Cambridge: Cambridge University Press.

Eckersley, R. (1992) *Environmentalism and Political Theory: Toward an Ecocentric Approach*, London: UCL Press.

Elster, J. (1983) *Sour Grapes: Essays in the Subversion of Rationality*, Cambridge: Cambridge University Press.

—— (1991) 'The Possibility of Rational Politics', in D. Held (ed.) *Modern Political Theory*, Cambridge: Polity.

Goodin, R. (1992) *Green Political Theory*, Cambridge: Polity.

Habermas, J. (1987) *The Philosophical Discourse of Modernity*, Cambridge, Mass.: MIT Press.

Hardin, G. (1968) 'The Tragedy of the Commons', *Science* 162: 1,243–8.

Heilbroner, R. (1980) *An Inquiry into the Human Prospect*, 2nd edn, New York: Norton.

Irvine, S. and Ponton, A. (1988) *A Green Manifesto: Policies for a Green Future*, London: Optima.

Kymlicka, W. (1990) *Contemporary Political Philosophy: An Introduction*, Oxford: Clarendon Press.

Ophuls, W. (1977) *Ecology and the Politics of Scarcity*, San Francisco: Freeman.

O'Riordan, T. (1981) *Environmentalism*, 2nd edn, London: Pion.

Osterfeld, D. (1989) 'Radical Federalism: Responsiveness, Conflict and Efficiency', in G. Brennan and L. Lomasky (eds) *Politics and Process: New Essays in Democratic Thought*, Cambridge: Cambridge University Press.

Paehlke, R. (1988) 'Democracy, Bureaucracy and Environmentalism', *Environmental Ethics* 10: 291–308.

Passmore, J. (1993) 'Environmentalism', in R. Goodin and P. Pettitt (eds) *A Companion to Contemporary Political Theory*, Cambridge: Cambridge University Press.

Pearce, D., Turner, R. K., O'Riordan, T., *et al.* (1993) *Blueprint 3: Measuring Sustainable Development*, London: Earthscan.

Porritt, J. (1984) *Seeing Green: The Politics of Ecology Explained*, Oxford: Blackwell.

Rawls, J. (1972) *A Theory of Justice*, Oxford: Oxford University Press.

Roberts, A. (1979) *The Self-Managing Environment*, London: Allison & Busby.

Saward, M. (1993) 'Green Democracy?', in A. Dobson and P. Lucardie (eds) *The Politics of Nature: Explorations in Green Political Theory*, London: Routledge.

Tannsjo, T. (1992) *Populist Democracy: A Defence*, London: Routledge.

7

DEMOCRATISING GREEN THEORY

Preconditions and principles

Andrew Dobson

As the aims and claims of the environmental movement have come (slowly) to the attention of political theorists, several aspects of the green prospectus seem particularly worthy of investigation. One of the main ones is the claim made by greens (often implicitly) that ecologism is necessarily a democratic political ideology. A large proportion of the attention paid to green theory has been devoted to exploring the relationship between the aims it espouses and the processes by which it seeks to achieve them. The dominant opinion at present, it seems, is that there is no necessary connection between the two to the extent that green processes need to be democratic processes. In what follows I shall outline the problem as it has been expressed in work by Goodin (1992) and Saward (1993), and then explore John Dryzek's work on discursive democracy and Robyn Eckersley's on rights and autonomy to see whether green and democratic thinking can be brought more closely – and necessarily – together than Goodin and Saward suggest they can. This leads to an 'argument from preconditions' and an 'argument from principle', both of which contain significant insights, but neither of which can do without the other. I show how a combination of the two simultaneously democratises green theory and sensitises democratic theory to environmental concerns.

THE PROBLEM

Saward argues that the grounds on which greens have derived democratic principles from other – more obviously ecological and therefore apparently fundamental – aspects of their thought are shaky. He suggests that attempts, for example, to derive democracy from a particular reading of the natural world founder on the fact that multiple readings are possible, and that therefore no determinate political practices – and certainly not democratic ones – can uncomplicatedly be derived from them (Saward 1993: 69).

He also suggests that the urgency with which greens say we need to deal with environmental problems, and which is usually seen as one of their strongest suits in terms of political persuasiveness, can also work against them in terms of debates over political agency. This is because if the situation really is so dire, and if what is at stake is survival, then surely any means – even (or perhaps especially) authoritarian ones – can be justified in order to produce such a desirable end (Saward 1993: 64–5). Saward argues that the only outcomes that are proscribed by the logic of democracy are those that imperil democracy itself. The problem for greens is that a number of proscribed outcomes can be derived from the green value-set, and that these go beyond those proscribed by the principles of democracy (Saward 1993: 66).

It is also Saward's view that (some) greens' insistence upon the intrinsic value of nature produces too many hostages to fortune as far as anything of contingent value is concerned. For if it really is the case that nature has intrinsic value, then items of contingent value will necessarily come off second best in the case of a clash of values and associated policies. It is easy enough to see the implications of this for democracy (contingent value) in the instance of a clash with nature (intrinsic value) (Saward 1993: 66).

Goodin's approach is somewhat different from Saward's but he ends up in roughly the same place. His book is about green theories of value and green theories of (political) agency. After discussing the possible connections between these two realms of green thought, he decides that there are not any. More particularly, he argues that the green theory of value is so fundamental to the movement's intentions that it is not worth sacrificing it on the altar of this or that seemingly preferable form of political agency. He argues that 'core green concerns are consequentialistic at root' (Goodin 1992: 120), and goes on to suggest that 'In cases of conflict . . . the green theory of value – and the ends that it would have us promote – simply must, within the logic of the green's own theory, take priority over the green theory of agency' (Goodin 1992: 120).

Goodin's intention is to wean greens away from commitment to happy-sounding but ultimately unproductive theories and practices such as pacifism. Other forms of agency should also come under scrutiny if they prove not to deliver the goods: 'if the green theory of value really does take priority, within green theory itself, over the green theory of agency – then in insisting on rotation in office greens might be pursuing a lower priority goal in preference to a higher priority one' (Goodin 1992: 146).

The trouble with this neo-toughness, though, is that it can be taken stages further than Goodin probably intends. If the green theory of value and green theories of agency really are separate, and if the former is so overridingly important, then it can be made to sound as though any theory of agency – again, even (or perhaps especially) an authoritarian one – will do as long as it brings about the desired end; in this case, the instantiation of the green theory of value. Goodin poses the problem succinctly: 'To advocate democracy is to advocate procedures, to advocate environmentalism is to advocate substantive outcomes: what guarantees can we have that

133

the former procedures will yield the latter sorts of outcomes?' (Goodin 1992: 168). Goodin appears to feel that no such guarantees are available – although some interpretations of discursive democracy suggest otherwise, as will become clear.

The consequences of all this for green theory and its theorists are plain to see. Saward and Paehlke, among others, have pointed out that while most contemporary greens will profess a commitment to democracy, a glance at the history of environmentalist thinking reveals that a number of en- vironmentalists of the not-too-distant past, such as William Ophuls and Robert Heilbroner (Saward 1993: 71; Paehlke 1988: 291–5), have shown a penchant for getting problems solved without too much regard for scoring democratic points. This, it is suggested, is *de facto* evidence for a big hole in green political thought where democracy ought to be. Much has been made of this in the realm of real-world politicians and their respective think-tanks: Andrew McHallam, writing in a series run by the Institute for European Defence and Strategic Studies in London, has argued that the changes that greens envisage could 'only be achieved by central planning and coercion on a massive scale' (McHallam 1991: 41).

It has been possible to raise these questions about the place of democracy in green political theory because it seems as though democracy is not *intrinsic* to green political theory. On the face of it green thought is about issues other than political agency. According to taste, it is about (for example) preserving wilderness and ensuring sustainability, and when the question of agency arises (i.e. *how* to preserve wilderness or ensure sustainability), the choice is based not upon the intrinsic worth of one or other form of agency, but upon which works *best*. In this context I take it as read that contingent (or 'weak') arguments for democracy can be made on behalf of greens – arguments that suggest that democratic procedures are more likely to produce environ- mentally responsible policies than authoritarian ones. Is there any way, though, of linking green and democratic thinking in anything more than a contingent fashion? In what follows I want to canvass two possibilities – what I call the 'argument from preconditions' and the 'argument from principle'. The argument from preconditions suggests that there are ecological pre- conditions for the practice of democracy that tie green and democratic thinking closely together, and the argument from principle suggests – simply – that green values are fundamentally democratic ones. I take John Dryzek's work on discursive democracy to be exemplary of the first approach, and Robyn Eckersley's work (particularly her chapter in this collection) to be representative of the second.

Discursive democracy

As described by John Dryzek, 'Discursive democracy is woven . . . from the threads supplied by a classical (Aristotelian) model of politics, participatory democracy, communicative action, practical reason, and critical theory' (Dryzek 1990a: ix). Following the tradition developed by critical theory, Dryzek wants to restrict the claims of instrumental rationality – which he defines as 'the capacity to devise, select, and effect good means to clarified ends' (Dryzek 1990a: 3–4) – to its proper realm. Likewise, he proposes the complete rejection of 'objectivism' – 'the idea that rational choices concerning theories and beliefs about matters of fact, and even about values and morals, should be made through reference to a set of objective standards that are equally applicable – and accessible – to all individuals' (Dryzek 1990a: 4).

Instrumental rationality is criticised by Dryzek on a number of counts (Dryzek 1990a: 4–7), chief among which is that its extension into the realms of culture and social interaction is inappropriate for a form of reason that deals in means rather than ends. Dryzek also claims that instrumental rationality is undemocratic, repressive and 'ineffective when confronted with complex social problems'. Some of these criticisms need more substantiation than Dryzek gives them, but my worries could not be pursued here without detracting from the main task, which is to examine discursive democracy in the light of green thinking.

Dryzek's fully functioning discursive democracy would operate according to the principles of communicative – as opposed to instrumental – rationality, about which he has the following to say:

> Communicative rationality clearly obtains to the degree social interaction is free from domination (the exercise of power), strategizing by the actors involved, and (self-) deception. Further, all actors should be equally and fully capable of making and questioning arguments (communicatively competent). There should be no restrictions on the participation of these competent actors. Under such conditions, the only remaining authority is that of a good argument, which can be advanced on behalf of the veracity of empirical description, and understanding and, equally important, the validity of normative judgements.
>
> (Dryzek 1990a: 15)

What can be made of this as far as greens and democracy are concerned? Two problems suggest themselves at the outset. The first is contained in Dryzek's contention that, 'We should bear in mind that communicative rationality is best thought of as a *procedural* standard, dictating no *substantial* resolution about values to be pursued' (Dryzek 1990a: 54; emphasis in the original). In the light of what we established earlier, this seems to put discursive democracy as much at odds with green thinking as is possible – Dryzek is stressing procedure over product to the point where it seems impossible to incorporate the end-oriented nature of green thinking.

The second difficulty comes with Dryzek's observations on consensus. He is sensitive to the charge (often made against Habermas for similar reasons) that the conditions for communicative rationality are set up in such a way that consensus is inevitable, and that therefore communicative rationality (and its conditions) are coercive. Dryzek resists this conclusion on the grounds that participants in communicative action will have such irreducibly different perspectives that consensus is unlikely: 'even in the ideal speech situation consensus could not be expected. If participants hold to different fundamental values and interpretations, then one should expect them to disagree on practical questions too' (Dryzek 1990a: 42). If Dryzek is right about this, then how will greens react? Is it not one of their points that disagreement about the desirability of, say, a sustainable society is irrational, and that therefore the lack of consensus about it is to be regretted?

These two possible green objections to the implications of discursive democracy are obviously linked, and I should like to explore them in some detail so as to see whether there is anything in the discursive democratic project that can tighten the link between green and democratic thinking. Much of what Dryzek himself says about the possibility of consensus and/or substantive outcomes is ambiguous, and there is some room available here to bring green and (discursive) democratic thinking together.

THE ARGUMENT FROM PRECONDITIONS: DISCURSIVE DEMOCRACY

While it is clear that discursive democracy privileges procedures above products, Dryzek also says 'I shall . . . argue that pure proceduralism is incoherent, for a commitment to the procedures of communicative rationality implies approval of certain broad kinds of political institutions even as it allows greater plurality in other realms of life' (Dryzek 1990a: 18). What this amounts to is the contention that there are certain preconditions (in this case, institutional preconditions) that need to be fulfilled for discursive democracy to be possible. It would therefore be contradictory for the procedures of discursive democracy to take precedence to the point where those procedures throw up decisions that endanger the procedures themselves.

The notion of the 'self-bindingness' of democracy is not new, of course, and it is referred to by Saward, following Salecl: democracy 'restricts itself, or proscribes certain types of outcome, in order to preserve itself' (Saward 1993: 66). Democracy – and discursive democracy in particular – cannot therefore be purely procedural. It is concerned with outcomes, either negatively in the sense of proscribing those that endanger it, or positively in terms of encouraging those that enhance it. In our context the point is to say that there may be *environmental* preconditions for the practice of discursive democracy, and that the fulfilling of them will involve discursive democrats in being less than neutral as far as policy outcomes are concerned. In this way it is clear that the distinction between democratic thinking (procedure) and green thinking (product) is too starkly drawn by Saward and Goodin, and that the two can be brought closer together via the notion of self-bindingness.

Similarly, while Dryzek says that consensus is unlikely, he also recognises the possibility (even the likelihood) of the existence of what he calls 'generalizable interests', and he writes that, 'In offering an argument on behalf of a candidate for generalizable status, an individual is in effect claiming that rational, uncoerced, and knowledgeable individuals would subscribe to it in the situation at hand' (Dryzek 1990a: 55). Since it is precisely the point of the ideal speech situation that underpins Dryzek's notion of discursive democracy that individuals are rational, uncoerced and knowledgeable, it is hard to see how consensuses on generalisable interests would *not* emerge. Anyone who did not agree with the dominant view would have to be regarded as one or another of irrational, coerced or ignorant – and in the ideal speech situation people are none of these things. One can imagine all kinds of 'generalizable interests' but Dryzek's own example is particularly interesting in our present context: 'The continuing integrity of the ecological systems on which human life depends could perhaps be a generalizable interest par excellence' (Dryzek 1990a: 55).

The point is that all rational, uncoerced and knowledgeable individuals (i.e. all individuals in the ideal speech situation participating in the procedures of discursive democracy) will come to the conclusion that the ecological systems upon which human life depends should be protected. This amounts to saying that sustainability is a generalisable interest, and that the procedures of discursive democracy will always produce decisions in favour of it. The upshot of this is that while discursive democracy is an affair that stresses procedures over products, it is possible to conceive of the procedure as always giving rise to a special type of product ('generalizable interest'). Moreover, it is possible to conceive of some (at least) of these products as ones that will satisfy the environmental constituency. In this way, again, the gap between procedure and product is closed, and the apparent distance between democratic and green thinking likewise.

HIATUS I

It will be clear from the discussion so far that there is an assumption about the nature of green value theory which helps to drive a wedge between it and the values of democracy. The assumption is that green value theory is driven by notions of the good rather than the right. On this view, the outcome of decisions is generally more important than the way they are taken, and that is why democratic processes look as though they must take second place to the 'correct' outcomes. It has emerged that one way of dealing with this is to point out that it is wrong to view democracy as a purely procedural affair. The internal logic of the (continued) practice of democracy is such that some outcomes will be proscribed and/or others will be encouraged. Even assuming it is correct, therefore, to characterise green thinking as concerned with the good rather than the right, democracy can be brought closer to the realms of the good than might seem possible at the outset.

Of course it is always possible that the 'good' of democracy will clash with the 'good' of green thinking. We might establish that they can be talked of in the same breath, as it were, only then to experience a kind of theoretical halitosis that renders them incompatible. What if, for example, the 'good' of democracy (the expressed wishes of a majority of whaling nations) were to clash with the 'good' of green thinking (the banning of commercial whaling)? The discussion of proceduralism and generalisable interests in discursive democracy above, though, seems to suggest that at a high enough level of generality the goods of both democratic and green thinking can be made to match. The good in question is (for example) the sustainable society – a basic aim of green thinking, as well as a precondition for the practice of democracy, and a generalisable interest that discursive democrats (at least) would unanimously recognise.

The problem with working at this level of generality, though, is that it is possible to use it to endorse virtually any process of decision making. It is as true of authoritarians as it is of democrats that they need an ecologically viable society within which to operate. So just as democracy is self-bound not to endorse decisions that endanger the practice of democracy, so is authoritarianism – a sustainable society is as much a generalisable interest for authoritarians as it is for democrats.

Without apparently realising it, Dryzek himself runs into this sort of trouble when providing an answer to his own question, 'How might one go about establishing the special claims of ecology upon human communication?' (Dryzek 1990b: 205). His answer – working from the preconditional logic outlined above – is: 'One could start by arguing that intersubjective discourse presupposes some ecological – and not just linguistic – standards' (Dryzek 1990b: 205). He goes on to say that any communicative act 'is made possible' by the ecological system within which we live, and while this is an unfortunately transitive way of putting things, the point is clear: without an ecological system functioning in such a way as to sustain human life, the communicative act of which Dryzek speaks is impossible. To this extent, a functioning ecological system is a precondition for communicative practice.

But that is just the point – a functioning ecosystem is the precondition for *any* sort of communication, and Dryzek appears not to see that in underwriting the environment for the sake of the possibility of democratic communication, he must also be underwriting it for the sake of the possibility of authoritarian communication. Put differently, while we might agree that a functioning ecosystem is a precondition for human communication, it is radically indeterminate – it seems – as regards types of communication.

So one way around the procedure–product conundrum is to say that democracy cannot concern itself only with procedures because a certain kind of product is necessary for the procedures to take place at all. This brings green and democratic thinking together by stressing the end-oriented nature of them both, and by showing (or purporting to show) that the ends they have in mind are of the same type. This, in brief, is the 'argument from preconditions', but it does not exhaust the contribution that discursive democracy can make to this debate. It is possible to argue for the strongest possible necessary connection between (discursive) democracy and green thinking by showing that democracy is a necessary condition for the emergence of green values and the instantiation of a sustainable society. The argument runs as follows.

HIATUS II

We presume that advocates of green values believe that they are the 'right' values, and that advocates of the sustainable society believe that it is the 'right' kind of society in which to live. Such advocates, then, should prefer the kind of decision-making procedure which is most likely to come to these conclusions – conclusions which represent the truth about values and societies. In this connection, Saward points out that an attractive feature of democracy is that the open-ended nature of democratic argument inclines us to the belief (for reasons advanced by John Stuart Mill)[1] that truths are more likely to emerge from its processes than from those characterised by discursive closure (Saward 1993: 76). So if political ecologists are right about what they say, then the more democracy there is, the more likely their message is to emerge and be delivered.[2]

From one point of view, this perspective turns green worries about democracy (or worries imputed to greens) on their head. The worry was that democracy is so much a matter of procedures that the outcomes that greens want might be endangered (or at least not sufficiently guaranteed) by following them. The point now, though, is that it is supposed to be a peculiarity of democratic procedures – and particularly those carried out in the pristine conditions of communicative rationality and discursive democracy – that they will produce the 'right' answers. To the degree that there is a determinate answer about the 'right' values and the 'right' kind of society in which to live (and greens, in the round, believe that there is), then greens should be committed to democracy as the only form of decision making that – for Millian reasons – will necessarily produce the answer. As Tim Hayward has argued in this connection: 'If ecocentrism is "true", then this is a truth, like any other, which will be proved in practice' (Hayward 1995: 98). In this context, procedure is made to matter in a very important way: it is the method by which ecological truths will be revealed. At this point democracy looks to be of necessary, rather than merely contingent, value.

It is also worth saying that if this is right then it goes some way towards allaying green fears concerning the implications of the work of Jürgen Habermas. It has been pointed out that Habermas appears simply to hope that the right thing would somehow be done by the natural world under conditions of communicative rationality, and he has endorsed Joel Whitebook's view that, 'the proper norms for regulating the relation between society and nature would *somehow* follow from the communicatively conceived idea of the human good life without reference to nature as an end-in-itself' (Habermas 1982: 247; my emphasis). I have written elsewhere that therefore, on the face of it, 'Even where the public sphere is invigorated in the way that Habermas demands, there is no guarantee that the free and equal conversations that ensue will grant a more valued status to the non-human natural world than it has at present' (Dobson 1993: 198). This is something that worries Robyn Eckersley too: 'Under Habermas's framework, ecological rationality (as defined by Dryzek) is merely a *potential* by-product of communicative rationality' (Eckersley 1990: 759). On the reading given above, though, Whitebook, Eckersley, myself (and Habermas?) may have underestimated the likelihood of a determinate answer emerging from the pristine procedures of discursive democracy. And not only is this answer likely to be determinate, but if greens are 'right', then – for Millian reasons again – the answer will be a green one.

To the delight of the collector of curios, then, we seem here to have an example of greenery which is concerned at least as much with the right as with the good. We saw earlier that we can push democracy from the realm of the right towards that of the good by employing the notion of pre-suppositions, and now we see that green thinking can be pushed in the opposite direction. From both points of view the distinction generally drawn between the two (green thinking: good; democratic thinking: right) now seems too stark and unsubtle, and from the point of view of legitimacy there may be advantages for greens here. At present the legitimacy of green claims derives from the substantive content of the message they purvey. The notion of the good inherent in this message competes with many others in a fluid and highly contested fashion, and consequently the legitimacy of the message is by no means assured. If, on the other hand, it could be shown that the green message (the good) was implicit in procedures (the right) that have a legitimacy which is virtually unrivalled (democracy), then the legitimacy of the good piggybacks on the legitimacy of the right in a way which greens should find advantageous.

One objection might be entered against this view: the conditions necessary for truth to emerge in this way are very stringent. Particularly, the conditions are those not just of any old democracy but of discursive democracy, in which undistorted communication is the rule. This, we remember, is communication in the context of social interaction which is 'free from domination (the exercise of power), strategizing by the actors involved, and (self-) deception. Further, all actors should be equally and fully capable of making and questioning arguments (communicatively competent)' (Dryzek 1990a: 15). It is hardly original to say that these conditions do not obtain in actually existing democracies, and that there-fore in such democracies the green-sounding outcomes that seem guaran-teed by the procedures of discursive democracies are not at all guaranteed in real ones. This observation has the effect of – once again – widening the gap between procedures and outcomes that had apparently been closed under the hypothetical conditions of discursive democracy.

At this point discursive democrats have two options. They can either produce a programme for pushing real democracies in a discursive direction,[3] or they can say that discursive democracy bears no more relation to the real world than John Rawls's 'original position', and that its function is no more (and no less) than to provide a hypothetical and superior comparator for decisions and decision making in real democracies. That real democracies will be found wanting is precisely the point – and (more important for greens) the decisions taken in real democracies will come into question too. In this way the very conception of a discursive democracy provides greens with a tool for criticising non-green decisions in actually existing democracies. Further, the criticism that discursive democracies do not exist and that therefore discussion of them bears no relation to the real world forgets the point that discursive democracies are themselves *trans-formative* – transformative of the real world. To the extent that discursive democratic practices are approximated to at all they are an incitement to deliberation: to the testing of views against the benchmark of the better argument. Discursive democrats do not merely express their preferences, they test them first, and in doing so may transform them.

So far we have taken as read that green thinking is consequentialist, that it is more interested in outcomes than in how to arrive at them. This is what sets up an apparent tension between democratic and green thinking in that the former is procedural while the latter – fundamentally – is not. Our discussion of discursive democracy showed that it is possible to view democracy in partly consequentialist terms, and this enabled us to pull green and democratic thinking closer together. I hinted above at another strategy: to reject the implication that green thinking is necessarily end-oriented, and to bring ecological and democratic concerns together by focusing on their common procedural core. Robyn Eckersley takes this further by referring this procedural core to a common value base, and it is to this that I now turn.

THE ARGUMENT FROM PRINCIPLE: AUTONOMY

To recapitulate, the success of the 'argument from preconditions' within the context of discursive democracy appears equivocal. The argument seemed destined to produce a tight bind between democratic and green thinking, but the preconditions have to be drawn so generally that while they *can* produce a tight bind, this is bought at the cost of producing it for other forms of decision making too. Eckersley, on the other hand, trades on Saward's claim (1993: 69) that there is a 'natural compatibility between liberalism and democracy' and asks whether 'green values can be reformulated in ways that might be more compatible with democracy' (in her contribution to this volume) by linking green values with liberal ones. The way to do this, she suggests, is to ground them in 'a critique of domination (of humans and other species) and a general defence of autonomy (the freedom of human and non-human beings to unfold in their own ways and live according to their "species life")' (in her contribution to this volume). At this point, she continues, 'the connection between ecology and democracy [is] no longer merely contingent . . . authoritarianism is ruled out at the level of green principle (rather than on purely instrumental grounds) in the same way that it is ruled out according to basic liberal principles: it fundamentally infringes the rights of humans to choose their own destiny' (Chapter 11: 223).

There are a number of things that can be said about 'revisiting the rights discourse' in this way.[4] The first is that the rights in question need to be carefully specified before we can pass judgement on whether reformulating green values in terms of them helps or hinders the project of bringing green and democratic thinking together. Not all rights are preconditions for democracy – not even all liberal ones, as the chequered history of property rights in this context shows. One is looking for rights that are *constitutive* of democracy such that, if violated, a democracy cannot (be said to) exist. The rights in question are rights to freedom of speech, freedom of association and so on[5], and it is not clear that the rights to which Eckersley refers in this volume and elsewhere (1996) have this constitutive sense required of them. For instance, she talks of environmental rights as 'rights in support of a kind of "negative freedom", that is, "a freedom from" harmful ecological actions at the hands of other human agents' (in her contribution to this volume). This is an important right, no doubt, but it is not any more constitutive of democracy than it is of any other system of decision making. It is, in other words, too general, just as the 'generalizable interests' discussed above in the context of Dryzek were too general to do specifically democratic service. Elsewhere Eckersley refers to 'the right to exist' (Eckersley 1996), but this rather compounds the problem of excessive generality: once again it is a right (unless generously interpreted otherwise) that is as preconditional for authoritarian as for democratic practices.

The best general formulation of the right we need is that provided by

Eckersley above – in terms of autonomy. This word (suitably modified to take account of the fact that it is strictly problematic for greens in a technical sense as the Kantian carrier of distinction between the human and animal realms) is a recognisable feature of green discourse as well as a precondition for democracy, in the sense that greens can be said to be putting a 'normative argument in favour of extending the principle of autonomy to all life-forms'.[6] Such a formulation stresses the deontological aspects of green thinking in contrast to more consequentialist interpretations like that of Robert Goodin who, as we remember, writes that 'To advocate democracy is to advocate procedures, to advocate environmentalism is to advocate substantive outcomes' (1992: 168). Eckersley's deontological approach confronts Goodin's consequentialist one head on: democratic and green thinking are (for Eckersley) linked by the common core notion of autonomy, in that the defence and extension of autonomy are what green thinking is about, while a belief in autonomy underpins defences of democracy.

On the face of it, this 'argument from principle' links green and democratic thinking more successfully than Dryzek's 'argument from preconditions' in that the former rules out authoritarian decision making in a way that a 'generalizable interest' in the integrity of ecosystems appeared not to do. Yet the notion of autonomy cannot uncomplicatedly be pressed into service since, for a series of reasons most recently canvassed by Ted Benton (1993) (and recognised by Eckersley in her contribution to this volume), the bare liberal notion of autonomy is subject to an 'immanent critique' that suggests that making good the right to autonomous development involves the presence of appropriate (material) conditions. In the socialist tradition these material conditions are often seen in terms of the satisfaction of basic needs, which in turn refer to the universal provision of food, clothing, shelter and so on. What the environmental insight adds to this is that ecological security is at least as fundamental as social security – and this should remind us of Dryzek's remark concerning one sort of 'generalizable interest': 'The continuing integrity of the ecological systems on which human life depends could perhaps be a generalizable interest par excellence' (Dryzek 1990a: 55). In this respect the 'argument from principle' needs to be buttressed by the 'argument from preconditions': the practice of the principle is only possible given the presence of the necessary preconditions.

Yet this works both ways, for while Dryzek's formulation of an ecological generalisable interest rightly stresses the ecological preconditions for the practice of democracy, it does not stress the democratic preconditions for such practice – it does not stress the precondition of autonomy, without which normative arguments in favour of democracy would not make sense. So the 'argument from preconditions' needs to be reminded of the importance of principle (autonomy), and the 'argument from principle'

ANDREW DOBSON

needs to be reminded of the importance of preconditions (ecological and social). Dryzek's conclusion might therefore be reformulated in the following way: 'The continuing integrity of the relevant social and ecological conditions on which the autonomous development of all life-forms depends could perhaps be a generalisable interest par excellence'. This now rules out the possibility of Dryzek's formulation being interpreted as equally favourable for democracy and authoritarianism, since it is not now just a question of the defence of the conditions necessary for the continuance of human life, but of the autonomous life, by whomever or whatever it is lived.

At least one problem remains, however. The interest referred to will be a trans-species interest for discursive democrats only if they are interested in furthering the autonomy of *all* life-forms, and not just the human version. The difficulty is that both Dryzek and his source of inspiration, Habermas, make it clear that only one species possesses the qualities necessary for the practice of communicative rationality, and that is the human species: 'all actors', writes Dryzek, 'should be equally and fully capable of making and questioning arguments (communicatively competent)' (Dryzek 1990a: 15). Once communicative competence is defined in this way – the capacity to 'make and question arguments' – other forms of communication imputed to some animals (e.g. dolphins) so as to close the gap between humans and animals are disallowed, thereby rigidifying the species boundary and making it clear that the actors in question can only be human actors.

Elsewhere, Dryzek tries to show that 'communication' can be understood in such a way as to view aspects of the non-human as capable of communication. For example he refers to the biosphere in the context of James Lovelock's Gaia and asks us to accept that it possesses an 'intelligence' with a 'rough equality in communicative ability' to human beings (Dryzek 1990b: 208). More recently Dryzek has sought to 'rescue communicative rationality from Habermas' by 'treat[ing] communication, and so communicative rationality, as extending to entities that can act as agents, even though they lack the self-awareness which connotes objectivity' (Dryzek 1996). He recognises, of course, that verbal communication cannot extend beyond the human but claims that 'greater continuity is evident in nonverbal communication – body language, facial displays, pheromones, and so forth' (Dryzek 1996). Dryzek (1996) observes that 'it may often be hard to prove these positions scientifically' but is not unduly bothered by this because no democratic theory has ever been founded on scientific certainty. He is right, of course, but it is my view that seeking continuity across the species divide (for this is what is at issue) via such a contentious issue as communication is asking for unnecessary trouble. I think it is much more fruitful to reserve communication to human beings, and to ensure that the representation of other species' interests is catered for by communicatively competent humans. But how are we to ensure that these interests are represented? What other bridge across the species divide might we suggest?

144

I take it that we have no trouble with the idea that while non-speaking, non-human entities might not qualify as morally considerable subjects, they can certainly qualify as morally considerable objects, and that there is nothing intrinsic about the primacy of human speech acts that disqualifies other species from having their interests represented by humans. It is hard to see why 'Habermas's delineation of the sphere of communication is such that the discursively adjudicated norms are restricted to serving the interests of speaking *human* participants' (Eckersley 1990: 759). Eckersley is surely right to say that 'The fact that the nonhuman world cannot participate in human speech should be no barrier to their special interests always being *considered* and respected by those who can participate in the dialogue' (Eckersley 1990: 761).

The real worry concerns not whether interests other than the human *can* be taken into consideration, but the strength of the guarantee that they *will* be. In one sense the guarantee can be no stronger than that for the interests of any community of people in a democracy. Once the representation of those interests is given institutional form, one hopes for a consensus on points of view recognised as correct by rational, uncoerced and knowledge-able individuals. That is the only possible nature, and indeed the fullest extent, of the democratic guarantee. The question then revolves around the institutionalisation of the representation of the autonomy claims of beings other than human ones.

I think that the best way to ensure that these claims are represented is to ground them in a theory of justice which has a naturalistic basis. This naturalism stresses the common interests of humans and other species in a way which Ted Benton has described as follows:

> The starting point for the analysis is the recognition of an attribute or requirement which is common to both human and many non-human animals. The specification of the distinctly human then proceeds not by identifying some further, *sui generis* class of attributes or needs possessed only by humans, but, rather, by identifying the species-specific ways in which humans exhibit attributes or meet needs which they share with other species.
>
> (Benton 1993: 54)

If we take 'autonomy' to be an example of such an attribute, and 'the relevant social and ecological conditions' to be the requirement for the practice of autonomy, it is clear how this naturalism buttresses the present argument. The attribute of autonomy crosses the species divide rather than being confined to one side of it, and so the ecological and social require-ments for its practice refer to non-human as well as human requirements. The formulation produces problems of its own, of course. It would be foolish to underestimate the complexity of arguments regarding *which* non-human animals are to be taken into account, or the trade-offs between

145

interests which would inevitably have to take place. But it is enough to say for now that a discursive democracy operating in a naturalistic context would necessarily take all autonomy claims (including those of non-humans) into account: it would be self-contradictory for humans to recognise an attribute (autonomy) common across species but make it count only in their own case.

CONCLUSION

The problem outlined at the beginning was that democratic and green thinking seem opposed in that the former is concerned with means and the latter with ends. I suggested that the two can be brought closer together by speaking of the preconditions for democracy, in that this suggests that democracy must concern itself with outcomes and cannot be purely procedural. It seemed, though, that for this 'argument from preconditions' to work, the preconditions need to be so widely drawn (in ecological terms anyway) that many modes of decision making (not all of them democratic) can be slipped in. The 'argument from principle' based on the common concern for autonomy in democratic and green thinking seemed less equivocal in binding the two together, but autonomy is somewhat empty without the material conditions for its practice. In this way the 'argument from principle' points us back to the 'argument from preconditions': the former democratises green theory and the latter sensitises democratic theory to environmental concerns.

ACKNOWLEDGEMENTS

This paper was read at the Department of Government at the University of Essex and to members of the Oxford Centre for Environment and Society, in January and September 1994. I thank all who attended for the comments they made on these occasions. Reactions of colleagues in the ECPR workshop itself made me rethink a number of points, and I am particularly grateful to Wouter Achterberg, John Barry, Brian Doherty and Robyn Eckersley for their detailed remarks. John Dryzek made a number of helpful criticisms of an earlier version of the paper to which I have tried to respond.

NOTES

1 'the opinion which it is attempted to suppress by authority may possibly be true. Those who desire to suppress it, of course deny its truth; but they are not infallible' (Mill 1859/1972: 79).
2 One problem for Saward with this is that it stands in some tension with his earlier worries about direct democracy, and his subsequent endorsement of indirect

forms. For if it is true that the truths of the ecological position are more likely to be arrived at through open-ended debate, then the more open-ended debate there is, the better. And if *that* is true, then the discursive closure implied by the Burkean theory of representation, argued elsewhere by Saward to be useful to greens, now appears to work against getting greens and democracy together. In other words, one of Saward's arguments pushes green theory in the direction of indirect forms of democracy, and the other pushes it towards direct forms.

3 In this context Dryzek makes much of the 'new social movements' which he believes represent 'real-world approximations' to the ideal of discursive democratic practice (Dryzek 1990a: 49).

4 One is that there may be a technical difficulty with deploying rights in this way. In order for rights to 'trump' in the way they are expected to, they must be seen to be more than the expression of a certain set of preferences – they must be morally compelling. As far as human beings are concerned, the possession of reason is held to ground the ascription of rights in a morally compelling way because reason is the precondition for moral behaviour. Following Plant following Gewirth we might say that A has a right to B against C in virtue of D (Plant 1991: 260). For humans the filler for D in the 'in virtue' clause is furnished by 'the rational faculty'. For non-humans, Eckersley suggests that D be understood as 'possession of the property of autopoiesis' (self-production) (see Eckersley 1996). Is autopoiesis as compelling as reason as a foundation for the ascription of rights? Is it any more compelling as a common characteristic than, say, the possession of toes? This question is, of course, parasitic on the large debate regarding the ascription of rights to non-human beings. Eckersley (1996) along with many others feels that rights can be ascribed to non-human beings, and her contribution to this volume trades on this. If they cannot (or at least if there is no presuppositional and compelling reason for them being so ascribed), then revisiting the rights discourse might lead up a blind alley.

5 These are rights gathered under Articles 19 and 20 in the 1948 UN Declaration of Human Rights, leading to Article 21 – the 'right to democracy': 'Everyone has the right to take part in the government of his country, directly or through freely chosen representatives'.

6 Robyn Eckersley, personal communication.

REFERENCES

Benton, T. (1993) *Natural Relations: Ecology, Animal Rights and Social Justice*, London: Verso.

Dobson, A. (1993) 'Critical Theory and Green Politics', in A. Dobson and P. Lucardie (eds) *The Politics of Nature: Explorations in Green Political Theory*, London: Routledge.

Dryzek, J. (1990a) *Discursive Democracy: Politics, Policy and Political Science*, Cambridge: Cambridge University Press.

—— (1990b) 'Green Reason: Communicative Ethics for the Biosphere', *Environmental Ethics* 12, Fall: 195–210.

—— (1992) 'Ecology and Discursive Democracy: Beyond Liberal Capitalism and the Administrative State', *Capitalism, Nature, Socialism* 10, June.

—— (1996) 'Political and Ecological Communication', in F. Mathews (ed.) *Ecology and Democracy* (special issue of *Environmental Politics*).

Eckersley, R. (1990) 'Habermas and Green Political Thought', *Theory and Society* 19.

—— (1996), 'Liberal Democracy and the Rights of Nature: the Struggle for

Inclusion', in F. Mathews (ed.) *Ecology and Democracy* (special Issue of *Environmental Politics*).

Goodin, R. (1992) *Green Political Theory,* Cambridge: Polity.

Habermas, J. (1982) 'A Reply to my Critics', in J. Thompson and D. Held (eds) *Habermas: Critical Debates,* London: Macmillan.

Hayward, T. (1995) *Ecological Thought: An Introduction,* Cambridge: Polity.

McHallam, A. (1991) *The New Authoritarians: Reflections on the Greens,* London: Institute for European Defence and Strategic Studies.

Mill, J. S. (1859/1972) *Utilitarianism, On Liberty and Representative Government,* London and New York: Dent & Dutton.

Paehlke, R. (1988) 'Democracy, Bureaucracy, and Environmentalism', *Environmental Ethics* 10.

Plant, R. (1991) *Modern Political Thought,* Oxford: Blackwell.

Ravitch, D. and Thernstrom, A. (eds) (1992) *The Democracy Reader,* New York: HarperCollins.

Saward, M. (1993) 'Green Democracy?', in A. Dobson and P. Lucardie (eds) *The Politics of Nature: Explorations in Green Political Theory,* London: Routledge.

Part III

THE INSTITUTIONS OF A GREEN DEMOCRACY

8

ECOLOGICAL CITIZENS AND ECOLOGICALLY GUIDED DEMOCRACY

Peter Christoff

Issues of political participation and representation are especially challenging when one considers environmental concerns. Consider the case of a chemical factory to be built on the banks of a river flowing through five countries. A serious accident at this factory would affect not only people living in the country in which it is sited but also inhabitants of the other countries, future generations of humans and other species. Who, then, should participate in decision making about the factory's construction?

By virtue of their regional and global impacts, environmental issues have expanded both temporally and spatially beyond the conventional borders of political decision making. They point to the need for new approaches to the protection of the environment and environment-related rights. As David Held (1991) argues,

> the very idea of consent, and the particular notion that the relevant constituencies of voluntary agreement are the communities of a bounded territory or a State, become deeply problematic as soon as the issue of national, regional and global interconnectedness is considered and the nature of a so-called 'relevant community' is contested.
>
> (Held 1991: 203)

So how are we to respond to the problem for 'green democracy' that 'democratic theory can no longer be elaborated as a theory of the territorially delimited polity alone, nor can the nation-state be displaced as a central point of reference' (Held 1991: 223)? Ideally, ecologically sensitive decision making would encompass a well-developed public recognition of the implications and impacts of human activities over time and over large distances. Such decision making would therefore depend on active citizens and a state better organised to facilitate democratic participation. For both democracy and the environment to flourish, we now need to elaborate further upon what Held (1989: 167ff) has called 'double democratisation' – the revitalisation of civil society and the related re-structuring of the state.

In this chapter, I want to concentrate upon the first aspect of 'double democratisation', on the new demands made by environmental concerns on citizenship and civil society. In doing so, I will make only brief reference to the larger, companion arguments for 'ecologically guided democracies' based around constitutional and legislative guarantees of strong democracy and of 'universal' ecological principles. These relate to the second part of the 'double democratisation' problem – the reconstruction of the state to enable ecological requirements to be met nationally and internationally.

UNBOUNDED DEMOCRACY?

Consider, first, the general problems posed by globalisation for citizenship. The relationship between citizen and nation-state is now one of considerable tension. While formal citizenship must be attached to an identifiable and legally bounded political community, citizenship no longer seems tied exclusively to any one nation-state. A number of factors contribute to this tension.

The past two centuries have been called the period of the Great Migration by Enzensberger (1991). He estimates that more than 20 million recent immigrants live in western Europe (over 5 per cent of total population). Others suggest that up to 20 per cent of residents in most European countries were born beyond their borders.[1] The flow of refugees in Africa and Asia is on a similar scale, and about 25 million Russians are also now 'ethnic exiles' following the collapse of the Soviet empire.

> [Yet] it could be even claimed that modern migration has, so far, been rather limited, especially if measured against the absolute increase in the world's population (the United Nations forecasts estimate a growth of almost one billion for 1990–2000). This invites the conclusion that only a small fraction of the potential migrants has actually set itself in motion: the real migration of peoples is yet to come.
>
> (Enzensberger 1991: 40)

These modern population movements, some the result of war but most of them labour market driven, have reshaped – in some cases constituted or substantially reconstituted – the social basis of most industrialised capitalist nation-states. No western industrialised country retains the level of ethnic homogeneity it had 150 years ago. The United States, Australia and Canada have largely been constituted by such immigration. Their founding myth is, as Enzensberger observes, the *tabula rasa* created by the violent expropriation of their indigenous populations, or *terra nullius* in the case of Australia, where the prior ownership of the land by its original inhabitants was not even given legal recognition. The imploding empires of Britain, Holland, Portugal and France have led to an influx of their former colonial subjects to the metropolitan centre. Imported 'cheap labour' from the

South (Southern European, African, Asian and Latin American countries) has left the North (Northern American and Northern European countries such as Germany, Sweden and Switzerland – and, anomalously, oil-rich Middle Eastern countries such as Kuwait and Yemen) with significant communities of settled 'guest workers'. The opening up of the former socialist states of the Eastern Bloc has also initiated a similar process of translocation.

One consequence of such mass migration is the diminishing capacity of nation-states to restrict the flow of people from one state to another, especially as nation-states are further integrated into larger economic blocs such as the European Union.[2] Another consequence has been the creation of multi-cultural societies with diverse ethnic communities coexisting within the boundaries of formerly ethnically homogeneous nation-states, challenging and reshaping the political and cultural identity of those states. Senses of ethnic identity, based on longing and loss, are often shaped and reinforced by cultural prejudice and political exclusion from the country in which migrants work. Consequently, with increasingly large and varied ethnic groups resident in many countries, the notion of national identity is called into question, or at minimum requires radical revision to incorporate its new multi-cultural dimensions. Second, it is clear that the ideological forces shaping nation-states and (former) empires have altered irrevocably. Traditional ethnic solidarity can no longer be called upon to define or bind the national 'community'. Formative 'national myths' based on ethnic solidarity have generally been weakened, often to be replaced by media-conveyed political and commercial appeals to caricatures of the same myths (vide Thatcher and the Falklands war). However, it is undeniable that in recent times there has been a conservative revitalisation of nostalgia for 'ethnically pure' states, which has inflamed conflict in the former Yugoslavia and fed tensions in other parts of Europe. Multi-culturalism makes problematic the notion of nationality as a constitutive force defining the political identity of the citizen within a democratic polity. Minorities within the boundaries of a nation-state increasingly have divided loyalties, allegiances and political-cultural expectations which differ from those dominant in their immediate political environment.[3]

A third consequence of migration is the separation of citizens from the states to which they have hitherto 'belonged', and the emergence of pressure to recast notions of democratic participation to take into account the disenfranchisement of those voluntarily or otherwise displaced as they move from one country to another in search of work or safe refuge. Until this is done, a large and perhaps growing population (more than one in twenty people in Europe, for instance) will remain disenfranchised. As one distressed correspondent to the weekly paper, *The European*, writes:

I belong to a probably growing body of EU citizens who have no voting

153

rights and therefore cannot take part in democratic life. As a Danish
citizen living in Germany and working for a German company, I have
no voting rights in Denmark, though I still own a small piece of land
there for which I pay property taxes. In Germany, because I am a
foreigner, I have no voting rights. I also have no voting rights to the
election of members of the European Parliament.

(Sorgensen 1994)

Sometimes formal citizenship extends beyond the territorial boundaries
of the nation-state, in the sense that 'expatriate nationals' may retain voting
rights – but not in their place of residence. It increasingly, although less
frequently, now extends to dual citizenship. Some have even sought to
stretch it to perhaps its apotheosis in the (defeated) proposal put before
the Italian Senate late in 1993 that emigrant and foreign-born individuals
of Italian descent may elect senators from their overseas communities – for
example, from among Italians in New York – to the Italian Parliament to
represent directly their cultural, social and economic interests in their
'homeland'.

But in most countries immigrants have no (or only limited) rights as
citizens, although this situation is changing in Europe as the Maastricht
Treaty offers all citizens of the European Union the right to vote and stand
for election in their country of residence as long as they were originally born
in a Member State. Limitations on full democratic rights for immigrants are
often found where formal citizenship is still bound to restrictive legal
definitions of national identity which are based on indigenous heredity,
ethnicity and race – where political competence is assessed against criteria
which are 'prior' to those of 'rational society'.

For example, in Japan, those of non-Japanese descent remain resident
'foreigners' for generation upon generation. By contrast, in some countries
citizenship is now accorded to those born within national borders, while in
'immigrant nations' like Australia, Canada, New Zealand and the United
States, it may be achieved by 'naturalisation' – demonstration of linguistic
competence and formal allegiance to the laws of the land.

As a general observation one can argue that the democratic content of
the concept of citizenship is increasingly being dissociated from its strict
legal definition. For example, Habermas notes that in the Federal Republic
of Germany, 'the legal status of aliens, homeless foreigners and the stateless
has been adjusted to the status of citizens. Since the structure of the
Grundgesetz (Basic Law) is founded on the idea of human rights, *every*
inhabitant enjoys the protection of the Constitution' (1991: 13–14). However the changes do not always deliver full participation in the polity within
which individuals live. Thus resident foreigners share with citizens duties as
well as legal protection and certain other benefits – excepting the right to
vote and certain economic rewards bestowed upon 'native' Germans.

Nevertheless, increasingly, a key defining characteristic of the viable modern, or post-modern, democratic nation-state is that it, in Habermas' words,

> does not derive its identity from some common ethnic and cultural properties, but rather from the *praxis* of citizens who actively exercise their civil rights. At this conjuncture, the republican strand of 'citizenship' completely parts company from the idea of belonging to a pre-political community integrated on the basis of descent, a shared tradition and a common language.
>
> (Habermas 1991: 3)

As noted earlier, however, this remains an unrealised ideal, for full citizenship rights are rarely conferred upon all 'competent individuals' living within the bounds of the nation-state. That is, many – up to one in five – individuals are denied the possibility of direct participation in decisions affecting their lives, which is a fundamental requirement of a democratic system.

These incomplete developments – which move towards constitutionally enshrining 'universal' civil liberties and political rights at the legal core of the nation-state – identify the mechanisms which must work both within and across borders if they are to protect environmental rights and standards for all humans and other species, irrespective of their location or place of birth. I shall return to this point later.

EXTENDING INSTITUTIONS

So far, the discussion has focused on formal (i.e. legal) citizenship in relation to the bounded national community. It has addressed only the most accessible part of the environmental/citizenship dilemma, by suggesting reform of democratic systems to incorporate in political decision making all intellectually competent humans living within the bounds of the nation-state. The next steps towards 'ecological citizenship' are much more provocative: how then to incorporate those humans with a 'vital interest' in decisions made beyond their national boundaries?[4] Who ought to participate in such decisions? How would the facilitating structures be organised? Furthermore, how are the needs or rights of other species to be recognised?

Problems for citizenship and democracy increase as one moves outward to the international level. The role of the citizen has, to date, been institutionalised only at the level of the sovereign nation-state: the main actors in the international community are states, not citizens. Similarly, the notion of political community is assumed to work only up to the level of the nation-state: at present, the rest depends on increasingly remote and unpopular technocratic administration. To date, citizens seem to have little direct purchase or influence on transnational regulatory and administrative institutions which are governing or reshaping their lives. They have no effective formal means of debating international decisions or influencing decision-making processes at this level, other than through their national government.

This is especially a problem for ecologically informed decision making. Many green political theorists have defended deliberative democracy as a form of decision making which is superior to processes based on preference aggregation alone. Its proponents have extolled its moralising and pedagogical effect, and its potential to deliver decisions which are widely supported by the decision-making community.[5] But deliberative democracy is poorly suited – without considerable institutional innovation – to the determination of issues that affect an international constituency. How might we institutionalise stronger democracy – democracy which is equipped to deal with complex ecological decisions? Several possibilities suggest themselves.

Permanent quasi-federal regional parliaments – such as the European Parliament – could be established, in which elected representatives of regions or states voted on single issues of significance upon the advice of their local electorates or cantons. Separately, or additionally, states considering mutual environmental concerns could initially determine their positions on specific environmental issues through plebiscites of their populations. Alternatively, decision making could be based on plebiscites or referenda in which the total populace pooled across nation-states participated. Or, more radically, decisions could be made on the basis of direct democracy within a mobile or 'flexible' electorate, changing in composition according to the problem, including and enfranchising all its 'residents' on the basis of recognised vital interest and (usually) aggregated in terms of ecological units such as river catchments or airsheds.

It is not possible here to explore the full potentials and limitations of each of these approaches. Note, however, that each approach can be made more effective through (and the last approach depends on) an initial process of localised, deliberative decision making. Each would serve to enfranchise all residents affected by the potential ecological outcomes of their decision. In many of these cases, traditional political borders are made redundant. In other words, the 'environmental constituency' includes all those with an identifiable vital interest in the outcome.

Clearly, many problems remain. For instance, none of these decision-making models would in themselves guarantee ecologically sustainable outcomes – an issue addressed later in this chapter. Information requirements, the problems of media and interest-group distortions of information and the often problematic role of party politics would almost certainly complicate these approaches.

One key issue is that of agenda-setting. How would transnational associations of voters determine which environmental issues would be discussed?

An expanded system of national and international environmental laws, treaties and conventions – such as those governing protection of the North Sea, reduction of greenhouse gas emissions, elimination of CFCs, trade in wastes, harvesting of endangered species, which are now regarded as the responsibilities of signatory nation-states – could trigger action by encoding criteria for issue identification. This approach would rely upon the successful international mobilisation and integration of interests, and consequent co-operation between states, to encourage, enable or require individual states to recognise that actions within their borders have significant consequences for other citizens who therefore become formally recognised and empowered participants in decisions.

As the negotiations around the Montreal Protocol on ozone-depleting substances showed, identification of issues and effective co-operation to achieve their resolution is notoriously time consuming and awash with political compromise but not impossible. It is equally clear that – with regard to many relatively 'localised' issues of ecological concern, such as the example of the chemical factory at the start of this chapter – political processes would need to be flexible yet precise, rapid and also inexpensive. The constant redefinition of 'political communities' in relation to democratic decision making in areas of ecological concern merely adds to these challenges.

To begin to answer what are essentially questions of power and political will, it is helpful to look at notions of citizenship from a completely different angle, and turn to conceptions of citizenship based on moral responsibility and participation in the public sphere rather than those defined formally by legal relationships to the state. It is also necessary to consider additional dimensions of the environmental problem relating to other species and future generations.

THE ENVIRONMENTAL DIMENSION

'To be modern is to be part of a universe in which, as Marx said, "All that is solid melts into air"' (Berman 1983: 15). Ironically, this is now most literally evident when one considers the problems of air pollution and induced climate change. The spectre of environmental catastrophe is slowly overshadowing the vision of limitless plenty that was once offered by the ideology of industrialising progress. Human population growth, urbanisation, accelerating exploitation of natural resources and intensifying environmental degradation now threaten to produce an extinction of life forms unprecedented in the history of this planet (Meadows *et al.* 1992; UNEP 1992).

The extent, intensity and multi-dimensional nature of environmental destruction revealed since the 1960s have magnified existing problems for democracy and for citizenship, making them both more elaborate and more urgent. That such problems and threats require urgent resolution, and efficient international mechanisms for doing so, are well recognised. Environmental degradation – such as the pollution of groundwater aquifers, radioactive contamination, or induced climate change – may take decades to reveal itself and may also persist for hundreds or thousands of years, affecting many generations of humans and other species and altering the time-frame over which the consequences of decisions must be assessed. We decide not only for ourselves and our children, but often for our children's children. Yet the information required for ecologically sustainable decisions about production, consumption and environmental protection increase in complexity as the intensity or scale of human intervention increases. Decisions must be informed by evolving scientific understandings of the intricate behaviour of fragile ecosystems, and of the environmental implications of human activity. These informational demands exacerbate tensions relating to the limited capacity of representative democracy adequately to reflect informed environmental choice.

There is an emerging consensus, underlying the arguments presented in the Brundtland Report (WCED 1987) and Agenda 21, that several principles need to be observed in decisions with potential environmental impacts if ecological sustainability is to be achieved and maintained. These principles include:

- the precautionary principle
- the principle that biological diversity must be preserved, for ecological, economic and ethical reasons
- the principle of intergenerational equity
- a procedural principle relating to the need for reflexivity in decision making.

Realisation of these principles depends on expanding both legal and practical notions of citizenship to require a duty of care towards non-human species and unborn generations, and a corresponding reconfiguration of the state to provide widespread guarantees of environmental rights.

EXTENDING CITIZENSHIP: CITIZENS AS ECOLOGICAL TRUSTEES

Earlier, I referred to some of the more provocative questions posed by environmental issues for democratic theory. What to do about the rights and needs of non-humans? Fish cannot raise their fins to vote nor the unborn express their potential desires. So how then can their needs and rights be included in democratic discourse? Whether representative or deliberative, democracy remains dependent on decisions by humans who are capable of articulating and considering their individual and collective opinions, needs, rights and interests. Yet to shy away from the epistemological challenge of 'representing' non-humans and future generations is to shy away from taking responsibility for their fate. Indeed, we can, as Dryzek (1993) suggests, move some way beyond our species' limitations if we consider 'signals' emanating from the natural world – even if, ultimately, we do not escape our human bounds.

The principles of ecological sustainability require that we defend ecological values and the rights of future generations and other species just as we are morally obliged, and increasingly legally required, to consider and protect the rights of those humans who cannot be defined as 'morally competent' (children, intellectually disabled people, and so on). To become ecological rather than narrowly anthropocentric citizens, existing humans must assume responsibility for future humans and other species, and 'represent' their rights and potential choices according to the duties of environmental stewardship.

This concept of ecological citizenship – of *homo ecologicus* – adds challenges to those noted earlier in relation to the consequences of globalisation. The apparent paradox caused by the increasing de-linkage of the citizen from the modern nation-state is accentuated by environmental concerns. We have seen that the citizen's 'political community' – which, for other issues, may remain that of the nation-state – is profoundly reshaped by an ecological emphasis which generates additional and occasionally alternative transnational allegiances ranging from the bio-regional through to the global, as well as to other species and the survival of ecosystems. The simultaneous cosmopolitanism and localism of the slogan 'act locally, think globally' becomes paradigmatic for 'green activists' who best represent an expression of this realignment. While other public concerns will coexist with ecological ones to shape the public 'identity' of the citizen overall, in cases of conflict, ecological imperatives provide the boundaries for other concerns. More important than national allegiance and as important as formal or legal definitions of citizenship, then, is the further development of the notion of citizenship, based on the praxis of individuals seeking to promote environmental concerns through their political engagements on the basis of 'ecological loyalties'.

ECOLOGICAL CITIZENS, THE GREEN MOVEMENT AND CIVIL SOCIETY

The creation of ecological citizens depends on material preconditions – the impetus to social change caused by the deteriorating environment. It also depends upon the related emergence of a culture of environmental solidarity with its new forms of association (in particular, the green movement), as well as upon the changing opportunities afforded by the state.[6]

Since the 1970s, new social movements have sought to 'rescue' civil society from the administrative and regulative incursions of liberal-capitalist and 'actual-socialist' states.[7] At the same time, they have sought to revitalise the public sphere and to democratise both the state and (occasionally) the economic sphere, to make them more responsive, transparent and intelligible to emancipatory demands relating to issues of environment, race, gender, sexual desire and so on.[8]

In most western industrial nations, the green movement has transformed the public sphere by enabling citizens to present the state with ecological-ethical demands which are increasingly seen as an extension of existing civil, political and social rights. It has forced ecological concerns on to the formal political agenda either through existing political parties or through the creation of new green parties. Its critique of the colonisation, exploitation and destruction of nature has sought recognition of the importance of the biological world in the calculus of political and economic decision making. This emancipatory impulse represents an attempt to define or redefine, for the first time, human aspirations in an ecological context. The movement has also encouraged a critique of liberal-democratic and socialist states as institutions articulated around modernist notions of industrialising progress, and has challenged the legitimacy of specific capitalist and socialist governments over their promotion of resource exploitation and their inability to resolve environmental problems.

Despite the transnational aspect of ecological citizenship, the state remains an exceptionally important focus of concern for ecological citizens and their organisations seeking to refashion its activities; to have it enshrine protection of generalisable environmental interests in legislation guaranteeing environmental standards, the protection of ecosystems and species; and to provide the legal and material support for further (ecological) democratisation.

However, partly because of the nation-state's territorial boundedness, ecological citizens also increasingly work 'beyond' and 'around' as well as 'in and against' the state. For instance, ecological citizens focusing on community action to halt or repair environmental degradation have deliberately mobilised within civil society, with the state as the secondary rather than primary focus of their attention. And through its use of the media, the green movement has sought to create a public space apart from the state, in which ecological issues – alongside and in relation to other concerns of green politics, such as social welfare – might be debated, and directly influence private life and the economic sphere (e.g. by changing consumer behaviour and industry's investment patterns).

Environmentalists have, with limited success, sought to use international forums, treaties and conventions to articulate environmental rights and to create tools to strengthen opportunities for action at the level of the nation-state. Increasingly, there is also a 'shadowing' of international government agencies by the organisations of the developing international public sphere. The United Nations Environment Program (UNEP) is increasingly ambiguously placed between government and non-government organisations at the international level. The Earth Summit was also the focus for the first major gathering of non-government environmental organisations – the Global Forum. The G7 Economic Summit is regularly accompanied by a parallel meeting of activists and representatives of interested non-government bodies, at what is now called The Other Economic Summit (TOES). Rosenau (1993) sees a trend here toward the 'bifurcation of world politics', with the traditional state-centred structure of the international system now coexisting with a (weaker), more decentralised, poly-centric system comprised of non-governmental organisations and other transnational actors.

Indeed, recent technological innovations have enabled the creation of 'virtual communities' which are combinations of face-to-face and abstract networks, transnational and linked through their interests by computers, telephones, video, television, faxes, magazines and jet travel. The new global communication technologies have become increasingly important determinants of the efficacy of those engaged in political activity, whether in social movements or in political parties. This is particularly the case for the green movement, which is increasingly reliant upon rapid transfer of information between global networks of activists, scientists and environmental organisations and consequently increasingly capable of transnational political interventions.

Together, these developments reshape the definition of the 'relevant community' and the 'relevant actors' for democratic participation and representation of environmental issues. They emphasise the growing disjuncture or dislocation observed earlier between moral citizenship (as practised in individual and 'community' action and moral responsibility) and legal citizenship as defined by the nation-state. They force a redefinition of what constitutes global political action, operating as they do on several levels simultaneously. And they increase pressure for more universalistic, inclusive constitutional guarantees of citizens' rights and for definitions of ecological responsibility which tie local and international levels together through the conduit of the nation-state's apparatuses.

It is now possible to draw together some of the essential characteristics of ecological citizenship, including those which – depending on which form such citizenship takes – challenge, extend or alter existing notions of social and political citizenship.[9] Ecological citizenship is centrally defined by its attempt to extend social welfare discourse to recognise 'universal' principles relating to environmental rights and centrally incorporate these in law, culture and politics. In part, it seeks to do so by pressing for recognition of the need actively to include human 'non-citizens' (in a territorial and legal sense) in decision making. It also promotes fundamental incorporation of the interests of other species and future generations into processes of democratic consideration. This leads to challenges to extend the boundaries of existing political citizenship beyond the formerly relatively homogeneous notions of the 'nation-state' and 'national community' that to date have determined 'formal' citizenship.

The focus on a broadly ecological notion of welfare also increases demands for appropriate institutions for delivering such welfare. The state is under increasing pressure both to provide environmental education, regulation, expenditure and remediation, and to reduce its contradictory facilitation of resource exploitation for traditional economic growth. As an extension of social citizenship, ecological citizenship establishes demands for environmental welfare.[10] These demands at minimum reshape, and often work against, the requirements of capital reproduction and accumulation (capitalist or state socialist). It therefore has an impact on the capacity of the welfare state to pursue its social welfare functions where these conflict with longer-term social and ecological needs. Nevertheless, it remains unclear whether ecological citizenship in practice opposes capitalism, stands in tension with it by merely inhibiting the market, or supports it by believing that capitalism can be made truly 'green'. All three strands may presently be seen in competition with one another in the green movement. This ambiguity perhaps relates more to the different tactics of green and wider environmental movements and their different political and economic analyses rather than the normative construction of ecological citizenship as such.

For its success, the emancipatory project which is shaped by – and in turn constitutes – ecological citizens depends on the revitalisation and extension of civil society. It depends upon the active transformation of private life through creation of a 'green conscience', and increased democratic influence over the economic sphere through the actions of 'green workers', 'green producers' and 'green consumers'. This is reflected in the high value which green theorists and activists place on self-rule. This value includes the moral priority given to 'self-restraint' within civil society and also to active citizenship as defined by individual (self-) development beyond a merely instrumental relationship to the public sphere; a sense of active responsibility for representation and protection of environmental rights, and the individual and collective use of the public sphere and the state to provide the formal opportunities and protection for the institutions of ecologically guided democracy. This reiterates the importance of 'double democratisation' – the development of the state and a counter-balancing public sphere – for ecological democracy.

In addition, ecological citizens and their organisations have increasingly focused attention on the economic sphere to force the recognition of 'hidden' environmental impacts and 'externalities' – the uncosted use or loss of resources and environmental functions – and to dispose of the social arrangements which exclude open consideration of economic practices in terms of their environmental impacts. In its radical expression, this version of environmental politics seeks to extend civil rights to the economic sphere by calling for industrial democracy – a recognised problem for liberal democratic theory. (I am not certain, however, that this is an essential feature of ecological citizenship and of course, in itself, industrial democracy need not inevitably deliver ecological outcomes and may potentially lead to conflict between proponents of productivist and ecological values.)

Finally, however, it is apparent that at present the notion of post-national ecological citizenship – the idea of becoming a 'citizen of Planet Earth' – is still largely metaphorical, despite the growing influence of environmentalists at the local, national and international levels on government policies, the evolution of transnational environmental organisations, and the growing number of international conventions and treaties.

ECOLOGICALLY GUIDED DEMOCRACY

In the limited space available, I can only touch upon the essential, complementary part of 'double democratisation' – relating to the state – which bears upon how the *structural foundations* for ecological citizenship may be formalised. Clearly none of the proposals discussed above, such as the enfranchisement of ecological citizens and consideration of the needs of other species and future generations, will in themselves guarantee ecological outcomes. At best, the ecological crisis focuses attention on how 'bounded democracies' have to date enabled parochial and short-term – 'narrow' – human interests to overwhelm ecological requirements.

How can the tenets of ecological sustainability be realised through democratic decision-making processes? The tension between 'liberalism' and 'democracy', and the paradox of the need to protect liberal democratic values by placing constraints on unbridled individualism and 'free choice', are exceedingly familiar to democratic theorists. Yet in practice, legal restraints are often used to prevent violence and protect against individuals, groups and power structures which would diminish or infringe upon citizens' civil rights and to ensure neglected social groups are afforded consideration or redress. This conception of a constrained or self-protective democracy is the foundation for constitutions which enshrine the civil rights of minorities against the tyranny of the majority, protect electoral systems and their participants against the cynical manipulations of totalitarian and racist groups, and have outlawed slavery and child labour. Its survival as a democratic system depends, of course, on an active political culture which preserves liberal democratic values in practice.

What is proposed here is a 'hierarchy of value', in which universal ecological values or principles (like conservation of bio-diversity, the basic needs of future generations) are given priority over particular ecological values (such as protection of individuals of a species) and 'narrow' anthropocentric values (such as the right of individual humans, classes or nations to

163

'subdue the Earth', by destroying ecosystems, exterminating other species and consuming a disproportionate share of global resources). Without doubt, with the acceptance of such a hierarchy, liberal democracy has been compromised. As Habermas (1991) has suggested in another context, to go the next step and establish a legal duty to make active use of democratic rights – for instance, here, to compel custodial consideration of ecological values – would have something seemingly authoritarian or at least paternalistic about it. Yet I would hold that 'ecologically guided democracy' requires just this.

On the basis of mounting environmental evidence, we can argue that untrammelled freedom of human action and the destruction of the environment infringe upon the welfare – the rights and the actual, implied or potential needs and choices – of present and future generations of humans and present and future non-human species. Defending general-isable ecological values and rights against narrow anthropocentric concerns therefore may be regarded as a profound expression of liberal democratic principles, in which liberal democracy and green concerns are linked through the expansion of the constituency to which the notion of welfare refers (see Eckersley 1994).

Lowi (1979) offers an insight into the institutional requirements for protecting ecological needs in the context of 'green democracy'. He defines problems for democracy associated with interest-group liberalism – relating to the ways in which the negotiations and informal bargaining of interest groups blur the implementation of policy and derail the ability of a demo-cratic government to stick to formal procedure – which are similar to those associated with the dominance of short-term social and economic interests over longer-term ecological and social ones. To counter these tendencies he opts for juridical democracy in which the rule of law dominates, defines and guides the administrative and executive aspects of government.

> Juridical democracy is a public philosophy which rejects informality as a criterion. . . . The juridical principle would build a public phil-osophy around the state, including the judiciary, and would concern itself with how and why the state must limit itself in the use of its powers of coercion.
>
> (Lowi 1979: 298)

Lowi emphasises that the terms 'juridical' and 'democracy' must not be separable: 'while the juridical stresses form and the real impact of form, democracy stresses particular forms and particular contents'.

One can point to existing examples – all inadequate by ecological criteria – of such juridical states. The (formerly West) German *Rechtsstaat* is one such instance.

> Liberal principles, the protection of individual liberties and civil rights, are enshrined by the normative force of the *Rechtsstaat*, a state

164

bound by the rule of law. What characterises the [German] Basic Law more than any other feature is the expression given to the doctrine of 'constitutionalism' – that is, limited government, checks and balances, and a dispersion of decision-making authority. . . . The result is that policies can be agreed and carried out only if at some stage an integrative solution is forthcoming. A consensus need not be present at the outset – party positions may be sharply opposed and the interests of the *Länder* quite divergent – but it is in the way the structures are designed and operate that agreed solutions are found. *The institutional structures provided in the Basic Law amount to a set of consensus-inducing mechanisms: it is the process which helps fashion the consensus, rather than the latter being present beforehand.*

(Smith 1992: 39–40; my emphasis)

The distinctly ecological value of such a system would depend on the integration of legal guarantees of deliberative democratic processes with the means and rights legally to challenge actions which contravene ecological principles enshrined in law and constitution. However the 'strong green state' must be framed simultaneously by the essential, restraining guarantees for 'strong democracy' – constitutional, legal and regulatory guarantees of the rights, powers and resources for citizens to engage in a variety of deliberative democratic actions – and, separately, by the principles of ecological sustainability and environmental rights, similarly established at the heart of the legal and constitutional mechanisms of such a state.

Again, there are instances of evolution in this direction. For instance, in Norway legislation ensuring public access to information and participation relating to environmental issues is supported by an amendment to the Constitution which states that 'citizens are entitled to be informed of the state of the natural environment and of the effects of any encroachments on nature that are planned or commenced' (OECD 1993). Article 110b of the Norwegian Constitution states that 'Every person has the right to an environment that is conducive to health and to natural surroundings whose productivity and diversity are preserved. Natural resources should be used on the basis of comprehensive long-term considerations whereby this right will be safeguarded for future generations as well' (see also Paehlke 1990). An increasing number of countries are enacting bio-diversity and endangered species legislation which – where accompanied by rights enabling third parties (ecological citizens) to activate the legislation – can serve to obstruct or ban 'threatening processes'.

Building on such examples, one can begin to construct an ideal outline of the green state which, while denying the specific political texture and historical basis of actual states, may serve to suggest the panoply of mechanisms which would both facilitate and guarantee ecologically guided democracy. A green facilitative state – one which enables ecological citizens

165

to use the law to protect environmental rights – would need to be framed
and guided by constitutional or legal definitions of ecological principles and
of environmental as well as social/democratic rights, including legal protection for the survival of species, biological diversity, etc. It would also need
to provide legal guarantees for deliberative democratic processes (including
in the workplace) and associated 'triggers' and resources to enable these
processes to work. Resources and legal support would be required for
deliberative mechanisms such as citizen-initiated public inquiries, referendums and plebiscites, for related organisations such as civil and environmental rights-related non-government bodies, and for independent
environmental auditing and defenders' offices. Guarantees of freedom of
information and of independent environmental auditing, assessment and
regulatory enforcement of environmental standards would also be needed:
monitoring of the state of the environment would be essential to the
development of informed public and policy makers' opinions about necessary environmental actions and policy. The green state needs to 'learn'
reflexively, as well as to apply powerful sanctions against those who step
outside the bounds of the ecologically guided democratic framework.

Finally, the transnational nature of environmental issues must be again
emphasised here. The international dimension of the environmental crisis
discussed at the start of this chapter would need to be accommodated, for
'Ecological Sustainability in One Country' is no more feasible than 'Socialism in One Country' and the need for international ecological co-operation
is therefore profound. The nation-state would need to be constitutionally
enabled to act as a facilitator and focus for community discussion about
acceptable levels of international exposure or integration and as a conduit
for democratic response to international treaties and conventions which
require domestic legitimation for their legal efficacy. Processes which
encourage environmental solidarity could also enable national communities to reject the severe external economic pressures (such as threats of
capital flight and economic destabilisation) which will confront any attempts at significant environmental policy reforms. They will also enable
the extended 'ecological community' to promote, endorse and implement
strong policies as well as strong international treaties and conventions for
environmental protection.

Together, these developments suggest a desirable new relationship
between states, communities and individuals – one which integrates formal
political processes and state-regulatory controls over market forces with a
self-limiting culture of moderation and responsibility, producing individuals and corporate actors whose environmental awareness would morally
and materially confine their actions to those producing ecologically sustainable outcomes.

Beck (1992) has called this new formation the 'risk society' – a society
which has shed the romantic gloss of productivist progress and replaced it

with scepticism about the benefits of science and technology, and an anxiety about the (ecological and social) consequences of its actions. It is a self-reflexive society but also a more autonomously responsible society, in which individuals as actors are 'revalorised' and 'government regulation can at best offer points of orientation to them, but it cannot assume sole responsibility for setting and enforcing norms'. Interpreting Beck, Offe writes that

> a risk society is so arranged that constitution, law and state politics, as protectors and trustees of collective reason, generally play a diminishing and sometimes a negative role. . . . At the very least, they need to be supplemented by an increasing participation on the part of citizens whose actions and self-binding are oriented toward enlightenment, solidarity and responsibility.

> (Offe 1992: 67)

The radical changes necessary to achieve 'ecologically sustainable development' within the next three to five decades will have profound economic and social impacts. First World communities in particular will need to accept declining material living standards, the elimination of employment in certain industry sectors and geographic regions (even if compensated for by growth in other areas), and significant transfers of resources back to the Third World. Representative democracy alone, depending as it does on passive involvement of citizens in the public sphere, cannot generate the metaphoric 'brakes and shackles' on social and environmental activity we now require. Rapid industrial and ecological transition will depend on the creation of states, political cultures and international institutions which are able to consider, reach agreement about and implement such changes. These will depend upon the work of ecological citizens operating within a web of constitutional environmental rights and legal responsibilities which passes through, over and beyond the nation-state itself, binding those citizens in and between individual states.

ACKNOWLEDGEMENTS

I am grateful to Robyn Eckersley for comments on an earlier draft of this chapter, which was first delivered at the ECPR Conference, in Madrid, April 1994.

NOTES

1 See Council of Europe (1991).
2 Although it may be countered that there have been concerted attempts in recent times further to limit migration between blocs, and from South to North.
3 Notions of citizenship and nationality are often complicated by histories of conquest, colonisation and incorporation of minorities which nevertheless preserve their ethnic or religious solidarity (for example, the Irish, Scottish and

Welsh in the British Isles; East Timorese and West Papuans in Indonesia; Tibetans in China; and indigenous peoples such as Australian Aborigines, North and South American Indians, and Penan tribespeople, in their respective countries.

4 I am using the term 'vital interest' here in the negative sense in relation to those decisions which would damage the health or threaten the lives of humans and other species. This clearly is barely adequate, as it does not address precisely those issues which globalised economic systems throw up – for instance, whether citizens in State A can dictate how agriculture is undertaken in State B.

5 See Dryzek (1987, 1993).

6 Talking about 'the environment movement' as if it were a homogeneous social actor is, of course, problematic. As Falk (1992: 129) writes 'the new movements are exploratory and include quite a wide range of outlooks among their adherents. Perhaps it is questionable to group disparate initiatives within an issue area (say, environment or human rights) in an aggregate of the sort implied by the seeming coherence and solidity of the term "movement".'

7 The term is used in the Habermasian and Gramscian sense of public sphere, to mean – 'a social realm in which all cultural institutions within which opinion is formed are included' (Honneth 1993: 20).

8 See, for instance, Keane (1988) and Cohen and Arato (1992).

9 See, for instance, Turner (1993) and Hindess (1993).

10 It is also possible to argue that the lasting recognition and protection of environmental rights requires concomitant action to address the issue of economic inequality (particularly between First and Third World nations), and therefore incorporates and depends on achieving demands for economic justice.

REFERENCES

Beck, U. (1992) *Risk Society: Towards a New Modernity*, London: Sage.

Berman, M. (1983) *All that is Solid Melts into Air*, London: Verso.

Cohen, J. and Arato, A. (1992) 'Politics and the Reconstruction of the Concept of Civil Society', in A. Honneth, C. Offe and A. Wellmer (eds) *Cultural-political Interventions in the Unfinished Project of Enlightenment*, Cambridge, Mass.: MIT Press.

Council of Europe (1991) *Recent Demographic Developments in Europe 1991*, Strasbourg.

Dryzek, J. S. (1987) *Rational Ecology*, Oxford: Blackwell.

—— (1993) 'Green Democracy', unpublished MS.

Eckersley, R. (1994) 'Liberal Democracy and the Environment: The Rights Discourse and the Struggle for Recognition', unpublished MS.

Enzensberger, H. M. (1991) *Europe, Europe: Forays into a Continent*, London: Pan.

Falk, R. (1992) *Explorations at the End of Time: The Prospects for World Order*, Philadelphia, Pa: Temple University Press.

Habermas, J. (1991) 'Citizenship and National Identity: Some Reflections on the Future of Europe', *Praxis International* 12, 1: 1–19.

Held, D. (1989) *Political Theory and the Modern State*, Stanford, Calif.: Stanford University Press.

—— (1991) 'Democracy, the Nation-State and the Global System', in D. Held (ed.) *Political Theory Today*, Cambridge: Polity.

Hindess, B. (1993) 'Citizenship in the Modern West', in B. S. Turner (ed.) *Citizenship and Social Theory*, London: Sage.

Honneth, A. (1993) 'Conceptions of "Civil Society"', *Radical Philosophy* 64, summer: 19–22.

Keane, J. (1988) *Democracy and Civil Society*, London: Verso.

Lowi, T. J. (1979) *The End of Liberalism: The Second Republic of the United States*, 2nd edn, New York: Norton.

Meadows, D. H., Meadows, D. L. and Randers, J. (1992) *Beyond the Limits*, London: Earthscan.

Offe, C. (1992) 'Bindings, Shackles, Brakes: On Self-Limitation Strategies', in A. Honneth, C. Offe and A. Wellmer (eds), *Cultural-political Interventions in the Unfinished Project of Enlightenment*, Cambridge, Mass.: MIT Press.

Organisation for Economic Co-operation and Development (OECD) (1993) *Environmental Performance of Norway: Main Report*, Paris: OECD.

Paehlke, R. C. (1990) 'Democracy and Environmentalism: Opening a Door to the Administrative State', in R. Paehlke and D. Torgerson (eds) *Managing Leviathan: Environmental Politics and the Administrative State*, Ontario: Broadview Press.

Roche, M. (1992) *Rethinking Citizenship*, London: Polity.

Rosenau, J. N. (1993) 'Environmental Challenges', in R. D. Lipschutz and K. Conca (eds) *The State and Social Power in Global Environmental Politics*, New York: Columbia University Press.

Smith, G. (1992) 'The Nature of the Unified State', in G. Smith, W. E. Paterson, P. H. Merkl and S. Padgett (eds) *Developments in German Politics*, London: Macmillan.

Sorgensen, B. (1994) 'Citizens Who Have No Voting Rights', correspondence, *The European*, 14–20 January.

Turner, B. S. (1993) 'Contemporary Problems in the Theory of Citizenship', in B. S. Turner (ed.) *Citizenship and Social Theory*, London: Sage.

United Nations Environment Programme (UNEP) (1992) *Saving Our Planet*, Nairobi: United Nations.

World Commission on Environment and Development (WCED) (1987) *Our Common Future* (Brundtland Report), London: Oxford University Press.

9

SUSTAINABILITY, COMMUNITY AND DEMOCRACY

Wouter Achterberg

The main thesis of this chapter is that sustainability cannot be achieved without institutional changes in liberal democratic societies. The institutional changes explored have been proposed in other contexts by theorists of associative democracy and are supposed to broaden and enhance the democratic character of society. Two approaches to sustainability are discussed in the first section – the concepts of a sustainable society and of sustainable development. There is something common to these different concepts: both share an inescapable moral commitment, particularly to intergenerational and intragenerational justice or fairness. Realising sustainability could therefore imply a heavy burden of redistribution for rich countries. Because social acceptance of substantial redistribution requires mutual identification between all concerned and because the ties of community or, at least, mutual identification between citizens are rather weak in contemporary societies, the required redistributive measures might turn out to be a serious stumbling block on the route to a more sustainable and more just society. The importance of community for the realisation of sustainability will be explored in the second section.

In the third section, associative democracy will be discussed. I consider associative democracy to be mainly an institutional supplement to liberal democracy, which I take to mean representative democracies with market economies that are regulated to some degree. Nevertheless, different conceptions of associative democracy have been proposed, some of which have a more liberal inspiration while others draw more on socialist or social-democratic ideas. I will discuss two representative variants: the theory of Cohen and Rogers (1992), which represents the liberal perspective, and the more ambitious theory of Hirst (1994), which betrays a clearly socialist inspiration. The hypothesis will be put forward that the institutional changes proposed by adherents of associative democracy, which are sometimes rather minimal, will strengthen community ties and thereby make it more probable that sustainability will be achieved.

SUSTAINABILITY

Since the publication of the Brundtland Report *Our Common Future* (WCED 1987) sustainable development has broken through internationally as the umbrella objective of environmental policy. The glorious career of sustainable development reached a height at the United Nations Conference on the Environment and Development (UNCED, also known as the Earth Summit; Rio de Janeiro 1992). But, in the mean time, the meaning of the concepts of sustainability and sustainable development has become, if anything, more unclear. For a clear understanding of what is at stake in pursuing sustainability, it might be helpful to go further back in time than 1987. Important aspects of the meaning of this idea will be unearthed in this way.

Roughly, we can distinguish two lines of development in the history of sustainability, both going back at least to the beginning of the 1970s. The first line starts with increasing concern in western countries about environmental degradation and the incompatibility between our industrial way of life and the continued existence of a safe, healthy, clean and rich environment. The other dates from the United Nations Conference on the Human Environment (Stockholm, 5–16 June 1972). At this conference, the poorer countries stubbornly resisted a view of the environment and of desirable environmental policy which bore too much of the stamp of western concerns. The first line has emphasised a sustainable society and a stationary economy. The second line resulted in a conceptual compromise, that is, the concept of sustainable development, which allowed for some economic growth.

The sustainable society

The concept of the sustainable society had its origin to a great extent in debates about the limits to growth of the economy and population which raged in the early 1970s. The stationary economy was often connected with the thought of zero economic growth or at least zero growth of material production. Somewhat defensively, some participants in the debate went on to soften zero growth to limited or slow or selective growth. There is no end yet in sight to this debate about the compatibility of economic growth (which and how?) with a sustainable use of the environment. In the mean time through the influence of the Brundtland Report (WCED 1987), it has become enriched with peculiar ideas such as sustainable growth. A prominent thought in that report is that economic growth is necessary, though more so in poor countries than in rich, to pay the costs of environmental policy and to achieve sustainable use of the environment.

Basic to the original idea of a sustainable society was the presupposition that a partially or completely different society to contemporary capitalist or

171

industrial society would be necessary to cope successfully with the environmental crisis and to achieve sustainability. By now, this assumption has become marginalised and its remaining adherents are only to be found in the radical wing of the environmental movement. That is not as it should be and in this chapter a defence of the 'radical' presupposition will be offered. Nevertheless, a sustainable society is not a society which can survive indefinitely; no human society can do that. Instead, a sustainable society is a society arranged in such a way that the tendency to sustainable use of the environment is inherent to it, in much the same way as the tendency to unsustainability seems inherent to the capitalistic order. It was in this sense that the idea of a sustainable society was put forward by the *Blueprint for Survival*, written by the editors of the *Ecologist* magazine (Goldsmith 1972). It is worthwhile to recall some aspects of its vision.

The *Blueprint* begins with the summary judgement that 'The principal defect of the industrial way of life with its ethos of expansion is that it is not sustainable' (Goldsmith 1972: 15). This way of life will end therefore, according to the authors of the *Blueprint*, either 'in a succession of famines, epidemics, social crises and wars' or because we will manage to create in a controlled and humane way a 'sustainable society' and so ensure that deprivation and cruelty will not be the fate of our children (1972: 15). The sustainable society is a stable society, a society which 'to all intents and purposes can be sustained indefinitely while giving optimum satisfaction to its members' (1972: 30). The four main conditions of a sustainable society are minimal disturbance of ecological processes; as much conservation of energy and resources as possible; a stable population (only replacement will take place); and a social system in which the well-being of the individual is not lessened by the other three conditions. More specifically, a sustainable society will consist of 'decentralised, self-sufficient communities, in which people work near their homes, have the responsibility of governing themselves, of running their schools, hospitals, and welfare services' (1972: 30), in fact, of 'real communities', which will presumably contribute much to our well-being. The chances are that we will in these circumstances develop a real identity, find a meaning in life, have an ordered set of values and be proud of our own achievements and those of the community. These are all things difficult to be had in present-day mass societies. Clearly, the authors of the *Blueprint* see the environmental crisis as part of a much deeper crisis that challenges the whole industrial way of life.

One does not need to agree with these views to understand that without structural changes in industrial society a sustainable use of the environment will presumably not be achieved. Changes of individual lifestyle or changes of policy are not sufficient to realise sustainability. Structural changes concern the institutional pattern and/or the culture of a society.

Three basic assumptions ground the need for structural change: the fact that, in general, environmental capacity is limited or finite; the inherent tendency of industrial society, so far, to lose sight of these limits; and the moral insights that we ought to counteract this tendency and that society ought to fit within ecological constraints, not just for our own sake, or for the sake of our children, but also for the sake of future generations. It would be quite right to add: for the sake of nature. The addition implies that nature has a moral weight of its own, instead of being just a precondition for the existence and evolution of human society. But in this chapter I will limit myself to the institutional aspects of the environmental issue.[1]

Sustainable development

The second tradition of thinking about sustainability goes back to ideas which gained some international recognition at the Stockholm Conference. This tradition leads to the Earth Summit by way of the *World Conservation Strategy* (WCS 1980) and *Our Common Future* (WCED 1987), with a non-anthropocentric version in the form of the *World Charter of Nature* (1982) and *Caring for the Earth* (1991), the successor of the WCS. It suffices here to summarise the basic assumption of this way of thinking: sustainability ought not to be achieved at the expense of the legitimate aspirations of poor(er) countries to reach a level of development and welfare comparable to that of the richer nations. In other words, and because poverty is an important cause of environmental degradation, development is a moral and practical condition for achieving sustainability. Indeed, the point seems to be that it is simply a matter of justice if the rich, industrialised countries help the developing countries to catch up with them, preferably in ways which give the poor countries the opportunity and means to determine their own way of development. So, in addition to the basic assumptions of the first tradition, we have the principle that sustainable development is feasible and morally acceptable only *in tandem* with more just relations between rich and poor countries. Sustainability in one country is even more absurd, morally and practically, than socialism in one country! This means, in effect, that the main responsibility for 'taking off' to sustainability is placed with the rich countries. Besides providing aid to the poor countries, the rich should set a shining example in structurally changing their own societies, especially by making their pattern of production and consumption sustainable. All this is said or implied in the Declaration of Rio (in particular the principles 3 and 5–8) and, more elaborately, in Agenda 21.[2]

COMMUNITY

Whatever assessment is made of the Earth Summit (and perhaps the safest judgement is that the conference was not a complete failure), the Declaration of Rio at least expresses a broad moral consensus about sustainable development and about a demanding programme of action and policy to

173

implement the principles of sustainable development. We have much less reason to belittle this moral consensus, because basic principles of political morality lead to a similar vision. If we take as a starting point of political morality the view that people ought to be treated as equals and that they deserve equal concern and respect (Dworkin 1977: 180–2), then we have, according to Kymlicka (1990: 5), set foot on the 'egalitarian plateau', which he rightly says should be the basis of every acceptable modern political morality. The validity of this starting point as to its scope is not limited to some specific nation, culture or generation. It can be elaborated in either a consequentialistic manner, resulting in a theory which recommends 'protecting the vulnerable' (Goodin 1985), whoever they may be and wherever and whenever they live or will live, or in a deontological theory at the core of which are principles of inter- and intragenerational justice (Barry 1991). Moreover, according to both types of theory, redistribution may well be required morally in cases of an unequal redistribution of resources. Having accepted these starting points, we can leave moral theory and go on to consider the practical consequences of the pursuit of sustainability.

I take it that sustainability minimally implies establishing sustainable patterns of production and consumption. How and under what conditions will these patterns be achieved? From three different directions the answers to this question converge upon the role and importance of community in achieving sustainability.

First, the question of how sustainability is to be achieved. Regulation by central authorities and financial incentives (such as price signals) will be needed, but these cannot be the whole story. Central regulation and financial incentives are in fact the easiest part of environmental policy, at least so far as it is aimed at what has been called 'ecological modernization' (Weale 1992). For example, standards will have to be established for admissible pollution or for less intensive use of energy and more efficient use of resources, which means, among other things, recycling in production or, more generally, 'closing of substance cycles in the chain of raw material – production process – product – waste and the associated emissions', which in turn implies 'integrated life cycle management' (Ministerie van Volks- huisvesting, Ruimtelijke Ordening en Milieubeheer 1989: 12 and 17). Different industries need to find out how to meet these objectives in their specific circumstances of production. On the other hand, it is not clear how the relevant standards will be enforced when this is necessary. In short, there will have to be much more co-ordination by central (or regional or local) authorities or other (semi-) public bodies, but also voluntary co-ordination and co-operation between firms, branches of industry, and employers and employees. Furthermore, achieving sustainable patterns of consumption cannot just be a matter of waiting for consumers to see the light, after exposure to specific media messages. Co-operation will therefore be necessary between producers and organisations of consumers, and between government agencies and producers. So far, we have hardly begun to deal with the questions of how to reorganise the transportation of freight and passengers, and the collection and processing of domestic waste. The required co-ordination and voluntary co-operation at different levels presuppose that citizens are sufficiently involved with each other, an involvement which, in turn, is based on a shared understanding of the meaning and value of sustainability in general, and of sustainability specific to particular contexts of activity. This type of mutual concern on the basis of a shared acceptance of certain values is an important component of what traditionally has been understood by community.

Second, there is another fundamental reason why pursuing sustainability presupposes community. This is because of the moral starting point mentioned earlier: even in the pursuit of sustainability people should be treated as equals. The implication is that a society should receive aid if it cannot manage to establish sustainable patterns of production and consumption. Making equality our starting point therefore implies solidarity and redistribution between rich and poor. And yet, at present, this is not a remote possibility if we recall that even the basic needs of a substantial part of the world's population go unmet. Indeed, redistribution already has a high priority on the list of conditions for achieving sustainability. After all, the pursuit of sustainability implies very limited or selective possibilities for economic growth. The usual political strategy in welfare states – of keeping the social peace by redistributive measures funded by a growing economy – will have to be abandoned almost completely. Moreover, environmental policy often has regressive effects. If we add to that the aid or compensation owed to poor countries, it becomes clear that there will be insufficient public support for the pursuit of sustainability in rich countries, which are themselves often confronted with increasing inequality: unless, the level of community among members in society is sufficiently high or the extent of their mutual identification is great enough; unless, that is, their solidarity is strong enough.

The crucial importance of redistribution for the solution of the environmental issue, at least in capitalist countries, is recognised by socialist or ecosocialist thinkers (see, for example, the descriptions in Eckersley 1992; Dobson 1990; Pepper 1993). But its significance was also pointed out very forcefully by the 'survivalist' Heilbroner (1974: 101–6) who saw it as the crucial test for capitalism.[3]

The relationship between achieving redistribution (on the basis of a principle of equality or distributive justice) and ties of community has been emphasised by communitarian philosophers like Sandel, Walzer and Charles Taylor. Walzer, for example, does not conceive of society as an organisation for mutual benefit. He proposes the following three principles: every political community ought to meet the needs of its members as they

WOUTER ACHTERBERG

collectively define these needs; there should be distribution according to these needs; and equality of membership for all members (1983: 184). Citizens need to reach an agreement about the extent of communal provision, 'the sphere of security and welfare'. This agreement is, in fact, a kind of social contract aimed at the redistribution of:

> the resources of the members in accordance with some shared understanding of their needs, subject to ongoing political determination in detail. The contract is a moral bond. It connects the strong and the weak, the lucky and the unlucky, the rich and the poor, creating a union that transcends all differences of interests, drawing its strengths from history, culture, religion, language, and so on. Arguments about communal provision are, at the deepest level, interpretations of that union.
>
> (Walzer 1983: 82–3)

A similar relationship is recognised by Sandel in his criticism of the way in which Rawls explains and justifies the Difference principle of justice (Sandel 1982: ch. 2), and by Taylor (1985). Taylor points out the 'legitimation crisis' which liberal democracies are undergoing at present: the maintenance of the welfare state requires increasingly large transfers by citizens of parts of their personal incomes. But they are increasingly less prepared to do that because, as Kymlicka summarises Taylor on this point, 'they share less and less with those for whom they are making sacrifices. There is no shared form of life underlying the demands of the neutral state' (Kymlicka 1990: 225).

I want to use this communitarian insight without endorsing the communitarian position *in toto*. That is to say, at this point I don't need to accept the underived value of community as an independent principle of political theory. For my purposes it suffices to adopt David Miller's (1989: 57) minimalistic argument for a certain kind of communitarianism as an essential part of socialism. Miller's point of departure is that freedom, in the sense of 'equality of effective choice' (1989: 51) is central in a modern, viable socialism. He argues that freedom in this sense depends on the distribution of resources.

> To equalize effective freedom, we need a system of distributive justice. But such a system can't be legitimized unless people see themselves as tied together communally. Politics enters the picture to prevent communal ties becoming merely traditional, to honour socialist demands for rationality.
>
> (Miller 1989: 72)

He adds to this argument the empirical proposition that the more egalitarian the desirable distribution, the stronger the ties of community should be (1989: 59). What scope does the community intended by Miller have?

He does not mean the more or less localised community, based on face-to-face relations and unified by a way of life or a conception of the good life, a community which determines the identity of its members to a large extent, such as Sandel's constitutive community (1982: 150). This type of community can be a marginal phenomenon only in modern industrial societies since these are predominantly market societies characterised by increasing individualism and commercialisation (Hirsch 1976), materialism and self-interest, and acquisitiveness (Dryzek 1987). But, nor does Miller's community embrace humanity in its entirety either. Although we could conceive of communities based on mutual recognition of impersonal principles of justice or beneficence, Miller says that this would ignore the particularism of communities (1989: 68). Miller's position seems correct to me, but I would add that the importance and strength of mutual identification, on the basis of a shared moral sense of the kind articulated in impersonal moral principles, should not be underestimated, especially in societies with ideological pluralism and chronic conflicts of interest (see also Hirst 1989: 55–6). We cannot afford the luxury of not invoking this minimal kind of identification, but it is also very doubtful whether identification of this minimal type is strong enough on its own to support cooperation and redistibution when strong conflicts of interest are rampant.

Lastly, Miller points out that communities are not available on demand. If their existence is required by some purpose, the only option is to build on the present ties of community. The most extensive communities nowadays, which could also legitimise 'effective practices' of distributive justice, are national communities. 'Nationality is the identity we have in common, an identity in large measure inherited from the past, and not fully open to rational scrutiny' (Miller 1989: 70).

Miller's arguments are plausible as far as they go. We have no reason to belittle the significance of mutual identification on the basis of shared nationality for voluntary redistribution between members of the nation; and some environmental problems can be solved only at the level of the nation-state. Some doubt, though, is in order if we remember the sheer burden of redistribution imposed on us by the pursuit of sustainability on a global scale. At the very least, a strengthening of mutual identification at the sub-national (for example, regional) level would be very welcome. But how is that possible if communities of the type described above are only marginal phenomena? The desired strengthening might be brought about in and by the institutional changes proposed by adherents of associative democracy (see pp. 179–85). On the transnational level the prospects are dim, to judge by the results of the Earth Summit. Perhaps one can find viable foci of international solidarity in the network of non-governmental organisations (NGOs), which were exuberantly active at the time of the Earth Summit.

There is a third direction from which the significance of community to the realisation of sustainability can be made clear. This third way has to do

177

with how we conceive of our relations to future generations. The problem here is clearly indicated by John O'Neill:

> The problem of obligations to future generations is a social and political problem concerning the economic, social and cultural conditions for the existence and expression of identity that extends across generations. At the heart of that issue is the problem which has been the focus of much social and political theory for the last two centuries – that of developing forms of community which no longer leave the individual stripped of particular ties to others, but which are compatible with the sense of individual autonomy and the richness of needs that the disintegration of older identities also produced. One part of a solution to that problem lies in those surviving practices and related associations in which individuals become part of a tradition. These persist despite the market. They form a necessary component of an ecologically rational social order.
>
> (O'Neill 1993: 42–3)

O'Neill's view of community is associated with another, less impersonal, type of ethical theory. Ethical theory of this type emphasises nested or otherwise related commitments and projects of varying scope. A good impression of its basic idea is given by Adams.

> I believe a better basis for ethical theory in this area can be found in . . . a commitment to the future of humanity as a vast project, or network of overlapping projects, that is generally shared by the human race. The aspiration for a better society – more just, more rewarding, and more peaceful – is a part of this project. So are the potentially endless quests for scientific knowledge and philosophical understanding, and the development of artistic and other cultural traditions. This includes the particular cultural traditions to which we belong, in all their accidental historic and ethnic diversity. It also includes our interest in the lives of our children and grandchildren, and the hope that they will be able, in turn to have the lives of their children and grandchildren as projects. To the extent that policy or practice seems likely to be favorable or unfavorable to the carrying out of this complex of projects in the nearer or further future, we have reason to pursue or avoid it.
>
> (Adams 1989: 472)

The commitments and projects referred to by Adams are typically shared. They are foci of as many nested or overlapping communal ties of varying scope. However, there might be normative problems in their interrelations. For example, to constrain group-egoism, a universal, but minimal morality, will remain necessary.

The absence of communities of the type referred to by O'Neill does not mean that we do not have obligations towards future generations. It can mean only that these obligations will then belong to the class of obligations that we have in some circumstances towards strangers; obligations of the kind illustrated in the parable of the 'Good Samaritan'. Good Samaritan obligations can be justified only on the basis of universal and impersonal principles of morality. These are important obligations and the mutual recognition of them is the basis for a minimal mutual identification. However, a more robust form of mutual identification might have a greater moral carrying capacity in seeing us through the period of transition to sustainability. How could such a more robust mutual identification be brought about?

ASSOCIATIVE DEMOCRACY

The central hypothesis of this chapter is that within the framework of liberal democracy institutional changes of the kind recommended by adherents of associative democracy might contribute significantly to the establishment of the more robust type of identification necessary to achieve global sustainability. Theories of associative democracies have not been designed specifically with this kind of problem in mind, but they would be much more interesting if they proved useful in explaining and confirming this hypothesis. Here, I cannot do much more than elucidate the hypothesis and indicate some of the ways in which the strengthening of communal ties and mutual identification might come about. This is because the theory of associative democracy has not yet been elaborated in great detail, and, what is more important, because the evidence necessary to corroborate the hypothesis is, as far as I know, not yet available either. Sufficient evidence will not be available, in the near future, because the recommended institutional changes can be introduced only gradually. Moreover, the circumstances under which the changes will have to take place are widely different between countries.

Another worry about associative democracy is that the gradual character of the intended transformation to it is a disadvantage from a moral and practical point of view. The question is whether we still have enough time and knowledge for the changes, in view of the urgency and the complex nature of the environmental problems. Can we morally and rationally afford incremental changes? The same question has to be asked in view of the inequality between rich and poor countries. Hirst's remark in connection with the last question merits quotation:

It would be foolish to abandon advocacy of reform and renewal in Western societies, as if the World's poor would gain by our maintaining the imperfections of our current institutions. That is self-defeating, but such advocacy of associationalist reform can only be honest if we do accept that in doing so we are better arranging the affairs of the rich and we know what lies beyond, in the world of the poor and that to its questions we have no ready and effective answers.

(Hirst 1994: 73)

One more caution is in order here. I do not mean to suggest that a society, associatively transformed, will on that account alone decide to pursue sustainability. My purpose is more modest: to argue that, if (a big if!) a liberal democracy has reached a clear and unambiguous political consensus about sustainability (on which see Achterberg 1993), the chances of achieving sustainability might be better in an associatively transformed liberal democracy.

What, then, are the core ideas of associative democracy? In answering this question I draw first upon Cohen and Rogers (1992) and then Hirst (1994), who has elaborated a rather more radical and leftist view of associative democracy.

Cohen and Rogers on associative democracy

These authors put associative democracy forward as a general strategy to curb the 'mischiefs of faction' (Hamilton *et al.* 1987) by making it possible for secondary associations to play a more positive part in the governance of a democratic society. Secondary associations are associations which are not primary, that is to say, all associations except the state, the family and the firm. Faction, to recall, is defined by Madison as:

a number of citizens, whether amounting to a majority or minority of the whole, who are united and actuated by some common impulse of passion, or of interest, adverse to the rights of other citizens, or to the permanent and aggregate interests of the community.

(Hamilton *et al.* 1987: 42)

Cohen and Rogers mainly have in mind minority faction or 'the exploitation of the many by the few' (1992: 465). They emphasise the 'artefactual' character of secondary associations (1992: 414; 425–30), and although associations are not completely products of politics, central government can influence them, or the 'associative environment of public policy' (1992: 425), by conventional public policy measures like taxes, subsidies and legal sanctions to such an extent that they in fact contribute better to the realisation of the norms of 'democratic governance' (1992: 425). In general, regulation by associations is an 'alternative to markets or public hierarchies' and 'permits society to realize the important benefits of cooperation among member citizens' (1992: 425). What associations can do is help 'to formulate and execute public policies and take on quasi-public functions that supplement or supplant the state's more directly regulatory actions' (1992: 425).

Alternate governance by associations would come in very handy in the case of environmental policy. In the first place, much information (from 'below') is needed to establish environmental standards, for example, concerning effluents, emissions and the use of resources, operational in the specific contexts of production. This information can be supplied only by organisations of producers, sometimes in co-operation with environmental organisations or environmental consultancies. Second, compliance with centrally imposed norms or levels needs to be enforced. This typically has to be done at many and at such diverse sites that the enforcement capacity of a central government would very soon be overloaded. Here also, there is an important role for associations. Third, the rearrangement of production processes in order to make them sustainable cannot take place without voluntary co-ordination and co-operation between branches of industry, firms within the same branch or across branches, etc. Associations will be central in this process of rearrangement.

A dense associative infrastructure is needed for the design, implementation and enforcement of an effective and efficient environmental policy. The same goes for public policy in general, for example in the areas of public health, employment, industrial renewal. According to Cohen and Rogers the construction of such an infrastructure requires more than just the consent of the governed. It also needs their active support, and that will be forthcoming only if an 'associative democracy connects with deeper aspirations to democratic order' (1992: 442). On this question I will look only at the way the associative infrastructure can contribute to achieving distributive justice and enhancing 'civic consciousness'. As I noted, I am interested in distributive justice because sustainability will not be achieved without meeting standards of inter- and intragenerational justice, and in civic consciousness because it bears on how citizens conceive of their relation to each other and to posterity.

The contribution of associative democracy to distributive justice is likely to be quite modest. On the one hand, the better organised might improve their incomes, working conditions and social benefits. On the other hand, poorly organised groups, and regional inequalities, would both require special compensatory measures. The contribution to civic consciousness is more impressive. Particularly at the level of the most encompassing groups Cohen and Rogers suggest that there would be an increasing social solidarity; and a growing awareness of interdependence. They cite De Tocqueville with approval on the educative value of associations under democratic circumstances: 'Feelings are recruited, the heart is enlarged, and the human mind is developed only by the reciprocal influence of men on one another' (Cohen and Rogers 1992: 424). This enhancing of civic consciousness can be expected to contribute substantially to the growth of solidarity and mutual identification, which liberal democracies will need if they are to achieve sustainability.

In summary, I conclude that the contribution of associative democracy, as conceived by Cohen and Rogers, to the strengthening of community would be uneven. Regarding how sustainability is to be achieved, the first of the three questions raised on p. 174, the contribution of associative democracy is impressive; but on the second issue of how to achieve a sufficient level of mutual identification and the third of how to achieve a viable identification with future generations it is less so.[4]

Associative democracy according to Paul Hirst

Hirst (1994) agrees with Cohen and Rogers (1992) that associative democracy is not a replacement for liberal democracy but, rather, a supplement. But he is also critical of them because they emphasise the artefactual character of associative democracy too much. Even if governments could take such an active part in forming associations, in practice, doing so would damage the force and legitimacy of the associations themselves. Hirst recommends instead that associations be set up 'from below', by the voluntary action of citizens. Moreover, strong associations could help the weak ones. This whole process implies a partial shift of power away from the state as the primary association because the associations would take over some of the tasks the welfare state has had so far, in particular in the areas of social and economic regulation and coordination, and of service delivery (education, health, care of elderly people and social security). To a certain extent the state will be decentralised and 'pluralized', while civil society will be in the same measure 'publicized' (1994: 74). A residual core of public tasks would remain which cannot be taken over by secondary associations, such as defence, policing, enacting and maintenance of common laws protecting the rights of individuals (against each other and against the association they have joined) and associations, environmental protection and management, and the maintenance of public health. What results is a more than minimal state which stands a reasonable chance of being more up to its remaining core tasks than the overloaded welfare state. The 'associationalism' defended by Hirst reverses so to speak the relation between primary and secondary associations, compared with the usual liberal democratic view of that relation which we have seen in Cohen and Rogers:

> Voluntary associations are regarded in modern liberal democratic theory primarily in terms of their role as the social foundation of a pluralistic politics, that is they provide articulation for the divergent interests in civil society and thereby prevent any tendency toward the formation of potentially tyrannical homogeneous majorities. Such voluntary bodies are viewed as 'secondary associations' and as important because they ensure the democratic nature of the 'primary

association', the state. Associationalism turns this relationship on its head. It treats self-governing voluntary bodies not as secondary associations, but as the primary means of both democratic governance and organizing social life. A self-governing civil society thus becomes the primary feature of society. The state becomes a secondary, but vitally necessary, public power that ensures peace between associations and protects the rights of individuals. It also provides the mechanism of public finance whereby those forms of provision that are regarded as necessary and available as of right to all members of society are administered through voluntary associations that those members elect to join to receive such services.

(Hirst 1994: 25–6)

The market would play an important part in the associative society, albeit that the social 'embeddedness' (Hirst 1994: 65) of it has to be improved by better co-ordination and co-operation, at different levels and between different social actors. Criteria for improvement concern not only efficiency and employment, but also more substantial principles such as equity, and something Hirst does not mention, sustainability. The improved social channelling of the market requires a society that is complementary to the market and also coherent and co-operative enough to regulate the market economy and to correct its results. In contrast to variants of market socialism (compare Bardhan and Roemer 1993), there is no fixation, in the theory of associative democracy, on specific property relations (Cohen and Rogers 1993: 236). As Hirst puts it: 'The new associative economic democracy will be neither "socialist" nor "capitalist" it will be able to accommodate very different forms of enterprise ownership and control within the same scheme of social governance' (1994: 109).

For Hirst, joining and leaving associations is purely voluntary. People join an association or set up an association because they understand that a common interest or purpose, as they see it, can be better served in that way. Enlightened self-interest is sufficient motivation to join an association; no special altruistic disposition or spontaneous tendency to form communities is assumed. Thus, the main normative starting point of associative democracy is that 'human beings ought to associate one with another to fulfill common purposes, and that they should be able to do so on the basis of free choice' (1994: 44). By participating in associations people are able to develop their capacities as rational and social beings.

In particular, the right to voluntary exit makes Hirst's associations functionally limited organisations which generate only a limited loyalty. Membership in an association determines the identity of the members only in *small measure*. So associations are 'communities of choice' and not 'communities of fate'. In communities of fate, also known as 'existential' communities, one normally lives one's life without having much choice in

183

the matter. Communities of fate, which are few and far between according to Hirst (1994: 54) – he mentions classes, religious and ethnic groups – *substantially* determine the identity of their members.

Individuals would typically be members of many associations. Thus there would be a considerable overlapping membership in the whole set of associations, much co-operation between groups and growing networks of formal and informal relations (1994: 69). What is more, 'associational governance may actually help to rebuild ties between groups, and facilitate the construction of national, regional or social foci of common identification' (1994: 68), and 'given sufficiently varied and overlapping planes of social identity and cleaving, most conflicts between groups could be contained by being parcelized' (1994: 67). In this way, I would add, the growth of mutual identification, national, regional or social, could be stimulated, without which the redistribution needed for sustainability will be so much more difficult.

A guaranteed basic income scheme (GMI) is crucial to associative democracy as conceived by Hirst (1994: 179–89). This would mean that every adult individual would have a right to a basic income which would be paid from general taxes. Its level would vary depending on general economic success and the level of unemployment, but at a minimum it would have to be (just) high enough to live on. This is so that it would encourage its recipients to look for work, without forcing them into it. Arguments for basic income show considerable variation and have been proposed by all shades of the political spectrum. Basic income has been justified on grounds of efficiency, freedom, equality, justice and community. According to Hirst this is

> a sign that it may answer very basic needs of social organization. It is the one reform that would make extensive associational experiments possible, since it provides a basic plank of universal income support on the basis of which large-scale experiments that led to diversity and heterogeneity in provision might be acceptable.
>
> (Hirst 1994: 180)

What is the significance of a GMI for moving towards a more just and sustainable society? This question cannot be answered by pointing out that many greens have also proposed some kind of GMI.[5] Here I can only indicate some core elements in the answer, in line with the moral commitment outlined in the first section and the importance of community emphasised in the second section above.

At the very least, the funding of a GMI from general taxation presupposes some measure of general redistribution of income in society, and it might contribute to an increasing social acceptance of the more thorough-going redistribution which is necessary for a sustainable society at the national and the global level. This is because establishing a GMI scheme expresses the recognition that all people should be treated as equals and therefore deserve social and economic security. Thus it expresses an elementary and general level of mutual identification between citizens. Moreover, as John Mathews, another leftist theoretician of associative democracy, puts it 'The GMI scheme would encourage a social climate in which holistic social practices and arrangements could be expected to take root and flourish – such as worker co-operatives, community co-operatives, and democratic citizen initiatives' (1989: 128).

In summary, associative democracy as conceived by Hirst may contribute to the growth of community for two reasons. These are, first, its potential for deepening solidarity through increased co-operation and co-ordination, and the expanding network of overlapping 'foci of common identification'. Second, the growing network of communities of choice may also lead to a stronger awareness of continuity and identity with future generations. This possibility is not mentioned by Hirst, although it is implied by what he says.

Comparing Hirst's view with the theory of Cohen and Rogers, we may conclude that associative democracy as viewed by Hirst gives us a better chance of making society more thoroughly sustainable. If Hirst's proposals work, the self-motivation of citizens in forming associations and the security provided by the GMI scheme may bring about a stronger mutual identification than the enhanced civic consciousness envisaged by Cohen and Rogers.

CONCLUSION

I have argued that achieving a more sustainable and just society will be more difficult, presumably much more difficult, without the institutional changes proposed by the theories of associative democracy. If my argument is correct, I have also made plausible the idea that putting into effect even a minimal conception of sustainability – establishing sustainable patterns of production and consumption (as recommended in Agenda 21) – is impossible without structural, even if modest, changes in a liberal democratic society; without, in other words, society itself becoming sustainable. And society itself becoming more sustainable implies in turn, as we have seen, a more democratic disposition, in the associative sense, and a more just arrangement of society. Of the two types of associative democracy discussed, the type represented by Hirst deserves pride of place, so it has been argued, because the institutional changes proposed by it promise to contribute more substantially to achieving a more sustainable and just society. The type represented by Cohen and Rogers, though, may well indicate an important, but modest, first step on the road to the more ambitious scheme proposed by Hirst.

ACKNOWLEDGEMENTS

I would like to thank the participants at the ECPR workshop on Green Politics and Democracy, Madrid, 16–22 April 1994 – in particular John Barry, Robyn Eckersley, Alf-Inge Jansen, Michael Saward and Stephen Young – for their criticisms and encouragement.

NOTES

1 Moreover, if moral respect for nature became more prevalent, it would be accompanied by a cultural change and this change would be compatible with various institutional contexts. This would satisfy Norton's convergence hypothesis: in which 'policies serving the interests of the human species as a whole, and in the long run, will serve also the "interests" of nature, and vice versa' (1991: 240). In fact, the hypothesis is an article of faith, as Norton also admits: with respect to each seeming conflict of interest between humanity and nature one can maintain that if one had taken a longer-term view or if one had taken a more enlightened view of the interests involved, especially of the human interests, then the conflict would have disappeared. Nevertheless, the hypothesis is in many cases correct and I will adopt it here for the sake of argument.
2 See the texts in Johnson (1992).
3 And Heilbroner has not changed his mind on it, judging by his new 'Afterword for the 1990s' in the 1991 edition of *An Enquiry into the Human Prospect*.
4 An improvement might be to add sustainability explicitly to the norms of democratic governance. In the theory of Cohen and Rogers sustainability seems to be implied by the norms of economic performance or distributive justice or both. The explicit addition would seem to be natural. Anyway, I take it that adherents of liberal democracy will want to maintain the democratic order across generations, even if *we* don't know whether later generations will think democracy as valuable as we do. Civic consciousness, defined by Cohen and Rogers as the 'general recognition of the norms of democratic process and equity and a willingness to uphold them and to accept them as fixing the basic framework of political argument and social cooperation – at least on condition that others do so as well' (1992: 420), would in this way express part of an identity that 'extends across generations' (O'Neill). Of course, in that case we have to delete the condition mentioned, which, after all, is not applicable in the intergenerational context.
5 See, for example, Dobson (1990: 111–16) and for different proposals and objections, Van Parijs (1992: 26–8).

REFERENCES

Achterberg, W. (1993) 'Can Liberal Democracy Survive the Environmental Crisis?', in A. Dobson and P. Lucardie (eds) *The Politics of Nature: Explorations in Green Political Theory*, London: Routledge.

Adams, R. M. (1989) 'Should Ethics be more Personal?', *Philosophical Review* 98, 4: 439–84.

Bardhan, P. K. and Roemer, J. E. (eds) (1993) *Market Socialism: The Current Debate*, New York: Oxford University Press.

Barry, B. (1991) *Liberty and Justice: Essays in Political Theory*, Oxford: Clarendon Press.

Cohen, J. and Rogers, J. (1992) 'Secondary Associations and Democratic Governance', *Politics and Society* 20, 4: 393–472.

—— (1993) 'Associative Democracy', in P. K. Bardhan and J. E. Roemer (eds) *Market Socialism: The Current Debate*, New York: Oxford University Press.

Dobson, A. (1990) *Green Political Thought*, London: Unwin Hyman.

Dryzek, J. S. (1987) *Rational Ecology*, Oxford: Blackwell.

Dworkin, R. (1977) *Taking Rights Seriously*, London: Duckworth.

Eckersley, R. (1992) *Environmentalism and Political Theory: Toward an Ecocentric Approach*, London: UCL Press.

Goldsmith, E. (1972) *A Blueprint for Survival*, Harmondsworth: Penguin.

Goodin, R. E. (1985) *Protecting the Vulnerable: A Reanalysis of our Social Responsibilities*, Chicago: University of Chicago Press.

Hamilton, A., Madison, J. and Jay, J. (1987) *The Federalist*, ed. and intr. by Max Beloff, Oxford: Blackwell.

Heilbroner, R. L. (1974) *An Inquiry into the Human Prospect* (1991), New York: Norton.

Hirsch, Fred (1976) *Social Limits to Growth*, Cambridge, Mass.: Harvard University Press.

Hirst, Paul (ed.) (1989) *The Pluralist Theory of the State: Selected Writings of G.H.D. Cole, J.N. Figgis, and H.J. Laski*, London: Routledge.

—— (1992) 'Comments on "Secondary Associations and Democratic Governance"', *Politics and Society* 20, 4: 473–80.

—— (1994) *Associative Democracy: New Forms of Economic and Social Governance*, Cambridge: Polity.

Johnson, S. P. (ed.) (1992) *The Earth Summit: The United Nations Conference on Environment and Development*, London: Graham & Trotman/Dordrecht: Martinus Nijhof.

Kymlicka, W. (1990) *Contemporary Political Philosophy*, Oxford: Clarendon Press.

Mathews, J. (1989) *Age of Democracy*, Melbourne: Oxford University Press.

Miller, D. (1989) 'In What Sense Must Socialism Be Communitarian?', *Social Philosophy and Policy* 6, 2: 51–73.

Ministerie van Volkshuisvesting, Ruimtelijke Ordening en Milieubeheer (1989) *To Choose or to Lose: National Environmental Policy Plan*, The Hague: SDU.

Norton, B. G. (1991) *Toward Unity Among Environmentalists*, New York: Oxford University Press.

O'Neill, J. O. (1993) *Ecology, Policy and Politics: Human Well-Being and the Natural World*, London: Routledge.

Parijs, Ph. van (ed.) (1992) *Arguing for Basic Income: Ethical Foundations for a Radical Reform*, London: Verso.

Pepper, D. (1993) *Eco-socialism: From Deep Ecology to Social Justice*, London: Routledge.

Sandel, M. J. (1982) *Liberalism and the Limits of Justice*, Cambridge: Cambridge University Press.

Taylor, C. (1985) *Philosophical Papers*, vol. 2, Cambridge: Cambridge University Press.

Walzer, M. (1983) *Spheres of Justice: A Defence of Pluralism and Equality*, Oxford: Blackwell.

—— (1990) 'The Communitarian Critique of Liberalism', *Political Theory* 18, 1: 6–23.

Weale, A. (1992) *The New Politics of Pollution*, Manchester: Manchester University Press.

World Commission on Environment and Development (WCED) (1987) *Our Common Future* (Brundtland Report), London: Oxford University Press.

10

THE ECOLOGICAL RESTRUCTURING OF THE STATE

Marius de Geus

> Reform or revolution? I envisage a change of revolutionary depth and size by means of many smaller steps in a radically new direction. Does this essentially place me among the political reformists? Scarcely. The direction is revolutionary, the steps are reformatory.
>
> (Naess 1989: 156)

In this chapter I want to investigate the extent to which the development of environmental problems has direct consequences for the role and structure of the state in contemporary society. In the first section I analyse the question of why most discussions of the environmental issue reach the conclusion that increased state interference in society is necessary. In the second section the proposition of William Ophuls that only the erection of an absolute state can protect humanity against a future environmental catastrophe is explored. In the third section, referring to the ideas of the anarchist political thinker Murray Bookchin, the radical green arguments for institutional decentralisation are outlined and the shortcomings inherent to this approach are examined. In the fourth section the three dominant models of ecological change in modern society are discussed. The fifth section deals with the question of what could be the basic principles of an ecological restructuring of western liberal democracy. In particular: what role does the state have to play and what kind of state is best suited to fight current environmental problems effectively? Finally, the main conclusion is drawn.

THE ROLE OF THE STATE

It is striking that in many discussions on the environmental issue the conclusion is reached that a growing interference of the state in society is absolutely necessary. A good example of this is found in the programmes of the PvdA (the Dutch social democratic party) and the radical Vereniging Milieudefensie (the Dutch branch of the worldwide environmental organisation Friends of the Earth International). In their programmes it is stated emphatically that a successful environmental policy requires a strictly normgiving, binding and effectively sanctioning state authority; a large, energetically acting and powerful state is a necessity (PvdA 1989: 4; Vereniging Milieudefensie 1991: 17). In large sections of society, social democratic, christian democratic, and also liberal, the state is seen as an indispensable actor and often as the essential problem-solver in respect of environmental problems. But why is this position commonly defended?

A first reason is that in the case of resource depletion and environmental degradation, generally questions of collective goods and free-rider behaviour play a crucial role. Clean soil, air and water are collective goods that people try to profit from, but are not prepared to pay for. A rationally calculating individual will try to make use of the available collective goods, but will not be prepared to make a contribution in order to remove the pollution that was caused by his or her behaviour. A typical example of the working of this mechanism is given by Michael Taylor (1982) in his *Community, Anarchy and Liberty*:

> Relatively straightforward and important instances of public goods and the free rider problem are to be found in connection with problems of resources and the environment. Consider for example a polluted lake, a receptacle for sewage and industrial wastes. Let us assume that an improvement in the quality of the water in the lake is considered to be a good by all the owners of houses and factories on its shore, who like to swim in it, sail on it, use it in their industrial processes, and so on, if it is sufficiently clean. If the water is well-circulated around the lake, such an improvement would be a public good for this group of people; it would be both indivisible (tending to perfect indivisibility with increasingly thorough circulation) and non-excludable (assuming that particular individuals cannot be or are not in fact excluded from using the lake). A lakeshore dweller or factory-owner could contribute to an improvement in water quality by taking his [*sic*] wastes elsewhere, treating them before discharging them into the lake or modifying his product. Making such a contribution to the public good is costly, and each member of the public good would most prefer everyone else to make a contribution while he has a free ride; but he would prefer everyone to contribute, including himself, to nobody doing anything about the polluted lake. Despite everyone having a common interest in a cleaner lake, nobody would voluntarily contribute to improving it if the costs of his doing so would exceed the benefits *to him* of the improvement in the water's quality which would result from *his* contribution.

> (Taylor 1982: 43)

In this case although everyone has an interest in the water becoming cleaner, none of the participants is prepared to make a substantial

189

contribution towards it voluntarily and the participants will not take any initiative of their own to prevent the pollution, unless the gains for individuals supersede the costs. According to many thinkers only some overriding power – a state – can see to it that this kind of behaviour can be broken and is able to enforce that all the participants contribute to the elimination of the water pollution.

In fact, this is the argument that one finds in a well-established form in Hobbes' *Leviathan*. According to Hobbes (1974) the unrestricted freedom of humans in the state of nature leads to an inherently unstable, disquieten-ing and dangerous situation. Because of individual striving for power and freedom the collective good of preservation of life and the security of existence cannot come about. In these circumstances there will be 'con-tinuall feare, and danger of violent death; And the life of man, solitary, poore, nasty, brutish, and short' (Hobbes 1974: 186). Only the erection of an encompassing central power, the state or *Leviathan*, can provide a way out of this impasse. The Hobbesian state can break the dilemma of 'rational' individual behaviour (the struggle between individuals for power) that leads to 'irrational' collective behaviour (a permanent state of civil war).

Garret Hardin (1973) has applied this chain of reasoning to the use that is made of the 'Commons' in our world. Individuals are likely to show parasitic behaviour with respect to the common spaces on the earth, since they are prone to reason with their own interests in mind. The egoistic actions of the participants will, according to Hardin, inevitably produce an environmental tragedy, unless people are prepared to consent to a system in which societally responsible behaviour can be 'enforced'. Coercion from above is in Hardin's view inescapable, but is bound to certain conditions:

> To many, the word coercion implies arbitrary decisions of distant and irresponsible bureaucrats; but this is not a necessary part of its meaning. The only kind of coercion I recommend is mutual coercion, mutually agreed upon by the majority of the people affected.
>
> (Hardin 1973: 145)

William Ophuls (1973) makes use of the same line of reasoning as Hardin when he stresses the necessity for a supra-individual decision-making power and the need for compulsory measures by the state in order to save the environment. According to him people have to choose between Leviathan or Oblivion:

> If scarcity is not dead, if it is in fact with us in a seemingly much more intense form than ever before in human history, how can we avoid reaching the conclusion that Leviathan is inevitable? Given current levels of population and technology, I do not believe that we can. Hobbes shows why a spaceship earth must have a captain. Otherwise, the collective selfishness and irresponsibility produced by the tragedy

of the commons will destroy the spaceship, and any sacrifice of freedom by the crew members is clearly the lesser of evils.

(Ophuls 1973: 224)

In his opinion we cannot escape from the fact of giving one person or group of persons absolute power over a considerable part of our actions. In general terms his conclusion is as follows: 'Now we have discovered that the logic of individualism creates conditions that require the reimposition of some kind of absolutism in order to avoid ruin' (Ophuls 1973: 228). Ophuls not only states that the existence of a state is a necessary condition to solve the current environmental problems, but also immediately adds that a state 'along absolutist lines' is essential.

A second reason to consider the state as an organisation of vital importance in order to tackle environmental problems is that industry forms a very strong centre of power in modern liberal democracy. Trade and industry will not voluntarily decide to decrease current levels of pollution. Only a robust centre of power – the state – will be able to resist the influence of organised trade and industry, whose primary goals are growth of production, increasing profits and long-term survival in a strongly competitive market economy, not protection of the environment. The power of enterprises, especially that of multi-nationals, can be neutralised only by the strong countervailing power of an energetic state organisation (or a strong supra-national organisation) that will take into account the interests of others, like those of individual citizens and future generations.

A third reason for a central role for the state is to prevent counter-productive relations of competition between enterprises. Often enterprises find themselves in a stalemate. Companies that are prepared to behave in a more environmentally friendly way run the risk of being eliminated from the market, because of the higher prices of their products. When they, as forerunners, opt for extensive environmental investments and the passing on of the so-called 'external costs', their products become comparatively too expensive. The competitiveness of companies that move too quickly with environmental policies can easily be endangered. Enterprises that continue to produce high levels of pollution have lower production costs and are thus able to offer their goods to the market more cheaply. The result of this mechanism is that companies that dare to take the initiative will be punished by the consumer, unless the environmentally friendly character of the products is decisive for the consumer, despite the price that has to be paid. When a state or a supra-national organisation exists that enacts uniform environmental rules and emission norms for all enterprises in a certain branch of industry, the above-mentioned counterproductive relations of competition can be avoided. Because similar demands are put on all companies, 'open and just relations of competition' will prevail and nobody can hide behind the argument that forerunners in the domain of environmental measures run the risk of being harmed by the consumer via the market mechanism.

A fourth reason for viewing the state as an essential actor in the field of the environment is that there is a strong need for impartial expertise and the formulation of boundary conditions for sustainable development (e.g. what is a responsible and sustainable utilisation of the environmental wealth of the biosphere per inhabitant). What is needed is a collection of expertise to measure the level of pollution caused by certain specific kinds of behaviour, to decide what are 'safe' emission levels and norms, to set criteria for environmentally dangerous substances, and to collect relevant information concerning the possibilities for preventing and combating different kinds of pollution. These are complicated tasks that require large-scale and expensive application of funds, which can be provided only by a state with sufficient financial strength standing above the parties concerned. Taking into account the interests that are implied in environmental policies, it is of the utmost importance that this expertise is of an independent character and is not in the grip of highly influential societal groups, like trade and industry. In green critiques the state is often seen as structurally committed to adopting a pro-business stance. The impartiality that is needed must go so far that criteria, norms, measures and solutions are adopted which are necessary for environmental protection, even when they are disagreeable for, or even detrimental to, certain influential interest groups.

For these four reasons, at least, the call for a central role for the state and increased interference and regulation by the state organisation is explicable. Yet, how does this longing for an actively intervening, norm-giving, controlling and sanctioning state relate to individual liberties, including the highly valued right of 'free choice' to consume? There seems to be an acute tension between the carrying of active environmental policies and the individual's freedom of choice. The question then arises what alternatives might both introduce effective environmental policies and simultaneously maintain individual liberties?

THE PROBLEMS WITH OPHULS' SOLUTION

Is it possible to save the environment without installing an ecodictatorship à la William Ophuls? His proposition that the sacrifice of individual liberties is clearly the lesser of evils compared to the annihilation of our spaceship earth and that only the introduction of an absolute state can preserve humankind from an approaching ecological catastrophe may sound plausible at first instance, but turns out to be untenable at closer analysis. Ophuls overlooks the following three questions: Who are exactly the main polluters in modern society? What do the individual liberties of the citizens constitute? What is the difference between an 'absolute state' and a 'powerful and actively intervening state'? ˙

192

First, Ophuls implicitly assumes that the individual citizens are the main polluters within society, not private companies and state enterprises. On the basis of this fundamental assumption he argues that individual freedoms must be restricted in order to secure the survival of humankind. This line of argument is flawed, however, when one notices the fact that in western liberal democracy the private companies and state enterprises are responsible for the overwhelming part of environmental pollution, and *not* ordinary consumers themselves. The emission of greenhouse gasses (e.g. CO_2, CH_4, N_2O), acidifying emissions (e.g. NH_3, NO_x, SO_2), ozone-depleting chemicals (like CFCs and Halons) in the Netherlands are caused for the major part by chemical industries, oil refining works and electricity power stations (taken together) (Adriaanse 1990: 75–94). The introduction of strict environmental regulations for these polluters does not have to infringe on the individual liberties of citizens – following Ophuls' reasoning – but means only that the main polluters in society are held responsible. No freedoms of citizens need to be affected by these kinds of measures. (The figures also show that it is most effective to introduce stringent environmental measures for industry, rather than for the individual citizens: Adriaanse 1990: 75–94.)

Second, Ophuls starts from an ill-considered conception of 'freedom' and 'individual rights'. He suggests that every infringement on the freedom of choice of the citizen in fact puts an end to the 'freedom' of the individual in the state. When, for instance, the state regulates that car drivers have to collect their motor oil carefully, this does not imply the end of their 'freedom' and 'individual rights', nor is this the case when returnable deposit systems on bottles, refrigerators, cars, etc., are introduced. Ophuls overlooks the fact that the essence of individual liberty in western liberal democracy does not primarily exist in an unlimited freedom of choice or consumption, but in having a right to participate in politics and to enjoy a protected position with regard to the state. Freedom of the citizen is first constituted by having social and economic rights in addition to the civil liberties of participation, assembly, conscience, etc. (positive freedom). Further, the liberty of the citizen takes shape by the enjoyment of a secured position. Being a member of a free political community, the citizen obtains protection from the state. The state will guarantee the citizen a sphere of privacy, a restriction of its domain of authority. Through this the individual is safeguarded against abuses of state authority. From a legally secure position citizens can actively call on their constitutional rights in relation to the state. In this conception the state is strictly bound by its own laws and the private sphere of the citizens is respected (negative freedom) (Berlin 1971: ch. 3). This positive and negative freedom that makes up the very heart of the liberal constitutional state, in principle does not have to be affected when the state adopts actively intervening and regulatory behaviour in order to tackle the environmental crisis.

Third, Ophuls pretends that there is no substantial difference between

193

an 'absolute state' and a 'powerful and actively intervening state'. He does not seem to realise that an absolute state is governed by some unrestrained ruler or group of rulers, not bound by constitutional law, who can impose 'any policies' and who can restrict and violate the private sphere of the individual as they see fit. However, a state can just as well take stringent measures in the area of the environment, without adopting the characteristics of an absolute Leviathan. One can imagine a democratic constitutional state in which the rulers are freely chosen, are bound by the rule of law, and can initiate active environmental policies, while observing the private sphere of the individual. In this respect one can better speak of a freedom-oriented and strong ecostate, instead of a Hobbesian and absolute political structure.

GREEN ARGUMENTS FOR INSTITUTIONAL DECENTRALISATION

As Robert Goodin has noted: 'if there is anything truly distinctive about green politics, most commentators would concur, it must surely be its emphasis on decentralisation' (Goodin 1992: 147). In order to analyse the radical green argument for institutional decentralisation I will refer to the work of the influential anarchist political philosopher Murray Bookchin. He gives three main arguments for a fully fledged decentralisation of society (Bookchin 1988: 88).

First, decentralisation is absolutely necessary in order to be able to create political entities on a human scale. According to him only small-scale and surveyable communities render it possible for citizens to know each other personally and to participate jointly in the decision-making process in public meetings. The second argument is that decentralised communities can be sensitively tailored to natural ecosystems. Small decentralised communities do not destroy the natural landscape and can live in harmony with the surroundings. The third argument emanates from the 'logistical' advantages of decentralisation. Bookchin mentions for example energy supply and transport. In his opinion a megalopolis uses immense amounts of resources in the form of oil, gas and coal. Sustainable forms of energy, however, like sun, wind, and tide energy, that he greatly prefers, in most cases can be provided only in relatively small quantities and for that reason are less suited for large cities:

> If homes and factories are heavily concentrated, devices for using clean sources of energy will probably remain mere playthings; but if urban communities are reduced in size and widely dispersed over the land, there is no reason why these devices cannot be combined to provide us with all the amenities of an industrialized civilization. To use solar, wind and tidal power effectively, the megalopolis must be decentralized. A new type of community, carefully tailored to the

194

characteristics and resources of a region, must replace the sprawling urban belts that are emerging today.

(Bookchin 1990: 96–7)

Also in the field of transport Bookchin finds decentralisation highly advantageous. In small decentralised communities distances are shorter and it is easier to make use of noiseless, clean and safer electrical vehicles, that have a relatively restricted radius. In his opinion air pollution is primarily a consequence of combustion engines in motorcars and of a high population density. The millions of people that are concentrated in our large cities inevitably produce serious forms of air pollution by their daily activities. In the cars, houses and factories huge quantities of fossil fuels are burnt, which unavoidably produces severe local pollution.

This plea for decentralisation is not uncongenial in itself, but it turns out to be not well thought out on closer inspection. Bookchin raises the suspicion that he sees decentralisation as a panacea for the ecological crisis. He does not pay any attention to the following three disadvantages of decentralisation with regard to environmental questions.

First, many environmental problems cross the borders of small political entities. Air, water, and soil pollution do not take any notice of borders. Whenever one wants to prevent and control these kinds of pollution, an intensive and well-designed policy will be necessary on a local, regional, national, and international level (see pp. 206–7 for an elaboration of this argument). The attention of green anarchist thinkers like Bookchin, however, is in general primarily focused on the level of local communities. The anarchist model of society seems to be vulnerable with respect to the effective 'coordination and adjustment' of the environmental policies of decentralised communities. In a certain sense these communities will be able to function in efficient ways. The decisions are always taken at the lowest possible level and on the basis of the most directly available information and expertise. The channels of communication are short, open and little distorting and the local decisions can therefore be quick, flexible, and well adapted to circumstances. Only, will the whole federative system function in an ecologically responsible way? The local communities lack the general overview of the 'total ecological situation' and will probably also miss out on the complicated (and expensive) expertise in environmental matters that can be generated far more easily by large-scale centralised organisations. One may have considerable confidence in spontaneous co-ordination and self-regulation, but the danger of societally and ecologically irresponsive behaviour is always a threat. On the one hand a decentralised social organisation is more responsive to 'feedback mechanisms' and the people on the ground know more about the situation than those in control. On the other hand there is the problem of local communities attempting to 'free-ride' and avoid ecological policies. When there is insufficient mutual adaptation and a lack of centrally guided co-ordination of environmental policies there is a danger that the vulnerable ecological equilibrium of society might be violated (Goodin 1992:166).

Second, decentralisation in many cases has considerable drawbacks: one can think of several significant examples in which centralisation is highly advantageous. An obvious example can be found in the area of energy supply. According to the anarchist principle of decentralisation, does every household or commune have to be provided with (often disfiguring) windmills and sun collectors? Or is it more sensible to found – far out of sight and in the most windy areas – large-scale windmill parks and to place large numbers of sun collectors on the most empty and sunny spaces? The choice does not seem a difficult one.

Another example can be found in the area of industrial production. Should one not be content that the manufacturing of specific products like chemicals, medicines, and all kinds of sophisticated and complicated medical instruments is concentrated in large-scale industrial complexes, where the funds, instruments and know-how can be generated which are indispensable for high-tech industrial research? This can never be provided by a small-scale local producer or commune. Moreover, the localisation of several industries in one specific area has the advantage that only one landscape is spoilt instead of a whole range, and that the risks of fire, explosions and unforeseeable emissions of poisonous gasses are concentrated in one sparsely (or even not) populated region.

A third disadvantage of fundamental decentralisation seems to be the danger of parochialism and especially the very short distance between governors and those being governed. In small communities a tendency to give priority to one's own interests and to consider the outside world as hostile can easily arise. This could lead to the inclination to try to pass on the locally produced pollution to the surrounding area, as was argued above regarding the free-rider dilemma. As pointed out by Robyn Eckersley:

> historically most progressive social and environmental legislative changes – ranging from affirmative action, human rights protection, and homosexual law reform to the preservation of wilderness areas – have tended to emanate from more cosmopolitan central governments rather than provincial or local decision making bodies. In many instances, such reforms have been carried through by central governments in the face of opposition from the local community or region affected – a situation that has been the hallmark of many environmental battles.
>
> (Eckersley 1992: 173–4)

The short distance between governors and those being governed which is the direct consequence of decentralisation implies that the former might be reluctant to take disagreeable measures. Because of the close contacts between 'rulers' and 'ruled' it is difficult for the former to take a detached view, and this is fertile ground for the favouring of acquaintances, closing of eyes to abuses, and cover-ups. It was shown in the Netherlands that municipalities (in particular) are not very strict with the granting of permits to pollute to factories, farmers, and small traders and that in general the local officers do not tend to punish transgressions of environmental laws according to the official rules (Groen 1991: 6).

In the southern Dutch provinces like Noord Brabant and Limburg, investigations showed that the predominantly christian democratic mayors and aldermen have had the utmost difficulties – to say the least – in maintaining the quite strict national environmental regulations which they have to impose on their voters (the farmers and agriculturists who are their neighbours and friends, and who make up their own constituency). The Dutch national policy to restrict the production of manure, and to curtail the extensive use of fertilisers, insecticides, pesticides, and herbicides, has become a complete failure for that reason. Higher levels of government, like regions or provinces, are more distant from the local population, but this makes them far less vulnerable than decentralised communities to local interests, favouritism, nepotism and the tendency to spare their own citizens (Wijkhuizen 1992: 10–15).

THREE MODELS OF ECOLOGICAL CHANGE

This study now turns to consider how changes to a society based on ecological constraints might be achieved. For this purpose, three models of ecological change can be distinguished: the piecemeal engineering model, the radical utopian model, and ecological restructuring as a model.

The piecemeal engineering model

As Karl Popper noted in the first part of *The Open Society and its Enemies*, most liberal democratic states rely on the principle of 'piecemeal engineering', of modest reforms and changes in order to solve the most acute problems: 'The piecemeal engineer will ... adopt the method of searching for, and fighting against, the greatest and most urgent evils of society, rather than searching for, and fighting for, its greatest ultimate good' (Popper 1974: 158). Liberal democracies are founded on compromises, the weighing of interests and on a careful policy of small steps. There is no room for large-scale, profound changes that focus on the reconstruction of society as a whole and that leave no part of it untouched. The confidence in encompassing utopias and radical ideologies has served its turn and is replaced by the idea that a liveable society can be reached by 'a long and laborious process of small adjustments'. Popper describes this approach:

197

In all matters, we can only learn by trial and error, by making mistakes and improvements; we can never rely on inspiration, although inspirations may be most valuable as long as they can be checked by experience. Accordingly, it is not reasonable to assume that a complete reconstruction of our social world would lead at once to a workable system.

(Popper 1974: 167)

The radical utopian model

Green radicals, however, stress that environmental problems require a different approach and that they may undermine the traditional assumptions of policy makers. From green parties and green movements has come the emphasis on the need for far-reaching changes and for a fundamental reconstruction of society as a whole in a sustainable direction. The green argument calls for sweeping changes to an ecological society that is often modelled after a utopian blueprint. This utopian method was commented upon by Popper as follows:

Utopian engineering recommends the reconstruction of society as a whole, i.e. very sweeping changes whose practical consequences are hard to calculate, owing to our limited experiences. It claims to plan rationally for the whole of society, although we do not possess anything like the factual knowledge which would be necessary to make good such an ambitious claim. We cannot possess such knowledge since we have insufficient practical experience in this kind of planning, and knowledge of facts must be based upon experience.

(Popper 1974: 162)

In various green party programmes references can be found to the ideas of anarchist-ecological thinkers like William Godwin, Peter Kropotkin, William Morris and Murray Bookchin on a future green steady-state society. The thoughts of these utopian philosophers may be instructive and fascinating, but they are certainly not flawless. The confidence in detailed blueprints and encompassing ideologies – also an anarchist-ecological one – is limited among most people. The general idea behind this is that 'the best is the enemy of the good'. An ecological society constructed after a blueprint will possess the uncertainties and dangers that are inherent to all-embracing alternatives: unforeseeable 'new' problems, unintended consequences, discrepancies between theory and practice.

However, the other approach of adopting an attitude of waiting, of not interfering too much, taking extremely cautious policy steps, contains a very high risk. Adhering to a passive attitude of 'muddling through' does not seem to be effective, nor does clinging to a totally divergent and new anarchist-ecological model of society. But then what is to be done?

My answer would be neither 'piecemeal engineering' nor 'utopian engineering', but well-designed forms of 'ecological restructuring', by which the shortcomings and setbacks of both approaches are avoided.

Ecological restructuring as a model

What do we understand by ecological restructuring? Restructuring is akin to transforming as opposed to abolishing the state and the status quo. It is not a dogmatic attempt to create a completely new world that knows no pollution at all and that is clean and beautiful in all respects. Ecological restructuring does not imply the attaining of a 'Nowhere à la William Morris'. The whole society does not have to be altered, not every stone has to be moved. It encompasses further-reaching changes and reforms on a middle to long term, that can be readjusted, that are aimed at the prevention and solution of the most aggravating forms of pollution and at acute forms of degradation of the environment. It deals with policy plans in the areas of production and consumption that can be tried out first under Popper's motto: 'If they go wrong, the damage is not very great and re-adjustment not very difficult' (Popper 1974: 159). This kind of restructuring will bear the character of compromise and will have to be accomplished in democratic ways. They must be the result of open discussions, of imaginative power, and of the preparedness to accept disagreeble measures. They will require courage and determination and will entail taking certain risks, but less considerable risks than are implied by acting only marginally or not at all (as is happening at present), or by aspiring to do it all at once (as the utopians envisage).

The comparison that suggests itself is that of the (re)building of a house (Van Gunsteren 1978: 143). The utopian engineer takes up the position of an architect who is designing a completely new and complex building. Starting from a specific set of ideals the engineer tries to build an architecturally sound and appealing edifice. In this respect Popper speaks of 'aestheticism': 'the desire to build a world which is not only a little better and more rational than ours, but which is free from all its ugliness: not a crazy quilt, an old garment badly patched, but an entirely new gown, a really beautiful new world' (Popper 1974: 165).

In the case of piecemeal engineering the house in principle is kept intact: heavy leakages are repaired, broken windows are replaced, generally the maintenance that is really necessary is carried out step by step. There is no need for an architect, there is no need for rebuilding, reconstruction or more drastic alterations. Reservedness, carefulness, doing no more than is strictly necessary, are the basic principles.

Somewhere in between lies the wide (and actually neglected) area of 'restructuring', the rebuilding of a house. It is not that a completely new house is erected – in order to prevent the annihilation of capital, the usually high costs, the unpredictable problems, disadvantages, and setbacks – but the existing house is more or less thoroughly altered, rebuilt, reconstructed, to comply with the newly formulated demands. An architect is needed only for certain stages, during the rebuilding one has a roof above one's head, when surprises arise (the sewer turns out to be in a worse condition than assumed, some beams need to be repaired, etc.) the plans can be re-adjusted, and one can still learn from earlier mistakes. The rebuilding does not primarily tackle the consequences of the obsolescence of the house, the leaking roof, the porous pipes, the woodrot in the window-frames, but alters the structure of the house itself. With great caution some of the walls are broken through, modern provisions are installed, new rooms are added, a dormer is constructed. In large part the house stays the same, yet simultaneously it undergoes a structural change.

In the case of environmental policy these are the kinds of choices that have to be made. The house is kept as it is, one tries only to prevent unacceptable deterioration and takes no measures to restrict water and energy consumption. One can also decide to demolish the house and replace it with a perfectly insulated, energy-saving and environmentally friendly built house, fitted with sun collectors and a compost lavatory. One can also – with far less cost and with reasonable results – insulate an existing house, install a highly efficient heating system, and take a range of water-saving measures (replacing the bath with a shower, replacing the outdated cistern with one of a small water volume, installing water-saving taps.)

I do not want to spin out this example endlessly. The vital point is that there is a whole world between 'piecemeal engineering' and 'utopian engineering' and that the introduction of middle-range reforms can eventually lead to structural changes in our modern unecological society. If applied with patience and perseverance, a combination of detached and surveyable alterations in itself can produce the highly needed ecological reconstruction of society.

BASIC PRINCIPLES FOR ECOLOGICAL RESTRUCTURING

We discovered that taking 'mouse steps' is ineffective and that a scheme based on 'elephant steps' will not withstand serious criticism. What remains is to try to introduce effective 'partial solutions and relatively modest experiments' that can lead to the ecological restructuring mentioned above: not wanting too much at one time, not trying to conceive of one all-encompassing strategy, but trying to make those choices that in the longer term will impinge on environmentally detrimental mechanisms and structures and to bring these with well-considered leaps – like an ibex finds its way in high mountains – towards the aim of the ecological restructuring of society.

200

What would be the basic principles of an ecological restructuring of western liberal democracy? In particular what role does the state have to play and what kind of state is best suited to combat actual environmental problems? In order to avoid the pitfall of utopianism I am not going to give an elaborated, detailed and compelling enumeration of principles and policy strategies, but I will indicate only a modest number of points that may form meaningful guidelines. The introduction of these guidelines will – in the middle to long term – imply a gradual, but not insignificant, structural change, through which our house would become more liveable.

First, on strictly pragmatic grounds, the maintenance of a free market economy, but explicitly under strict ecological limiting conditions. This system possesses a large capability to adapt to historic circumstances, it is less bureaucratic and more decentralised than socialist alternatives, and other alternatives – such as Murray Bookchin's – do not seem feasible. The free market economy has produced an immense increase in living standards, technological innovation, and unpreceded development of the productive forces; only this system has no built-in brakes. By taking a range of legal measures and by consequently introducing financial incentives the free market economy must be restructured in such a way that environmentally detrimental production will become unprofitable and that pollution will be prohibited or will cost a lot of money; for instance, high fines/penalties for the breaking of environmental laws; refusal to accept any longer the passing on of environmental costs, and making environmentally unfriendly products far more expensive and because of that more difficult to sell. A clear start must be made with an ecologically adjusted accounting system to include all ecological costs. Gradually the free market society can adapt itself to the demands of modern times and develop in the direction of an ecologically oriented market economy: 'a green market economy' (Eckersley 1992: 140–5; Eckersley 1993: 1–25). Only such an economy will be able to prevent the market's inbuilt imperative to exponential growth, its purely economic valuation of non-humans and its disregard of the future.

The second point introduces five basic principles for action on the different levels of society: the prevention principle; the precautionary principle; the judicial liability principle; the 'polluter pays' principle; the dealing with nature cautiously principle.

The prevention principle

The prevention of pollution should be preferred to the clearing away of waste; so, for instance, this would mean using less packaging, introducing returnable deposit systems and inherently clean production techniques,

201

closing production cycles and decreasing the consumption of goods in general.

The precautionary principle

The precautionary principle (*Vorsorgeprinzip*) must consequently be taken into account (Weale 1992: 79–93). A new attitude must be fostered so that measures are taken 'beforehand' to anticipate ecological damage in the future and to avoid risks. This principle also protects future generations. It follows that methods of energy supply, such as nuclear power and forms of production and chemical substances whose environmental safety cannot be made plausible in advance, should be rejected. As in the case of the approval of medicines, if the precautionary principle became the norm regarding ecological effects the producer would have to provide convincing evidence of the non-detrimental character of the fabricated substances. From this principle flows a systematic reversal of the burden of proof. Producers have to prove in advance that they are not going to pollute in unacceptable ways; the authorities do not have to prove that unacceptable forms of pollution will be created.

The precautionary principle will make sure that the producers cannot hide behind the usual argument that 'technological solutions to solve environmental problems will be found later'. The environmental pollution that is produced must – because of the many contingent factors – be controllable with the existing level of technology.

The judicial liability principle

If it is accepted that for purely pragmatic reasons the free market economy will be maintained, there are good reasons to provide ample opportunity for the appropriate 'liberal strategies' and to combat environmental degradation with the help of the notion of strict liability for property.

A strong defender of this approach is Murray Rothbard (1978) in his *For a New Liberty*. This book may be full of right-wing liberal rhetoric, but the reader who is prepared to look beyond this can discern several quite useful ideas to oppose pollution. Rothbard argues that a large number of environmental problems can be fought effectively by focusing on private property and legal liability. Take the example of air pollution:

> in the case of air pollution we are dealing not so much with private property *in the air* as with protecting private property in one's lungs, fields, and orchards. The vital fact about air pollution is that the polluter sends unwanted and unbidden pollutants – from smoke to nuclear fallout to sulfur-oxides – *through* the air and into the lungs of innocent victims, as well as onto their material property. All such emanations which injure person or property constitute aggression

against the private property of the victims. Air pollution, after all, is just as much aggression as committing arson against another's property or injuring him [*sic*] physically. Air pollution that injures others is aggression pure and simple. The major function of government – of courts and police – is to stop aggression; instead, the government has failed in this task and failed grievously to exercise its defense function against air pollution.

(Rothbard 1978: 256–7)

The idea behind this is that pollution is damaging private property and is injuring the bodies or possessions of innocent citizens. Where individual property rights are infringed – fully within the reasoning of traditional liberal thought – the victim has the right to go to court and to ask the judge for compensation, either financial or, for instance, in the form of a prohibition.

Some considerable problems are attached to the idea of punishing aggression against the private property of the victims of pollution. There is the problem of causality, the question of long-drawn-out lawsuits, the fact that the abatement of pollution always occurs retrospectively and the difficulty that a powerless injured party (a citizen with affected lungs) is expected to win against often extremely powerful organisations that are well able to provide themselves with the best legal defence available. Despite these obvious problems there seems to be room for an evident 'enlargement' of legal liability in cases of pollution. A preventive effect can be expected when companies and individual polluters realise that there is a good chance that injured parties will go to court to protect their property rights – in the form of a healthy body and the maintenance of possessions.

The 'polluter pays' principle

Apart from the enlargement of legal liability consequent steps must be taken to give substance to the 'polluter pays' principle. In numerous areas there is simply no adequate relation between the ecological costs and the price that is asked for a service or product. Whoever buys a car nowadays does not in any way pay for the energy that was needed to produce the vehicle, the pollution that is caused by the factory to the surroundings and the recycling of the automobile in the destruction phase. When citizens use their cars, they pay – entirely contrary to what the auto lobby is arguing – relatively little money for the air pollution produced, the damage to the landscape caused by the motorways, and of course the damage inflicted on national health (CEST 1988:10).

This is only one awkward and disagreeable example of the relatively low prices that have to be paid for environmentally polluting forms of production and consumption in western liberal democracies. In the end a serious start will have to be made with the assessment of ecological costs of services and goods and the passing on of these costs through prices (an ecotax). The consumers will then get a clear insight into the ecological soundness of their 'consumption' and will be stimulated to opt for those alternatives that are less of a burden on the environment. The advantages of an ecotax are as follows:

1 It is a market-oriented instrument that can be used to influence consumer behaviour.
2 It conforms to the 'polluter pays' principle.
3 It requires relatively few regulations and will create fewer maintenance and enforcement problems, as is the case in a system of 'command and control'.
4 The introduction of an ecotax will lead to the design and construction of products with reduced pollution levels (because these will be easier to sell).
5 An ecotax will reduce the pollution, while in principle the idea of individual freedom of choice in consumption is maintained.

The dealing with nature cautiously principle

As well as this it is worth emphasising the importance of attaching a central value to the principle of 'dealing with nature in a careful way'. As is also pointed out by Murray Bookchin (1988) and Arne Naess (1989), natural ecosystems are extremely untransparent, complex and elusive. Humanity should not cherish the idea of 'controlling' nature. In most cases the coherent knowledge that is required for adequate interference with nature is lacking. As Andrew Dobson (1990) has explained, this is an argument for treating the earth most carefully and cautiously and – in the field of interventions in nature – for adopting a modest and 'conservative' attitude:

> The implied impossibility of knowing enough is crucial to the Green suggestion that we adopt a hands-off approach to the environment. If we cannot know the outcome of an intervention in the environment but suspect that it might be dangerous, then we are best advised, from a Green point of view, not to intervene at all. In this respect Green politics places itself firmly against drawing-board design and thus in the realm of what is generally considered to be conservative politics – siding with Edmund Burke against Tom Paine, so to speak.
>
> (Dobson 1990: 79)

The third point is that a gradual restructuring of the liberal democratic state will have to take place, making use of valuable elements of ecological visions of 'anarchist' political thinkers like William Godwin, Peter Kropotkin, William Morris and Murray Bookchin. Yet, whoever opts for a green market

204

economy – as I have proposed – must also be prepared to renounce anarchist lines of thought in some respects. According to these ideas the centralised and pyramidally organised liberal democratic state must be rejected and abolished in principle. Anarchist ideas suggest a fully de-centralised, federally structured organisational form, that makes possible the self-government of individuals and local communities. Such an anarch-ist organisational structure emanates from individual freedom and auto-nomy and from the principle of providing opportunity for members of the organisation to govern their own lives and to share responsibility.

The anarchist political thinkers dare to dismantle the state organisation because of the fact that in their proposals the economic order undergoes a revolutionary change as well. In their vision the state organisation and the economic order are intricately related. Only after the introduction of a fully fledged anarchist economic order, which is based on communal ownership of the means of production and where self-governing labour associations take care of production, would the introduction of a completely anarchist political organisation be appropriate. Such a federalistic and decentralised organisation will, according to the anarchist thinkers, not have to play an extensive and coercive role. The main reason for this is that the ensemble of labour associations will not produce for profits, but only to meet the existing societal needs.

The unconditional introduction of a similar 'completely anarchist polit-ical organisation', in combination with a green market economy, is most unwise from the point of view of sound environmental protection. Capitalist enterprises will behave in a more environmentally friendly way only when they are persuaded by a strong and strictly norm-giving state that is prepared to prosecute, capable of doing so, and if necessary ready to impose severe punishment. Accepting a green market economy implies the need for a strictly regulatory state that establishes and sanctions the ultimate goals and conditions for a general environmental policy, in view of the earlier ascertained inherently environmentally hazardous behaviour of many producers, who will always try to avoid additional ecological costs. Taking this situation into account, an actively regulating state that also forms a strong countervailing power to the influence of the entrepreneurs is inevitable. The conclusion must be that the choice of a green market economy entails the rejection of ideas that are determined by the anarchist goal of complete abolition of the state. Consequently, the central question is not whether the liberal democratic state must be abolished, but how this state can be *adapted* in such a way that more effective environmental policies can be carried out and that it can become more democratic: how can the liberal democratic state be changed into an environmentally protecting and radically democratic state?

At the same time I would like to propose – in the line of reasoning of the American political scientist Robert Dahl – to continue to use the anarchist ideas as a critical touchstone and resource for inspiration. Dahl (1989) argues that the anarchists rightly point to the dangers of state coercion and to the problem that in practice it is impossible to rule on the basis of the 'consent' of all participants. According to him anarchism adequately shows that actually all states are imperfect. Anarchism provides an interesting criterium to 'judge' states. To what extent do they maximise 'consent' and minimise 'coercion'? He suggests:

> In my view, the best possible state would be one that would minimize coercion and maximize consent, within limits set by historical conditions and the pursuit of other values, including happiness, freedom, and justice.

> (Dahl 1989: 51)

What does this mean for the organisation of the state? In my opinion the direction for the future is that of a 'telescopic ecostate', which protects the environment to keep society liveable (in particular with a view to future generations, including non-human ones), which is maximally based on consent and which applies coercion minimally. What are the basic characteristics of such a telescopic ecostate?

This kind of state is flexible and can shove in and out like a telescope. In the starting position this type of state is pushed in, decentralised. Wherever this is possible, this state finds itself in a decentralised position. Centralisation is accepted only when it is really necessary. Perhaps this is the most important lesson of the anarchist-ecological thinkers; 'decentralisation if possible, centralisation if necessary'.

The scale of the environmental problems is decisive for the level of decision making in a telescopic ecostate. This state model offers the opportunity to solve small-scale and local environmental problems on a decentralised level, on the level of the municipality, the region or province. For national problems the national state will be the most adequate administrative unit. For cross-border environmental issues effective competence must be given to supra-national entities and for global problems international organisations must be created which must be able to implement efficacious environmental policies (Goodin 1992: 147–69).

Just like a telescope this kind of state can be 'attuned' precisely and is suited for fine-setting. After getting a first idea of specific environmental problems the state can either shove in or out. By 'trial and error' and deliberately 'experimenting' with the definition, it can be decided what policy areas and functions it is better to decentralise or to centralise. This means that in specific policy areas the state will find itself in the most shoved-in position and in other policy fields in the most shoved-out position (centralisation, the delegation of competence to international organisations).

In order to ascertain the democratic level of a telescopic ecostate, combinations of direct participation and political representation can be adopted. The opportunities for participation at a local level might be enlarged to give substance to the old but valuable ideal of citizenship; of public spaces of freedom, in which the members of the political community can exert influence. For the regional, provincial, national, and international administrative units, forms of political representation promise to be the most effective and to be the most workable proposition from a democratic perspective.

Similar to a shovable telescope this type of state is more inclined 'to give in', than to stay in a fixed and unyielding position, when one pushes on it. A freedom-oriented state that wants to avoid an ecodictatorship will have to approach the environmental problems via the use of coercive measures as little as possible, but will have to concentrate primarily on the creation of situations and conditions that will make it more attractive to the citizens to make environmentally friendly choices. This kind of state will not prohibit people from buying products that are detrimental to the environment, but will take care that the environmental consequences of certain goods and services will be systematically passed on to prices by way of levies and taxes, and that sustainable and recyclable goods become relatively cheap. In this way the individual's freedom of choice in consumption is upheld in essence, while the environment is protected.

Like a telescope this state model is focused on bringing closer what lies in the far distance. A telescopic ecostate has a longer time perspective and spots the interests of coming generations. Again and again the question is put – what does this policy decision imply for the longer term, for the generation that will come after us? This emanates from the consideration that we live on earth only temporarily and have responsibilities towards our descendants. In a telescopic ecostate the interests and rights of future generations are taken into account: 'our concern cannot be only for our children and grandchildren but must be for remoter generations and for the planet as a whole' (Naess 1989: 127).

The fourth point of departure for an ecological restructuring of society is a receptive (but not uncritical) attitude towards technological innovations. For several environmental issues adequate technological solutions are available, and it would be unwise not to make use of these opportunities. Why not deploy the most environmentally friendly, resource-saving and waste-preventing modern technologies? What is wrong with technological developments such as inherently clean production processes, efficient forms of energy generation, promising means of transport like electrical cars charged with energy from sun power stations or 'fuel cells'. In particular the 'ecotechnologies' that Murray Bookchin pays much attention to seem to have high potential (Bookchin 1990: 105–26).

Nowadays our daily lives are filled with technology, from the telephone

207

and desk lamp, to the personal computer we work with. Technology can be extremely useful and can be used for different goals. Initially computers, for instance, were a technology for the military, multi-nationals and large institutes. Computers have now become a technology for almost everybody, for students, journalists, scientists, hobbyists, and so on.

This may also happen to environmental technologies. The development of solar cells was stimulated by NASA (US National Aeronautics and Space Administration) in order to provide spacecrafts with sufficient energy. Now solar cells show a high efficiency, can be produced relatively cheaply and are useful to ordinary citizens. Builders of windmills have learned enormously from the findings of aircraft designers. In the Netherlands the bicycle manufacturers profit from the inventions which are made by chemical industries (e.g. carbon fibre), and apply environment- and energy-saving techniques that were developed by car manufacturers. However, a permanent discussion on the need and desirability of certain technological developments would be advisable in society: 'A public debate, lobbying and interference with the clash of interests provide an opportunity to influence technology. After all, technology develops like a social process' (Van der Pouw Kraan 1992: 82). The need for public, open and democratic debate on technological developments is of great importance.

Environmentally congenial technology can be stimulated by issuing strict ecological requirements for consumption goods. A good example of this is the Californian emission and consumption norms for road vehicles. These have provoked all kinds of technical improvements in engines and have paved the way for the introduction of effective three-way catalysts. The latest legislation in California stipulates that

> in 1998 2% of the cars sold must belong to the category of Zero Emission Vehicles (ZEV's) and only electrical cars can satisfy this norm. In 2010 at least 10% of the cars must belong to that category. If a manufacturer does not comply with these obligations, he will be excluded from the state.
>
> (Oosterbaan 1992: 20)

The consequence of all this is that car manufacturers, with the application of the most modern technologies, have started to design electro-cars, that have a high energy efficiency and a large range of action. In some cases it is very possible to exert influence on technology and to steer it in a socially and ecologically sound direction.

The last point of departure that I would like to formulate – after William Morris – is that of looking for well-balanced equilibriums and abandoning the hurried pace that characterises western society. It seems vital to find a balance between the tempo that is enforced by the economic system and the pace that seems more natural to humans. Economic growth has taken place at an accelerating speed which has caused imbalance between material development and environmental conservation. Often one discerns people that are ceaselessly restless and who are incited by unhealthy work pressures, a deeply anchored careerism, or a hard-to-restrain possessiveness (Macpherson 1975: chs 1, 5 and 6).

The restless character of our society is increased by the fact that often countries economically depend on foreign countries. A small country like the Netherlands is trapped into a competition battle with other industrial societies like Germany, France, Britain, the USA and Japan. But when every society is kept on the run by the competing countries to work harder, to produce more goods, to raise the tempo, ultimately the 'tempo spiral' will become disastrous. Let our societies set an example and search intelligently for well-balanced equilibriums between economy and ecology, exertion and relaxation, hurry and rest. Some day there must be a society that will break with the contemporary spirals of growth, frenetic pace and restlessness.

CONCLUSION: OPTING FOR A TELESCOPIC ECOSTATE

The central conclusion of this chapter is that the development of the environmental crisis must inevitably lead to consequences for the role and structure of the state in the future. The erection of an absolute power that can take all steps to protect the environment is in no way a feasible solution. In order to ensure a high quality of life the freedom of the individual is as essential as a clean environment. It is equally inadvisable, however, entirely to renounce a powerful state, centralisation, or the market economy, and to rely instead on a utopian anarchist organisation, radical decentralisation and a system of communal ownership of the means of production, in which small-scale self-governing associations take care of production. Such a radical green blueprint is likely to have detrimental effects on the environment. Despite my continued sympathy for these kinds of ideas, I have to conclude that the decentralised, participatory politics envisioned by the radical greens does not prove to be a plausible alternative. It presupposes a complete reconstruction of economy, society and state and will most probably produce all the well-known, negative (unintended) consequences of utopian engineering. Anyone who wants to steer in the direction of a sustainable society and prevent the drawbacks of utopian blueprints – either ecoauthoritarian or ecoanarchist – is bound to arrive at a position of consciously co-ordinated and well-designed reforming steps. In the longer term these will alter the ecological structure of society and will lead in the radical new direction of a green market economy, which, in combination with a freedom-oriented telescopic ecostate, will deal with potential environmental problems on the same scale that they occur; minimising coercion and maximising consent. Does this essentially place me among the political reformists? Scarcely. The steps are reformatory, the direction is revolutionary, as Arne Naess wrote (Naess 1989: 156). An ecological society is best not constructed according to a detailed blueprint, but will be the consequence of a well-designed and continuous process of experimenting and restructuring.

ACKNOWLEDGEMENTS

This chapter builds on earlier work on political philosophy, environment and the state, in particular my *Politiek, Milieu en Vrijheid* (Utrecht: Jan van Arkel, Utrecht, 1993). My thanks are due to Brian Doherty who read the first draft of this chapter and who made corrections to the English. John Barry and Grahame Lock gave valuable comments on a later version.

REFERENCES

Adriaanse, A. (1990) *Milieukerngegegevens Nederland*, The Hague: Uitgeverij Ministerie van VROM.

Berlin, I. (1971) *Four Essays on Liberty*, Oxford: Oxford University Press.

Bookchin, M. (1988) *Toward an Ecological Society*, Montreal: Black Rose Books
—— (1990) *Post-Scarcity Anarchism*, Montreal: Black Rose Books.

Centrum voor Energiebesparing en Schone Technologie (CEST) (1988) *Waardering van negatieve externe effecten van het autoverkeer*, Delft: CEST Press.

Dahl, R. A. (1989) *Democracy and its Critics*, New Haven, Conn.: Yale University Press.

Dobson, A. (1990) *Green Political Thought*, London: Unwin Hyman.

Eckersley, R. (1992) *Environmentalism and Political Theory*, London: UCL Press.
—— (1993) 'Disciplining the Market, Calling in the State', unpublished paper for the ECPR conference Leyden, 2–8 April 1993.

Goodin, R. E. (1992) *Green Political Theory*, Cambridge: Polity.

Groen, M. (1991) 'Milieu-inspectie', in *NRC Handelsblad*, Rotterdam: Dagblad Unie.

GroenLinks (1991) *Op weg naar een groene belastingheffing*, The Hague: Tweede Kamerfractie GroenLinks.

Gunsteren, H. R. van (1978) 'Politiek nieuws van het planningfront', in F. G. J. Derkinderen and J. Kooiman (eds) *Maatschappij geörienteerd besturen*, Leiden: Stenfert Kroese.

Hardin, G. (1973) 'The Tragedy of the Commons', in H. E. Daly (ed.) *Toward a Steady State Economy*, San Francisco: Freeman.

Hobbes, T. (1974) *Leviathan*, Harmondsworth: Penguin.

Macpherson, C. B. (1975) *The Theory of Possessive Individualism*, Oxford: Oxford University Press.

Naess, A. (1989) *Ecology, Community and Lifestyle*, Cambridge: Cambridge University Press.

Oosterbaan, W. (1992) 'Electrocar enige milieu-alternatief', in *NRC Handelsblad*, Rotterdam: Dagblad Unie.

Ophuls, W. (1973), 'Leviathan or Oblivion?', in H. E. Daly (ed.) *Toward a Steady State Economy*, San Francisco: Freeman.

Popper, K. (1974) *The Open Society and its Enemies*, vol. I, London: Routledge & Kegan Paul.

Pouw Kraan, P. van der (1992) 'Het revolutionaire potentieel van de schroevedraaier', in Writers' Collective Mascarpone (ed.) *Gebroken Wit, Politiek van de kleine verhalen*, Amsterdam: Uitgeverij Ravijn.

PvdA (1989) *Kiezen voor kwaliteit*, PvdA election programme, Amsterdam: PvdA Press.

Rothbard, M. (1978) *For a New Liberty*, New York: Collier.

Taylor, M. (1982) *Community, Anarchy and Liberty*, Cambridge: Cambridge University Press.

Vereniging Milieudefensie (1991) *Zicht op een beter milieu*, position paper, Amsterdam: Milieudefensie Press.

Weale, A. (1992) *The New Politics of Pollution*, Manchester: Manchester University Press.

Wijkhuizen, H. (1992) 'De mythe van decentralisatie doorgeprikt', unpublished seminar paper, Department of Political Science, University of Leyden.

11

GREENING LIBERAL DEMOCRACY

The rights discourse revisited

Robyn Eckersley

The apparent inability of western liberal democracies to provide a lasting resolution of the ecological crisis raises a question for greens that has long preoccupied democratic socialists:[1] if democracy is a non-negotiable element of green political theory, then how might greens secure their political goals by means of a decision-making framework that is supposedly open ended?

Liberal democratic theorists have generally not had to wrestle with this kind of problem. According to the conventional 'liberal line', no social group or class should decide the morals or prescribe the 'good life' of the citizenry – such action would be tantamount to totalitarianism. As Beetham reminds us, liberal democracy is anti-paternalistic, resting on the liberal epistemological premise that there is no superior knowledge or ultimate truth concerning the public good; it is up to citizens, and their elected representatives, freely to decide for themselves the meaning of the public good (Beetham 1992: 42). The institutions of liberal democracy must therefore be procedurally neutral and able to accommodate a diversity of opinion.

According to this standard liberal democratic view, there is really only one legitimate response that may be adopted by ecologically concerned citizens over and above their right to vote: lawful political persuasion. That is, ecologically concerned citizens may legitimately seek to enlist support for environmental goals through the exercise of the basic political rights of freedom of expression, movement and association along with the right to bring legal proceedings. In effect, this means utilising the conventional channels of political participation – public debates, the formation of citizens' campaigns and political parties, peaceful demonstrations, legal actions and so forth. However, at the end of the day, if a 'green majority' cannot be mustered at the crucial time of political voting (whether at general elections or in the representative assembly), or if democratically elected governments otherwise remain unpersuaded, then so be it – whatever the ecological consequences. People must be 'free' to make ecologically bad decisions; the alternative is ecological paternalism.

There are three interrelated lines of argument that might be offered in response to this standard defence of liberal democracy. The first is to argue that liberal democracy has not fulfilled its promise, that the practice of liberal democracy does not conform to the theory (this is the familiar socialist 'immanent critique'). A second response might be to argue that, in any event, the theory and practice of liberal democracy is far from neutral – it is anti-ecological. What is needed is a stronger, and more ecologically informed, theory and practice of democracy. A third response might be to take issue with the supposed distinction between political values/goals and democratic procedures. Here, it may be argued that there is no such thing as procedural neutrality when it comes to designing decision-making frameworks, decision rules or constitutions for that matter.

Combining and developing these three responses further, it might be pointed out that theories of democracy are intimately related to theories of human autonomy and justice, which provide the fundamental justification and ground rules of democracy while also constraining the range of choices open to citizens and representative assemblies. Given that liberal democratic ground rules were developed in earlier cornucopian times that no longer hold today, then perhaps it is time to re-evaluate and reframe notions of human autonomy and justice in ways that reflect our changed ecological setting and understanding. If it is accepted that some kind of re-evaluation and reframing of the basic principles of autonomy and justice are required, then it must also be accepted that some appropriate readjustment of the institutions and procedures of democracy may need to take place.

In debates about the possible greening of democracy, the green movement is presented with a kind of 'democratic paradox': any practical attempt to move towards a stronger and more ecologically informed democratic alternative to liberal democracy must necessarily begin by utilising existing liberal democratic institutions and regulative ideals. In short, it is necessary to rebuild the political ship while still at sea.

Such a project might begin by enlisting some of the fundamental regulative ideals and institutions of liberal democracy in ways that challenge and gradually transform not only the form, style and content of democratic deliberation but also society's relationship with the rest of nature. Such a strategy would combine an immanent ecological critique of liberal democracy with a creative refashioning of familiar liberal democratic institutions.

This chapter will take up the challenge of enlisting and refashioning one particular liberal democratic institution, namely, rights. In particular, the chapter will explore the possibilities of developing an environmental rights debate and associated political campaign. This discussion will be largely confined to human environmental rights. I have explored the possibilities and problems associated with enlisting the rights discourse on behalf of non-human species elsewhere (Eckersley 1996) and do not propose to develop this aspect of the argument here. Suffice to say that those who may be concerned about the predominantly human-centred focus of this chapter should consult the companion paper.[2]

The choice of the rights discourse has been prompted not simply by strategic considerations and by some of the inadequacies of popular notions of green democracy, both of which will be detailed below. The rights discourse has also been enlisted as a means of *connecting* democratic concerns and ecological concerns at the level of principle. That is, if it is accepted that the rights discourse has provided a means of connecting liberalism with democracy – morally, politically and legally – then could a reformulated rights discourse, grounded in a *prima facie* respect for the autonomy of *all* life-forms, also serve as a linchpin between green values and democracy? In taking up this challenge, attention will be directed to the adaptability of the form and composition of traditional arguments that have linked liberalism and democracy via a rights discourse, as well as the possible scope and content of environmental rights.

WHY RIGHTS?

To understand the appeal of the rights discourse to the green movement, and the service it may perform, it is necessary to understand both the ecological critique of liberal democracy and the brief history of green debates about possible democratic alternatives. I hope to show how environmental rights may partially redress a range of 'democratic deficits' in existing liberal democracies (this is the immediate, practical advantage) while also providing one plank in the theory of a stronger and greener democracy. As we shall see, the central challenge for green theorists is to find ways of ensuring that ecological concerns are given more systematic consideration in political deliberations. Meeting this challenge requires, *inter alia*, enhancing the opportunities for what Christoff (1994) has called 'ecological citizenship' – informed, democratic action in defence of the local, regional and global environment.

The central problem with the liberal democratic state is that it systematically under-represents ecological concerns. It does this in two ways. First, it represents only the existing citizens of territorially bounded political communities and therefore has no strong incentive not to externalise ecological costs, both spatially and temporally. In this respect, it is systematically biased against the interests of 'non-citizens', or what might be called 'the new environmental constituency', that is, all those who may be seriously affected by environmental decisions made within the polity but who cannot vote or otherwise participate in the political deliberations and decisions of the polity (I have in mind here non-compatriots, non-human species and future generations).

Of course, the ecological interests of non-citizens may be vicariously represented by citizens within the polity. Indeed, this is the only way in which they can be practically represented. However, the second problem with the liberal democratic state is that it provides very limited opportunities for such vicarious representation; indeed, it systematically under-represents not only the interests of 'non-citizens' but also the ecological welfare of its own citizens. That is, within the territories of liberal democratic states, the 'public interest' in environmental protection fares particularly badly in the political bargaining processes that characterise 'actually existing liberal democracies'. Environmental protection largely depends on public interest advocacy that is able to defend long-term, generalisable interests rather than short-term particular interests. However, liberal democracies pre-suppose partisan political competition between selfish actors in the struggle for 'who gets what, when and how'. Such partisan competition places groups and organisations that are well resourced, well organised and strategically located at a distinct advantage to poorly resourced, poorly organised and dispersed groups, such as community environmental groups. Those taking up public interest advocacy, such as environmental organisations, also become vulnerable to liberal democratic framing devices (employed by the media, political opponents and the state) that 'reduce' environmental claims into a format that is susceptible to compromise. That is, within the political bargaining processes that takes place between government and organised political elites, environmental organisations are characterised, like private lobby organisations, as merely pursuing the 'sectional' or 'vested interests' of their members. Such interests must therefore be 'balanced' against the claims of other interest groups in the corporatist negotiations, political compromises, and incremental policy shifts that characterise liberal democracies. The upshot is that the longer-term public interest in environmental protection is systematically traded-off against the more immediate demands of capital and (sometimes) labour.

Indeed, it is precisely this process (and expectation) of trade-off that has been inscribed into the state agencies and decision rules which govern environmental decision making. That is, the major innovations to en-vironmental law and administration that took place in the early 1970s in most OECD countries have largely followed a utilitarian rather than a rights-based path (see, for example, Tarlock 1988; Mackay 1994). Building on the analysis and framework of modern welfare economics, these innovations established new techniques of risk assessment or impact assessment based on cost-benefit analysis, while maintaining tight executive control of major environmental decisions. In Australia, for example, most environmental impact legislation confers considerable administrative and ministerial dis-cretion and extremely limited litigation rights on the part of the public.[3] Given the scientific uncertainty associated with many ecological problems, the many different perceptions of environmental risk, the difficulties in attributing blame and responsibility, the costs of the 'mopping up oper-ation', the existence of conflicting political priorities and the short time horizons of liberal democracies (corresponding, at most, to election periods) it is hardly surprising that the environment is regularly traded-off against what appear to be more urgent and/or straightforward political demands.

It is precisely this utilitarian framework of environmental decision making (which ultimately furnishes only 'advice' to the executive) that makes environmental rights a more attractive alternative. That is, pressing environmental claims as rights is intended to make such claims non-negotiable – or at least, less negotiable than they currently are. As Stone (1987: 54) points out, 'We do not conduct a cost-benefit analysis every time someone claims a right to free speech'; this is because the right to free speech is considered sacrosanct, whatever the cost. It serves to 'trump' competing claims for utility maximisation (Dworkin 1984). Similarly, whereas the cost of strict pollution prevention (as distinct from incremental abatement) might outweigh the benefits of unpolluted air and waterways in a utilitarian calculus, such costs could not be used as an adequate defence in an action based on the infringement of an environmental right to unpolluted air and water. The introduction of environmental rights clearly has the potential to alter radically the established framework of decision making in favour of 'the environment'.

Whether the potential of environmental citizenship rights can be realised remains, of course, an open question. This chapter seeks to canvass the possibilities and address some of the predictable objections to environmental rights while also showing how rights might serve to connect ecological and democratic concerns at the level of principle, rather than merely contingently or instrumentally.

THE GREEN RESPONSE: STRONGER DEMOCRACY

Many green activists have responded to the shortcomings of liberal democracy by disparaging and rejecting conventional liberal democratic channels of political participation and, in some cases, the rule of law. The growth of mass environmental protests, non-violent civil disobedience and direct action, which began in the 1960s and has continued through succeeding decades, is symptomatic of a deep and widespread frustration and dissatisfaction with the reactive and piecemeal environmental measures emanating from the liberal democratic parliamentary process. In some cases, most notably in the United States, this frustration has prompted the practice of 'monkeywrenching' or ecological sabotage (Foreman 1991).

Many of the contributors to the early wave of ecopolitical theorising in the 1970s have been similarly disgruntled with liberal democracy. However, some of these theorists (such as Ophuls 1973, 1977; Hardin 1972; Heilbroner 1974) looked to ecoauthoritarian solutions rather than to mass protests, civil disobedience or monkeywrenching. Reacting to the 'limits-to-growth' literature of the early 1970s, these 'doomsday' ecopolitical theorists warned that we faced a choice between 'Leviathan or Oblivion' (Ophuls 1973), that the urgency of the ecological crisis demanded tight, centralised government environmental regulation, energy and resource rationing, population control and a suspension of normal channels of political participation where these were seen to interfere with a swift and decisive governmental responses to the crisis (Heilbroner 1974).

However, by the time green political theory began self-consciously to develop in the late 1970s, the emphasis had shifted to finding 'stronger' forms of democracy than liberal democracy. The decision-making rules and frameworks that have been typically defended in green movement and party circles since that time have usually followed a string of variations on a participatory democracy theme (e.g., consensus, grassroots democracy, direct democracy, local and/or 'face-to-face' democracy). More deliberative, pedagogical forms of free and impartial public debate have been defended as being more conducive to securing long-range environmental protection than what Lindblom (1965) has called the 'partisan mutual adjustment' that is expected and encouraged in existing liberal democracies (Dryzek 1987). Deliberative or 'discursive' democracy is defended as superior because it seeks to educate through dialogue and transform political opinion through reasoned debate, rather than simply aggregate the sum of unchallenged individual desires. It is more demanding than liberal democracy; it requires more time, patience and information and it requires citizens to be generous and 'public spirited'.

According to Miller (1992), deliberative democracy is more likely to be achieved in small-scale communities or among trusted friends than in mass electorates (attended by competitive 'party machines'). Locally scaled decision-making structures are also defended as being more flexible and more attuned to feedback signals from the local environment (Dryzek 1987). However, Dryzek acknowledges that while 'small is beautiful' in terms of flexibility, resilience and local participation, radically decentralised decision-making units are unlikely to achieve the levels of co-operation and co-ordination that are required to solve complex transboundary problems beyond the local level (1987: 228).

Given the characteristics and optimal conditions of deliberative democracy, it is indeed uncertain how far it can be generalised for society (and international society) as a whole. As Held points out, 'The classical participatory model cannot easily be adapted to stretch across space and time' (1992: 19). While it promises to redress some of the anti-ecological biases of liberal democracy (i.e., by fostering debate over generalisable interests, by introducing greater flexibility, by calling on local knowledge and responsibility, and by lengthening the time horizon of, and time available for, deliberation), it fails to provide a robust model of co-ordination between what we might call 'deliberative communities'. Moreover, it is

217

sometimes difficult to determine whether deliberative democracy is meant to replace or merely augment liberal democracy or whether the models of democracy developed for the movement or the party are also meant to serve as models for society as a whole. There also remains considerable disagreement among green theorists as to whether the state is likely to play an enabling or disabling role in facilitating stronger forms of democracy (compare, for example the prescriptions of bio-regionalists and social ecologists to those of ecosocialists).

More significantly, however, many of the green arguments for stronger democracy fail to confront the question of power. Given existing social inequities and resource, knowledge and power disparities among different social classes and groups, it is unclear how the abstract norms of free and impartial public discussion will provide a check against the power and interests of elites. If it is accepted that small communities can be dominated by local elites – just as nation-states can be dominated by national elites – then should we not refashion democratic institutions in ways that acknowledge and seek to redress power disparities at both levels? That is, should not green institutional design start from the premise of power disparities rather than from a regulative ideal that is unlikely ever to obtain in practice? This point has also been made by feminist critics of the ideal speech situation (for a recent discussion, see Hayward 1994). Given that there are numerous practical obstacles in the way of free and impartial democratic deliberation, surely it is better to focus on the real, rather than the ideal, contexts in which political communication takes place (Hayward 1994: 3).

Political struggles for further 'democratisation' and liberation have often involved struggles for political recognition and inclusion via the extension of rights (in this respect, it is surprising how silent the green literature has been on this subject). The extension and development of the rights discourse has enabled more systematic political consideration to be given to the interests and concerns of hitherto marginalised groups and classes. In this chapter, I suggest that environmental rights might provide one institution that will enable more systematic consideration to be given to ecological concerns. However, before exploring the possible scope and content of such rights, let us first explore how the rights discourse has served classical liberalism.

RIGHTS AND LIBERALISM

The rights discourse has served a treble duty for liberalism – moral, political and legal. That is, it has provided a moral foundation for limited government by the consent of the people; it has provided a successful rhetorical device for the political recognition of a new, rising class (the bourgeoisie) and a political challenge to the existing class (the aristocracy); and it has provided a legal institution by which certain forms of conduct, or more precisely, certain social and economic relationships between people, have been sanctioned or penalised by the state.

For example, John Locke, in his *Two Treatises of Government* of 1690, argued that humans possessed 'natural' and 'inalienable' rights to life, liberty and property. Although these rights were held to belong to all human beings 'by nature', independently of positive law (this is the moral dimension of the argument), representative government gave them political and legal recognition. The construction of political and legal rights through the social contract thus facilitated the enjoyment, and protected against the infringement, of 'natural' or 'basic' rights. For Locke, rights provided both a justification for representative government and a limitation on government.

Of course, the moral, political and legal dimensions of rights are rarely separated out in practice and they are sometimes conflated in theory. It is well known that Bentham rejected natural rights as 'nonsense on stilts'. Rights, he argued, were created by convention and by positive law, not by God or Nature – an argument that is now widely accepted. However, Bentham's criticism applied only to the way in which Locke constructed his moral argument (indeed, Bentham's argument provided an explicit recognition of the political and legal applications of the rights discourse).

While the classical liberal rights discourse has served to challenge existing power relations, it has also been used to construct and sustain new power relations (Stammer 1993). It is precisely because the liberal rights discourse serves to connect liberalism with democracy that it has this 'double edge': it has been used as an ideological smokescreen to blur the differences between the theory and practice of rights and it has been used as a powerful critical tool to expose these differences. In particular, the liberal rights discourse has been used by socialists to wage an 'immanent social critique' of liberalism, which has exposed stark discrepancies between the formal existence of rights and the substantive enjoyment of rights.

Nowadays, partly as a result of the socialist 'immanent critique', the rhetoric of rights has expanded well beyond its classical liberal formulation. Rights now form part of ordinary language and a central part of the discourse of *Realpolitik*, providing a 'court of appeal' in which the justice of actions or proposed actions may be judged. As political rhetoric, rights are usually invoked not as something that is God-given or 'natural' but merely as statements concerning the standard of conduct that we should expect from citizens, communities or the state.

In the post-Second World War period, the human rights discourse has expanded well beyond the scope of the American Bill of Rights of 1787 and the 'Declaration of the Rights of Man and the Citizen' proclaimed by the French National Assembly of 1789. Alongside these more traditional political and civil rights (known as the first generation of rights) the 1948 United Nations Universal Declaration of Human Rights and the 1966

International Covenants on Civil and Political Rights and on Economic, Social and Cultural Rights have vindicated a much broader, second generation of human rights. These include a right to 'medical care and necessary social services' (Article 25) and a right to 'protection against unemployment' (Article 23). More controversially, the UN Declaration on the Right to Development (1986) has embodied the aspirations of developing countries (and more recently, Eastern Europe) in a third generation of 'development rights'.

These three generations of human rights (civil and political, economic and social, and development) reflect a discordant philosophical rights heritage that has been associated with three different political revolutions and associated philosophies: the bourgeois revolution of the late eighteenth century, the socialist revolution of the early twentieth century and the rise of the welfare state, and the anti-colonialist revolution of the post-Second World War years (Marks 1980–1). Would an environmental rights discourse provide perhaps a fourth generation of human rights that might also serve to recontextualise and qualify existing human rights in ways that reflect the late twentieth century political revolution and philosophy of environmentalism?

This last question is admittedly speculative but by no means unthinkable. While there is not (yet) any formal recognition of environmental human rights in international law, talk of such rights has certainly been in the wind for some time and there are now numerous examples of official and unofficial international declarations and drafts which embody the notion of a human right to a sustainable environment or an undegraded environment.[4] Moreover, the human rights discourse is an evolving discourse and there is an increasingly dynamic interplay between international, regional and national rights claims – an interplay which sometimes has an upward ratcheting effect on political expectations as discriminated groups appeal to the higher moral authority of international or regional human rights against discriminatory laws at the local or national levels.

However, these international questions are beyond the main burden of this chapter, which is to explore the scope of ecological citizenship rights within the liberal democratic state. After all, the practical realisation of the noble ideal of international human rights depends on the co-operation of nation-states and, ultimately, the enactment of appropriate regional, national and local laws. The question therefore remains: what kind of service can environmental rights perform for citizens in liberal democratic states?

CONNECTING ECOLOGY AND DEMOCRACY

We have seen that while both the 'doomsayers' and the 'eco-warriors' have shown a preparedness to sacrifice some measure of democracy at the altar of ecological principles, most green theorists and activists (including those

220

who have practised nonviolent civil disobedience) have defended democracy as a desirable form of decision making but have sought a style and
form of democratic communication that is more conducive than liberal
democracy to achieving environmental protection. What is common to all
of these responses, however, is that a distinction is made between the
desired outcome (environmental protection) and a range of possible social
choice mechanisms (the forms of action and decision making – nonviolent
civil disobedience, ecotage, authoritarian government, local community
consensus, etc.) that might conceivably produce the desired outcome.

Such a characterisation of the problem facing greens supports the
contention that there is no necessary connection between the principles and
procedures of green politics (Goodin 1992; Saward 1993). According to
Goodin, a distinction must be made between a green theory of value (which
is consequentialist rather than a deontological theory that is concerned with
particular outcomes, which Goodin interprets to mean the protection of
'natural values') and a green theory of agency (which must be understood
as a separate and subsidiary component of a green theory of value). A green
theory of agency would not insist, in advance, on any particular social
choice mechanism (including the forms of agency typically recommended
by greens). Rather, a green theory of agency would examine the available
means and choose those that are found to be most conducive to achieving
the desired outcome. According to Goodin's assessment, many of the
familiar green forms of agency (such as rotation in office, decentralisation
and locally scaled decisions) have served as obstacles to securing green
outcomes. If greens are not to remain 'an amusing parliamentary sideshow',
he argues, they must form parties of the standard kind, fight elections in
the standard way, compromise and enter into coalitions (1992: 171).

In a similar vein, Saward has pointed out that although 'grassroots
democracy' is generally included in the shopping list of green political
principles, the putative link between ecology and democracy is 'an artificial
unity'; democracy is supported on instrumental grounds, not on grounds
of green principle. Indeed, Saward (1993: 69) argues that there is a 'natural
compatibility between liberalism and democracy which does not obtain
between ecologism and democracy'. We must understand democracy as 'a
politics without certainty'; greens must stop claiming that there are ecological imperatives that override democracy and accept that 'persuasion
from a flexible position based on uncertainty can be their only legitimate
political strategy' (1993: 77). Consistent with this argument, Saward's
chapter in this volume seeks to build a 'pure' theory of democracy, arguing
from first principles. That is, he conscientiously sets out to avoid 'infecting'
democracy with green ideological baggage; on this view, it is impermissible
to compromise democracy by introducing ecological norms and values into
the decision-making principles and framework of democracy.

221

I think Saward's earlier claim that liberalism and democracy can be connected in principle (Saward 1993) is supportable, but that his claim concerning the impossibility of such a connection for ecologism (i.e., green theory) and democracy can be challenged. That is, I want to show how green values and democracy might also be connected at the level of principle, rather than merely instrumentally. In order to demonstrate such a claim, we need to understand how liberalism and democracy are connected, or rather, how (liberal) democracy flows from liberal principles. In short, liberal democracy would have no foundation were it not for the liberal principles of autonomy and justice. That is, liberal democracy is built upon the more fundamental principle of respect for the inherent dignity and autonomy of each and every individual. After all, if liberals rejected the principle that all (rather than only some) individuals are ends-in-themselves, and the best judge of their own affairs, then they would no longer be constrained to support the notion of one vote, one value or to support a legal framework that protects the civil and political rights of all citizens. In other words, liberal support for democracy flows from the liberal principles of autonomy and justice. The liberal principle of autonomy respects the rights of individuals to determine their own affairs; the liberal principle of justice demands that this respect be accorded to each and every individual.

Indeed, *contra* Saward, it would seem impossible not to develop a theory of democracy without also enlisting some kind of theory of autonomy and justice. The fundamental area of normative disagreement between greens and liberals, then, is not the meaning and form of democracy but rather the meaning and scope of autonomy and justice. In this chapter I do not intend to take on the full burden of this normative argument (it is briefly sketched below, but for a fuller introduction to ecocentric normative arguments, see Eckersley 1992: pt I). Suffice to say, such a critique would seek to expose the arbitrary and self-serving ways in which notions of 'inherent dignity and value' have been reserved exclusively for humankind. It would also point out how, as Benton (1993) has argued, the liberal notion of the atomistic individual, and the associated traditional liberal rights discourse, have ignored both the ecological 'embodiment' and 'embedded-ness' of individuals (both human and non-human). Here, however, I am primarily interested in the form rather than the content of the argument that might be used to connect ecological and democratic concerns. That is, if the immanent ecological critique of the liberal values of autonomy and justice is accepted (a big 'if', to be sure), then it must follow that our decision-making institutions and procedures must be appropriately adjusted to reflect the new understanding. Now rights, as we shall see, are not essential to this more fundamental debate (except for classical liberals who still accept the notion of 'natural rights'). Rather, they enter the picture only after the 'deeper' liberal principles of autonomy and justice have been subjected to an immanent ecological critique. For liberals and for greens, rights can provide one form in which fundamental political values may be expressed and institutionalised.[5]

Before exploring this mode of argument further, however, I should explain why I think greens ought to reject Goodin's formulation of, and distinction between, a green theory of value and a green theory of agency. Although Goodin's theory of value is non-anthropocentric and tightly argued, it is too narrow to serve as a basis for a green political theory because it applies only to the non-human world. Moreover, his green theory of value is formulated as a consequentialist theory of 'natural' values. This necessarily converts questions of agency and political strategy into instrumental/ utilitarian calculations – in short, greens are free to choose whatever means are most likely to secure their goals. It just so happens that Goodin judges liberal democracy to be the best available means of securing green goals. But this is a purely contingent assessment that others may not share. Monkeywrenchers, for example, would beg to differ: tree spiking is judged to be superior to lobbying and voting when it comes to the protection of old-growth forest.

The instrumental and contingent nature of this assessment may be avoided, however, if green values were to be grounded in a broader defence of autonomy (let us say, for the moment, the freedom of human and non-human beings to unfold in their own ways and live according to their 'species life') and, by association, a broader critique of domination (of humans and other species). If we are to give moral priority to the autonomy and integrity of members of both the human and non-human community, then we must accord the same moral priority to the material conditions (including bodily and ecological conditions) that enable that autonomy to be exercised. By widening the circle of moral considerability, humans, both individually and collectively, have a moral responsibility to live their lives in ways that permit the flourishing and well-being of both human and non-human life. This more inclusive notion of autonomy would necessarily involve the 'reading down' or realignment of a range of 'liberal freedoms' in ways that are consistent with ecological sustainability and the maintenance of bio-diversity. Such a formulation of core green values incorporates yet goes beyond the concerns of nature preservationists (Goodin's main focus) by encapsulating the basic, connecting principle underlying what are popularly understood to be the four pillars of green politics (ecological responsibility, social justice, grassroots democracy and nonviolence). Moreover, the connection between ecology and democracy would no longer be merely contingent. That is, authoritarianism would have to be ruled out at the level of green principle (rather than on purely instrumental grounds) in the same way that it is ruled out according to basic liberal principles: it fundamentally infringes the rights of humans to choose their own destiny.

But what kind of liberal democratic tradition might we be enlarging here,

223

and how might it connect with the case for environmental rights? According to C. B. Macpherson 'the justifying theory of Western [i.e., liberal] democracies rests on two maximising claims – a claim to maximise individual utilities and a claim to maximise individual powers [or individuality]' (Macpherson 1973: 3). The former claim may be traced to Bentham while the latter claim finds its most articulate expression in the writings of J. S. Mill. Both claims are liberal because they maintain that liberal democratic society enables the maximisation of individual human self-realisation. However, they are based on different maximising claims and different models of the individual. In short, utilitarians seek to maximise utilities while deontological theorists seek to maximise autonomy (or, in the case of J. S. Mill, individuality).[6] However, both approaches ultimately rest on a respect for the inherent dignity and value of each and every individual, an idea that remains basic to the democratic impulse.

It is a familiar argument within liberalism that a rights-based approach offers a more secure form of recognition, inclusion and protection for minorities against 'the tyranny of the majority' than its main rival utilitarianism. This argument can be extended to environmental concerns in a number of ways. For example, we have already noted how the dominance of cost-benefit analysis in environmental decision making has not augured well for the environment. However, there is also more theoretical mileage to be had from the rights-based argument. That is, as a justificatory basis for democracy, the rights-based strand of liberal democratic theory offers certain advantages over utilitarianism.[7]

Rights-based liberal theorists not only have provided the justification for a range of constitutional restrictions on what the legislature may enact, based on the prior recognition of certain fundamental rights. They have also defended general principles that qualify the ways in which both the state and individuals may exercise their powers and rights. These restrictions and qualifications are justified, as we have seen, on the ground that they maintain democratic processes and structures and thereby maximise individual autonomy for everyone.

There are several ways in which greens might seek to adapt this form of argument, working from a socially and ecologically contextualised notion of autonomy. One approach might be to argue – at the very minimum – that there are certain basic ecological conditions essential to human survival that should not be bargained away by political majorities because such conditions provide the very preconditions (in the form of life support) for present and future generations of humans to practice democracy. In one sense, they might be seen as even more fundamental than the human political rights that form the ground rules of democracy.

Although not enlisting the language of rights, the general idea that there may be environmental preconditions for democracy has been pursued by Bartlett (1986) and Dryzek (1987). For example, Bartlett has taken issue with Diesing's claim that 'Political rationality is the fundamental kind of reason, because it deals with the preservation and improvement of decision structures, and decision structures are the source of all decisions' (Diesing 1962: 88). According to Bartlett, 'ecological rationality' is a more fundamental kind of rationality than political rationality 'because the preservation and maintenance of ecological life support capability makes possible the preservation and improvement of decision structures and, hence, political rationality and all other forms of rationality' (Bartlett 1986: 235).

Similarly, Dryzek (1987) has argued that ecological rationality cannot be traded off against other forms of reason, at least in the long term. According to Dryzek, a decision-making system may be said to be 'ecologically rational' if it is able effectively and consistently to provide the good of human life-support. As Dryzek (1987: 204) explains, 'the human life support capacity of natural systems is *the* generalizable interest *par excellence*, standing as it does in logical antecedence to competing normative principles such as utility maximization or rights protection'.

However, care must be taken in pursuing this line of argument. After all, for some political prisoners, freedom may be more important than bread or fresh water. Moreover, as Dobson points out in his chapter in this volume, all social orders and all forms of government (from democratic to fascist) require a minimal degree of ecological integrity if they are to be sustained over time. The argument about ecological preconditions therefore does not lend any support for democracy. At best we might say that a minimal degree of ecological integrity is a necessary, but by no means wholly sufficient, condition for a democratic polity.

A second, and more fruitful way of connecting ecological and democratic concerns is to avoid postulating environmental rights as standing prior to political rights. As Benton has argued in the most sustained discussion of environmental rights to date, environmental rights and political rights are inextricably interlinked and therefore should be 'acknowledged alongside, and presupposed by the rights to freedom of worship of speech and so on' (1993: 175). According to Benton, any ecological consideration of rights and needs must begin from a 'naturalistic framework', which focuses on the points of continuity between humans and other animals. As Benton explains: 'Human/animal continuity points to embodiment and habitat as features of moral relevance. Basic interests in bodily development, sustenance, health and reproduction, and in the ecological conditions of these, can be recognised as shared features of human and animal life' (1993: 183).

These two dimensions of ecological 'embodiment' and 'habitat' would provide a basis for asserting a right to uncontaminated food, air, water, and soil. It is noteworthy that Saward (in this volume) also argues that environmental health rights – defined as the right not to be exposed to certain preventable environmental risks – are intrinsically (rather than externally) connected to democratic theory in so far as such actualised environmental health risks may impair the capacity of citizens to exercise basic democratic rights. However, he arrives at this conclusion on the basis of a more sceptical and parsimonious starting point concerning human fallibility (rather than by way of an immanent ecological critique of liberal autonomy and rights, which is the form of argument employed in this chapter).

Yet Benton has pressed his two dimensions of ecological 'embodiment' and 'habitat' even further, suggesting that they would also provide a basis for broader (and culturally specific) notions of environmental belonging and identity, such as psychological attachments to physical places (1993: 180–2). As Benton explains, such belonging needs would be grounded in the human requirement for a physically situated sense of self.

Benton's 'embodiment' and 'habitat' dimensions of environmental rights are broadly consistent with the ontology of internal relatedness upon which ecocentric political theory rests (Eckersley 1992). Both offer an ecologically recontextualised notion of autonomy, just as socialist theory has offered a socially recontextualised notion of autonomy. Although the social and ecological critiques of liberal autonomy (and associated liberal rights) differ in scope and application, they are structurally similar. That is, both proceed from the premise that the well-being of individuals is indissolubly linked with the well-being of the broader social and/or ecological communities of which they are part. Individuals do not simply enter into social and ecological relationships; rather they are constituted by these relations. In other words, social rights, environmental rights and political rights must be understood to be co-determining; both social and environmental rights must therefore be seen as part and parcel of citizenship rights.

But do ecological citizenship rights belong to individuals or communities? And how might we define the scope of such rights in ways that make them practically enforceable? And what about the problems of complexity, causation and proof? Each of these problems will be addressed in turn.

GROUP RIGHTS OR INDIVIDUAL RIGHTS?

What rights would flow from a socially and ecologically contextualised (let us say, green) notion of autonomy? Indeed, why should greens be interested in pressing their claims in the idiom of rights, given that their concerns are primarily collective in nature? The problem with rights is that they are ordinarily tied to individual interests, yet individual interests do not always coincide with the interests of larger social or ecological wholes. Surely it is the broader network of social and ecological relationships that should be the proper field of concern, rather than individual well-being?

In responding to these familiar objections it is necessary to point out that the ontology of internal relatedness upon which a green notion of autonomy would be based does not demand that we totally submerge or

226

obliterate the individual in the name of the collective good (whether social or ecological). Rather, it suggests the need for a mediation between these two mutually constitutive and co-evolving realms. One way of providing such mediation is to reframe a green notion of individual autonomy, and the associated rights discourse, in ways that are compatible with social and ecological well-being. Such rights would therefore belong to individuals not only as individuals but also as members of social and ecological communities. Infringement of individual environmental rights would also be an infringement of collective social and ecological interests. We are already familiar with class actions on behalf of particular individuals who bear a special connection to other individuals (e.g., women, ratepayers, injured workers, environmentalists, indigenous peoples). Indeed, this might be the most likely way in which environmental rights would be tested and defended.

However, an objection is sometimes raised against the notion that public goods (such as clean air) might become the subject of individual rights. According to the economic definition, public goods are goods which are indivisible and non-excludable, or jointly produced (or protected) and jointly enjoyed. The non-excludability of such goods means that if one person presses a claim, then all must benefit, whether they choose to press their claims or not. Moreover, such goods can be produced only by the collective action and co-operation of all or most members of society. Should the enforcement of a single person's environmental right justify the imposition of such a widespread duty (Raz 1984)?

Neither of these objections would appear to be fatal because similar objections may be raised against many existing rights. For example, legal action in defence of important political rights can often serve as a test-case which carries implications for large numbers of people who are not parties to the proceedings; the broader implications for others is not taken to be a barrier to the pursuit of such individual rights. And the protection of many existing political rights requires the maintenance of a costly public infrastructure and the co-operation of all or most members of society, yet such costs are not seen as a reason for foregoing the rights.

According to Waldron (1987), who has considered these objections and arguments, if the benefit to the individual remains the ground of the duty, then both objections can be sustained. The universalisability of the claim is across individuals, taken one by one (1987: 314). However, Waldron goes on to distinguish public goods from what he calls 'communal goods' (such as conviviality, language, culture), which can be enjoyed by people only as members of a social, linguistic or cultural community rather than as individuals. To the extent that 'goods' have such a communal character, he argues that it is inappropriate to make them the subject of rights claims (1987: 315). He argues that such duties that may exist in relation to communal goods are owed to the community not to the individual.

But why, then, should the community not possess the right? And why should not individual members of particular communities who seek to protect collective goods (whether public or communal) be made to demonstrate benefit to the individual before they are entitled to proceed with a claim? (As we shall see below, this argument is close to the common law rule which applies to actions by citizens to uphold legislation enacted for the public benefit.)[8] Indeed, in the case of some public environmental goods, such as bio-diversity, it is often hard to demonstrate any particular or direct benefit to the individual.

Of course, Waldron's distinction would enable many environmental goods to qualify as valid subjects of rights claims (clean air, for example, is a public good rather than a communal good). However, in many cases, it is not easy to make such a distinction – partly because many 'general goods' have a dual character (e.g., the 'environmental integrity' of the homeland of indigenous peoples is both a public and a communal good). In any event, as I argue below, when it comes to ensuring that public environmental legislation is implemented according to law, it should not be necessary for the plaintiff to show any private benefit in the matter at all.

It would seem that the main problem identified by Raz and Waldron concerning public and communal goods is not whether they may be the subject of justifiable individual claims, but rather whether it is possible to define the associated rights in ways that create identifiable duties which may be practically enforced. This problem of practical enforcement, it would seem, is the nub of the challenge facing the case for environmental rights.

THE SCOPE, CONTENT AND ENFORCEABILITY OF ENVIRONMENTAL RIGHTS

If individual rights cannot be abstracted from their social and ecological context, then how might we approach the task of defining the scope and content of environmental rights in ways that ensure that such rights are practically enforceable?

There are three dimensions to the problem of enforceability. The first relates to the presupposition of a strong political consensus in relation to rights claims; the second relates to the problem of justiciability (i.e, can environmental rights be formulated in ways that are capable of being determined by a court of law or quasi-legal tribunal?); and the third relates to the opportunities for, and practicalities of, enforcement.

As we have seen, the appeal of rights claims is that they are not amenable to trade-off. However, to succeed, such claims must attract a strong and continuing political consensus with regard to the inviolability of environmental claims *vis-à-vis* competing claims. While a political consensus might occasionally be possible in relation to particular environmental assets, a more systematic, *a priori* ranking of environmental rights and duties is unlikely to attract the necessary political consensus. Indeed, it is precisely this absence of consensus that has led environmental law down a procedural path that has largely been concerned with a pragmatic accommodation of interests rather than the vindication of particular environmental values.

However, such a response should not be taken as sealing the fate of the case for environmental rights. After all, there is an ongoing conflict among most of the existing liberal civil and political rights. Few would accept the proposition that we should dispense with, say, the right to privacy altogether because it sometimes comes into conflict with other cherished rights, such as the right to freedom of speech. Rather, it is generally understood that the relationship between liberal rights is one that is often conflictual, requiring constant adjustment by the courts and/or parliament (which can, whenever it chooses, override the rulings of the judiciary). Adding environmental rights to the existing rights repertoire may complicate matters, but that in itself should not be a reason against their introduction if the claims are otherwise important and justifiable.

Now some cynics may observe here that, in the process of balancing different rights claims, we have utilitarianism entering via the back door, only this time the trade-offs will be determined by judges rather than bureaucrats or ministers. It is certainly true that not all rights can remain sacrosanct all of the time and that some reconciliation and balancing between different rights is sometimes necessary. However, in so far as trade-offs must be made, it is better that they be made solemnly, reluctantly, as a matter of 'high principle' and last resort, and under the full glare of the press gallery and law reporters rather than earlier in the public decision-making process, via the exercise of bureaucratic and/or ministerial discretion that is presently extremely difficult for members of the public to challenge.

The second problem facing those seeking to defend substantive environmental rights concerns the question of definition and adjudication. Here, the basic problem is that abstract and general formulations, such as 'a right to clean air and water', are in a similar category to abstract claims for 'a right to employment'. Both claims are desirable, but it is not always easy to identify those who are responsible for 'causing' the problem of pollution or unemployment. Even in those cases where 'culprits' may be identified, they are likely to be far too numerous to join in legal proceedings. Moreover, plaintiffs are likely to face considerable hurdles in establishing causation and liability and the judiciary cannot make meaningful rulings in the absence of clear and settled standards of adjudication. Indeed, these objections provide the Achilles' heel of the case for environmental rights. Again, they also help to explain why environmental law has been more concerned with assessing risks rather than establishing causal links between particular activities and actual harm (links which are ordinarily required by courts of law).

Again, however, this problem need not end the matter. Rather, it suggests the need for a degree of realism in the selection and formulation of rights claims – a move that requires the establishment of clearer links between substantive and procedural claims. Instead of an abstract, ambiguous 'right to clean air and water', an environmental bill of rights (whether embodied in ordinary legislation or the constitution) might declare, say, that citizens have a right to ensure that environmental quality is maintained in accordance with the standards set by current environmental laws (standards which would undergo regular public review). In other words, the familiar problems of justiciability and enforceability may be addressed by formulating the substantive environmental rights of citizens in terms of the prevailing standards established by public environmental laws.

Such substantive rights, although apparently modest in their formulation, would provide a strong foothold for the establishment of a range of more incisive procedural environmental rights. Indeed, the effectiveness of any substantive environmental rights presupposes the establishment of a wide range of environmental procedural rights, which would facilitate the practice of ecological citizenship. Such procedural rights would need to include rights to know (i.e., a right to environmental information, including rights to government records and to independent ecological and health research which has a bearing on the ecological welfare, rights to be informed of development proposals); rights to participate in the determination of environmental standards; rights to object to ministerial and agency environmental decisions; and rights to bring actions against departments, agencies, firms and individuals that fail to carry out their duties according to law.

Such an interlinked set of substantive and procedural rights would not be calling on the judiciary to make environmental adjudications on the merits by deciding 'how much' or 'what is reasonable' (these, after all, are ethical, aesthetic and scientific rather than legal questions). Rather, they would seek to strengthen the supervisory role of the courts to ensure that the state is both more responsive to, and responsible for, the ecological welfare of its citizens and for the welfare of the new environmental constituency. Such procedural safeguards would not only help to redress the current under-representation of environmental interests but also provide a firmer guarantee of environmental decision making according to law – thereby redressing the pervasive 'implementation deficit' in environmental law and administration.

Citizens' environmental procedural rights, including broader standing rules *vis-à-vis* public environmental statutes, have already been introduced in some jurisdictions with considerable success. For example, the parliament of Ontario has recently enacted an Environmental Bill of Rights Act (EBRA) (Bill 26, 1993), the preamble of which declares that 'the people of Ontario recognise the inherent value of the national environment' and 'have a right to a healthful environment'. Although the Act does not create any new substantive environmental offences, it creates a range of new participation and litigation rights in relation to environmentally significant decisions, the combined effect of which is to increase the opportunity of the public to participate in environmental decision making and bring actions to ensure that the environmental laws of Ontario are upheld. The Act also provides for the creation of an electronic registry containing a computerised database of environmental policies, Acts, regulations and instruments accessible by modem from a home computer or public library. All citizens are free to access the registry for information or to 'post' a comment, request a review or lodge an appeal in relation to particular policies, instruments or decisions.

For those jurisdictions labouring under the common law rules of standing in relation to the enforcement of public environmental statutes (such as Britain and Australia), such provisions represent a democratic and an environmental breakthrough. Under the common law rules, environmentally concerned plaintiffs could bring an action to uphold environmental laws enacted for the benefit of the public only if they could show some personal stake in the outcome (usually the infringement of some pecuniary interest or proprietry right). The ostensible reason for this rule was to prevent a flood of litigation. The rule assumed that any 'implementation deficits' in general laws would be filled by the Attorney-General acting as guardian of the public interest – by taking action *ex officio* or by relation (i.e., granting permission to an individual to bring proceedings in the name of the Attorney-General). Rarely, however, have Attorneys-General exercised their discretion in this way in Australia (and their discretion is effectively beyond reproach by the courts). Indeed, as high-ranking members of Cabinet, Attorneys-General in Australia have usually been more concerned to legitimise rather than challenge the exercise of state power. Clearly, the supervisory function will be better served by an ecologically informed and legally empowered citizenry, perhaps supplemented by a well-resourced statutory body (such as an Environmental Defenders Office) that is relatively independent of the executive. After all, if environmental laws are primarily concerned to protect generalisable interests, it is both illogical and unreasonable to demand that 'ecological citizens' wishing to uphold the law for the sake of generalisable interests must demonstrate a personal stake in the outcome.

As to the problems of proof, there is already a well-established environmental decision rule – the precautionary principle – that has been designed to deal with the scientific complexity and uncertainty typically associated with many environmental problems. Since the mid-1980s, this principle has appeared in policy statements, legislation and international treaties and declarations, including the Rio Declaration. According to the latter Declaration,

231

> In order to protect the environment, the precautionary approach shall
> be widely applied by States according to their capabilities. Where there
> are threats of serious or irreversible damage, lack of full scientific
> certainty should not be used as a reason for postponing cost-effective
> measures to prevent environmental degradation.
>
> (Rio Declaration, Principle 15)

If widely and systematically applied as an evidentiary rule, no single decision
rule is likely to do more to represent the interests of both ecological citizens
and the 'new environmental constituency'. In any action against a public
authority for dereliction of duty it should be enough for ecological citizens
to establish a *prima facie* threat of serious or irreversible environmental harm
for the onus to switch to the defendant to show why preventive action should
not be taken.

Yet there is one further dimension to the problem of enforcing rights
that has long been pointed out by socialist and feminist critics of liberal
bourgeois rights: the legal system tends to favour those with money, power,
education and position. And, as Yeager (1991: 175) shrewdly points out, 'it
is in implementation that the law finally defines itself and the social order
of which it is part'. Although important, these criticisms should not be taken
as basis for rejecting the case for environmental rights since the class biases
of the legal system can be at least partially redressed through such
mechanisms as environmental legal aid and the establishment of a well-
resourced and independent Environmental Defender's Office empowered
to advise and act on behalf of citizens. In any event, it would be foolish to
abandon rights as an imperfect means of legal protection for none at all –
a point that is acknowledged by many rights critics (e.g., Young 1990).

Environmental citizenship rights within state jurisdictions might also be
linked with, and bolstered by, a developing international discourse of
human environmental rights. Whereas citizenship rights attach only to
those persons who qualify as citizens in particular countries, human rights
attach to every person by virtue of the fact that they are human – irrespective
of race, creed, gender or language. It is noteworthy that the growing human
rights consciousness of the post-Second World War era (sobered by the
experience of fascism) has recently intensified in the 'new Europe'. In
regions of increasing economic integration and political fragmentation,
such as Europe, many minority groups are becoming increasingly dependent on the protection afforded by rights. In terms of the formal
recognition of rights, Britain now stands somewhat alone in Europe as the
only state that insists that the UK Parliament shall be unhampered by formal
constitutional restrictions. In contrast, continental Europe is more sceptical
about this defence of an unfettered parliament, preferring written constitutions to this 'tyranny of convenience'. Indeed, two-thirds of European
countries have made the European Convention on Human Rights (adopted

in 1950 in the aftermath of fascism) part of their domestic law (Dworkin 1990: 18–19). The inclusion of both substantive and procedural environmental rights in human rights conventions promises further to empower citizens to take action to redress both local and transboundary environmental problems in regions such as Europe. Such 'transboundary rights' can serve as 'weapons of the marginal', as one means of protecting the environmental welfare of individuals, classes and groups irrespective of nationality and residence.

CONCLUSION

In an overview of the state of play in democratic theory, Barry Hindess (1993) has drawn attention to a new mood of political realism. Whatever the preferred model of democracy, there now seems to be a growing acknowledgement that representative democracy is inevitable (Hindess 1993: 131; Beetham 1992), that the nation-state is here to stay for the foreseeable future and that liberal democratic principles and institutions (such as the rule of law, the rights discourse, and the separation of powers) must inevitably serve at least as the starting point for those seeking institutional reform, further democratisation and/or 'liberation' from oppressive or unsustainable social and economic practices. Such a mood of realism – and the 'democratic paradox' outlined earlier – have informed and conditioned the case for environmental rights developed in this chapter.

Although I have defended environmental rights, it is important also to emphasise that they are not offered as a panacea for the green movement or for democracy. Rather, this chapter is primarily designed to fuel a debate, which has been recently activated by Benton (1993), on the possibilities of developing an environmental rights discourse and associated campaign. Clearly, environmental rights do not meet all of the ecological challenges presented to liberal democracy. However, they may prove to be one very important vehicle for providing more systematic consideration of ecological concerns while also serving as a basis for an immanent ecological critique and renovation of liberal democracy. It might even help to open a new debate about the foundations and institutional design of a 'green constitutional democracy'.

ACKNOWLEDGEMENTS

My thanks to Peter Christoff, Andy Dobson, Marius de Geus and Freya Mathews for valuable comments and discussion on earlier drafts of this chapter and to all the participants at the Madrid ECPR Workshop on Green Politics and Democracy in April 1994 for a stimulating exchange of ideas.

NOTES

1 I use the term 'green' (or 'green movement') to refer not simply to the environment movement but rather to a broader social movement (and its green party political offshoots) that is working to secure the so-called four pillars of green politics: ecological responsibility, social justice, grassroots democracy and nonviolence.

2 This companion paper applies the same form of argument (i.e., an immanent ecological critique of liberal democracy) to the question of representing the non-human community, but with somewhat different consequences.

3 The most significant exception is in the state of New South Wales, where third party civil enforcement rights are provided by legislation (see s. 123 of the New South Wales Environment and Planning Act 1979).

4 Examples include the 1972 Stockholm Declaration and the 1992 Rio Declaration. The Brundtland Report also recommended a set of legal principles for sustainable development, the first of which declared that 'All human beings have the fundamental right to an environment adequate for their health and wellbeing' (WCED 1990, Annex 1). In May 1994, an international group of experts prepared a Draft Declaration of Principles on Human Rights and the Environment, which has been endorsed by Ms Ksentini, Special Rapporteur on Human Rights and the Environment in her report to the UN Sub-Commission on Prevention of Discrimination and Protection of Minorities, the subsidiary body to the UN Commission on Human Rights.

5 In a companion discussion to this chapter, I have argued that the language of rights becomes especially strained and ungainly as we move from a consideration of human and human analogous cases (e.g., domesticated and captive animals) to a consideration of entire biotic communities and other ecological entities. Such a humanist discourse cannot possibly do 'ecological justice' (Eckersley 1996).

6 Mill reacted against what he saw as the crude utilitarian view of the individual as a mere consumer or bundle of appetites. According to Macpherson (1973: 5) this reaction revived older elements of the humanist tradition which saw humans as rational, purposive beings. Mill argued that a liberal democratic government should be concerned with enabling individuals to develop their own special human attributes, their own forms of excellence – in short, their individuality.

7 It is noteworthy that the model of liberal democracy that is rejected by defenders of deliberative democracy (e.g., Miller 1992; O'Neill 1993; Dryzek 1987, 1992) is the utilitarian model (based on individual preference aggregation) rather than the deontological model (which seeks to uphold individual autonomy) (Although Miller's (1992) discussion of deliberative democracy does not specifically address green democracy, his discussion of generalisable interests has a clear application to environmental problems.) These theorists have argued that when it comes to reaching agreed judgements about generalisable interests (such as environmental protection), individual preference amalgamation is inferior to deliberative democracy. Preference amalgamation merely registers the preferences of individuals (who may choose selfishly or magnanimously); deliberative democracy requires a preparedness on the part of individuals, acting as citizens, to have their preferences transformed through reasoned debate about generalisable interests.

8 One of the key common law authorities for this proposition is the case of *Boyce* v *Paddington Borough Council* (1903), ch. 109.

REFERENCES

Bartlett, R. (1986) 'Ecological Rationality: Reason and Environmental Policy', *Environmental Ethics* 8: 221–39.

Beetham, D. (1992) 'Liberal Democracy and the Limits of Democratisation', *Political Studies* 40: 40–53.

Benton, T. (1993) *Natural Relations: Ecology, Animal Rights and Social Justice*, London: Verso.

Christoff, P. (1994) 'Ecological Citizens, Ecologically Guided Democracy and the State', unpublished MS.

Diesing, P. (1962) *Reason in Society: Five Types of Decisions and their Social Conditions*, Urbana, Ill.: University of Illinois Press.

Dryzek, J. (1987) *Rational Ecology: Environment and Political Economy*, Oxford: Blackwell.

—— (1992) 'Ecology and Discursive Democracy: Beyond Liberal Capitalism and the Administrative State', *Capitalism, Nature, Socialism* 3, 2: 18–42.

Dworkin, R. (1984) 'Rights as Trumps', in J. Waldron (ed.) *Theories of Rights*, Oxford: Oxford University Press.

—— (1990) *A Bill of Rights for Britain*, London: Chatto & Windus.

Eckersley, R. (1992) *Environmentalism and Political Theory: Toward an Ecocentric Approach*, London: UCL Press.

—— (1996) 'Liberal Democracy and the Environment: The Rights Discourse and the Struggle for Recognition', in F. Mathews (ed.) *Ecology and Democracy*, London: Frank Cass.

Foreman, D. (1991) *Confessions of an Eco-Warrior*, Boston, Mass.: Harmony.

Goodin, R. (1992) *Green Political Theory*, Cambridge: Polity.

Hardin, G. (1972) *Exploring New Ethics for Survival: The Voyage of the Spaceship Beagle*, New York: Viking.

Hayward, B. (1994) 'The Greening of Direct Democracy: A Reconsideration of Theories of Political Participation', paper presented at the XVIth World Congress of the International Political Science Association, 21–25 August, Berlin.

Heilbroner, R. (1974) *An Inquiry into the Human Prospect* (1991), New York: Norton.

Held, D. (1992) 'Democracy: From City-state to a Cosmopolitan Order?', *Political Studies* 40: 10–39.

Hindess, B. (1993) 'Democratic Theory', *Political Theory Newsletter* 5, 2: 126–39.

Lindblom, C. (1965) *The Intelligence of Democracy: Decision Making Through Mutual Adjustment*, New York: Free Press.

Mackay, M. (1994) 'Environmental Rights and the US System of Protection: Why the US Environmental Protection Agency is not a Rights-Based Administrative Agency', *Environment and Planning* 26: 1761–85.

Macpherson, C. B. (1973) *Democratic Theory: Essays in Retrieval*, Oxford: Clarendon Press.

Marks, S. (1980–1) 'Emerging Human Rights: A New Generation for the 1980s?' *Rutgers Law Review* 33: 435.

Miller, D. (1992) 'Deliberative Democracy and Social Choice', *Political Studies* 40: 54–67.

O'Neill, J. (1993) *Ecology, Policy and Politics: Human Well-Being and the Natural World*, London: Routledge.

Ophuls, W. (1973) 'Leviathan or Oblivion?', in H. Daly (ed.) *Toward a Steady State Economy*, San Francisco: Freeman.

—— (1977) *Ecology and the Politics of Scarcity: A Prologue to the Political Theory of the Steady State*, San Francisco: Freeman.

Raz, J. (1984) 'Rights-based Moralities', in J. Waldron (ed.) *Theories of Rights*, Oxford: Oxford University Press.

Saward, M. (1993) 'Green Democracy?', in A. Dobson and P. Lucardie (eds) *The Politics of Nature: Explorations in Green Political Thought*, London: Routledge.

Stammer, N. (1993) 'Human Rights and Power', *Political Studies* 41: 70–82.

Stone, C. (1987) *Earth and Other Ethics*, New York: Harper & Row.

Tarlock, A. D. (1988) 'Earth and Other Ethics: The Institutional Issues', *Tennessee Law Review* 56: 43–76.

Waldron, J. (1987) 'Can Communal Goods be Human Rights?', *Archives Européennes de Sociologie* 28, 2: 296–322.

Yeager, P. (1991) *The Limits of the Law: The Public Regulation of Private Pollution*, Cambridge: Cambridge University Press.

Young, I. M. (1990) *Justice and the Politics of Difference*, Princeton, NJ: Princeton University Press.

INDEX